HEART OF PHOTOGRAPHY

Way of Seeing Volume II

Further Explorations in Nalanda Miksang Photography

BY JOHN MCQUADE
AND MIRIAM HALL

Heart of Photography
Further Explorations in Nalanda Miksang Photography
Way of Seeing: Volume II

by John McQuade and Miriam Hall

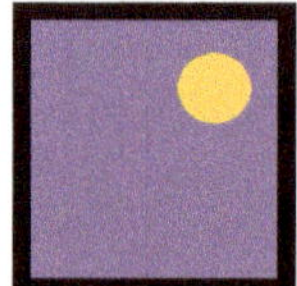

DRALA PUBLICATIONS

ISBN:1633934979
ISBN 13: 978-1-63393-497-9
Drala Publishing
Madison WI
www.miksang.org
www.miksangwayofseeing.org
www.dralapublications.com

All images in this work are the creations of either John McQuade or Miriam Hall, with
the exception of the author photo of Miriam Hall, which is by Gloria Merriam.

TABLE OF CONTENTS

For our teachers:

>Chögyam Trungpa Rinpoche
>Sakyong Mipham Rinpoche
>Vajra Regent Ozel Tenzin

From the *Aspiration of Shambhala* chant:

>May we courageously apply skillful means to squeeze out
>the golden nectar of luminosity inlaid in the fabric of phenomena.

ACKNOWLEDGMENTS

First and foremost, again, we acknowledge our teachers: Chögyam Trungpa Rinpoche, Sakyong Mipham Rinpoche, and the Vajra Regent Ozel Tenzin. Their tireless and loving dedication is the only reason these teachings were kept alive and vibrant for us to apply them to the skillful means of photography.

Collaboration is spicy and powerful, full of relationship juice and vigor, as well as fault lines we only find by continuing forward together. John and Miriam want to acknowledge each other, and the commitment each of us has put into these volumes, and into keeping this approach to contemplative photography electrically alive.

We also thank our spouses, Alice and Ilana.

Thank you to our donors, whose generous funding made the physical making of this book and ebook possible. The following are donors who gave $100 or more (please see the website for the almost one hundred others who gave smaller donations that added up to all we needed!):

Ray Ball, Lennie Birkett, Mary Braunagel, Michael Brouphy, Orlando Chiang, Malcolm Clay, Malini Dominey, Mark Edzards, Thomas Fitzpatrick, Angela Fletcher, Ann Hall, Gabi Helfert, Joey Johannsen, Margo McCarter, Luis Ochandorena, Mirella Vitrano, Rodney Weiss, Jessica Winslow, Mary Yamada.

Also we express much gratitude for our endlessly engaged students and social media participants, for incredible ongoing in-person and online community, and for the teachers who make all of it happen in so many locations around the world.

Carolyn Gimian and Oliver Glosband remain our permissions experts.

Finally, Jerri Hurlbutt jumped in with her good eye to polish the jewel of our two years of words into as-close-to-perfect as we can get, and John Koehler's crew made it all look so beautiful in the end.

Anyone we have missed—and because of interdependence, there are endless beings who made this book happen in direct or indirect ways— we thank you heartily as well.

DEDICATION TO MAXINE SIDRAN

John McQuade

In Nalanda Miksang, Maxine is my friend and conscience. As friend, she is someone I can be fully alive with in a free, insightful, and relaxed way. Although my relationship with Maxine is mostly Miksang, it is not all Miksang. We both have an avid interest in politics with left-liberal orientations. Maxine comes from a Jewish left-liberal tradition, and I come from a working-class union family. And Maxine—in her kind heart—rescues and organizes others to rescue stray and feral cats, to give them refuge and find them homes. That means there have always been cats in her home. I am allergic to cats. Somehow that worked out ok.

She is also a pure Nalanda Miksang practitioner and teacher, with me since the early days of Miksang. She is the real thing: she engages it in a contemplative way as a contemplative way.

In principle, I am a pure and true Nalanda Miksang practitioner and teacher. But I am also the co-director of Nalanda Miksang International. That means politics: the art of making the necessary possible, and the possible necessary. It means compromise. Maxine is not keen on compromise. She is keen on the pure contemplative. So many conversations with her over the years have helped keep me going in the right direction.

There are others within this intimate Nalanda Miksang way. There is my wife, Alice, the only Miksang student who has been with me the whole way. She is my main confidant and wisdom touchstone. But she is my wife. Enough said.

Miriam Hall holds the Nalanda Miksang teachings. We are very close, but I count on her to be the holder. So there is our friendship, and our being in this together, but also we have a formal, existential relationship. Together we serve something bigger: Nalanda Miksang as a feature of Shambhala Society.

I don't recall how Maxine first got involved; she will have to give her own account. At some point, we established a local Miksang monthly image show for the public. For many meetings, across many months, it was just myself and Maxine and a few interested others. Month after month we both showed up. Maxine was never discouraged when not many people showed up. She knew this was the real thing, and we could just go with it, and it would work out.

It did.

Now we are Nalanda Miksang International. We have Nalanda Miksang teachers and programs throughout North America and Europe. In large measure, this started with Maxine: Maxine practicing Nalanda Miksang; Maxine consistently showing up with her conviction, confidence, and good heart.

Maxine is a major practitioner and teacher in Nalanda Miksang. She is one of the first certified teachers and she taught for many years, when no one else other than me was teaching. She is also an innovator who opened an original and specific vector of Absolute Eye Photography. Absolute Eye Photography explores the perception connection of Nalanda Miksang and Modern American Art. In this context, Maxine revealed what we now call "The Secret Life of Mannequins."

So Maxine is a foundational figure in Nalanda Miksang—at all levels and in all dimensions.

Maxine is Maxine: a good friend and pure Nalanda Miksang practitioner who has helped keep alive Nalanda Miksang as a real contemplative practice and school. She is the real thing, and Nalanda Miksang is the real thing.

Miriam Hall

It just so happens that Maxine Sidran grew up in Wisconsin, like me, though she has lived in Toronto for most of her adult life. When I met her the first time, I simply knew she was important to John, and one of the only few other Nalanda Miksang teachers.

When Maxine and I met, it was a match made in heaven—sconnie sisters, truly of the same heart and eye. We poked around Kensington in Toronto for an entire afternoon, marveling at the different worlds we found on the exact same streets. We talked cats and politics, perception and photography. We got along famously.

Then John asked me to be co-director of Nalanda Miksang International. Subsequently, I found it a lot harder to relate to Maxine's purity. Living so far away, over so many emails, other aspects of our relationship got revealed: my desire to innovate rubbing up against her firm, traditional approaches; my excitement and enthusiasm as the kid sister irritating her long-standing, intimate relationship with our Miksang father; my focus on logistics and making things happen, pressing into her heart connection and need to preserve the view.

Yet, every time we met, whether in Wisconsin, Chicago, or Toronto, all those logistical emails fell away. Heart to heart, I could see that Maxine *saw*. As she shared notes with me from the decades, as she described the ways John's thinking evolved—

recounting the history of Absolute Eye, the endless hours of trying to absorb, often being the only person present —my heart broke with joy. Without Maxine and all those years of utter devotion, without her incredible good spirit and down-to-earth Wisconsin heart, it is possible we would have never made it this far.

Maintaining the high view of a practice like this is tricky. It's hard to, as John says, "Make the necessary possible, and the possible necessary," especially when the Internet, digital technology, and other advents—including newer generations of teachers with their own excitement and innovative ideas—cram into focus. The whole time I have felt Maxine like a lightning rod in the center, completely grounded and also totally appearing in the electrical energy that is the power of this practice. Wide open in space, while strong in the roots.

I grew up with two older brothers, no sisters. I have little romance about sisters; I know blood relations are often more complicated than we want them to be. However, I can't help but think Maxine and I are karmic sisters from somewhere far back in history. Maybe the dralas put the terma of Miksang in the ground, knowing that while men like Michael Wood and John McQuade would find it, a woman like Maxine Sidran and her little Wisconsin root sister would catalyze it wide open.

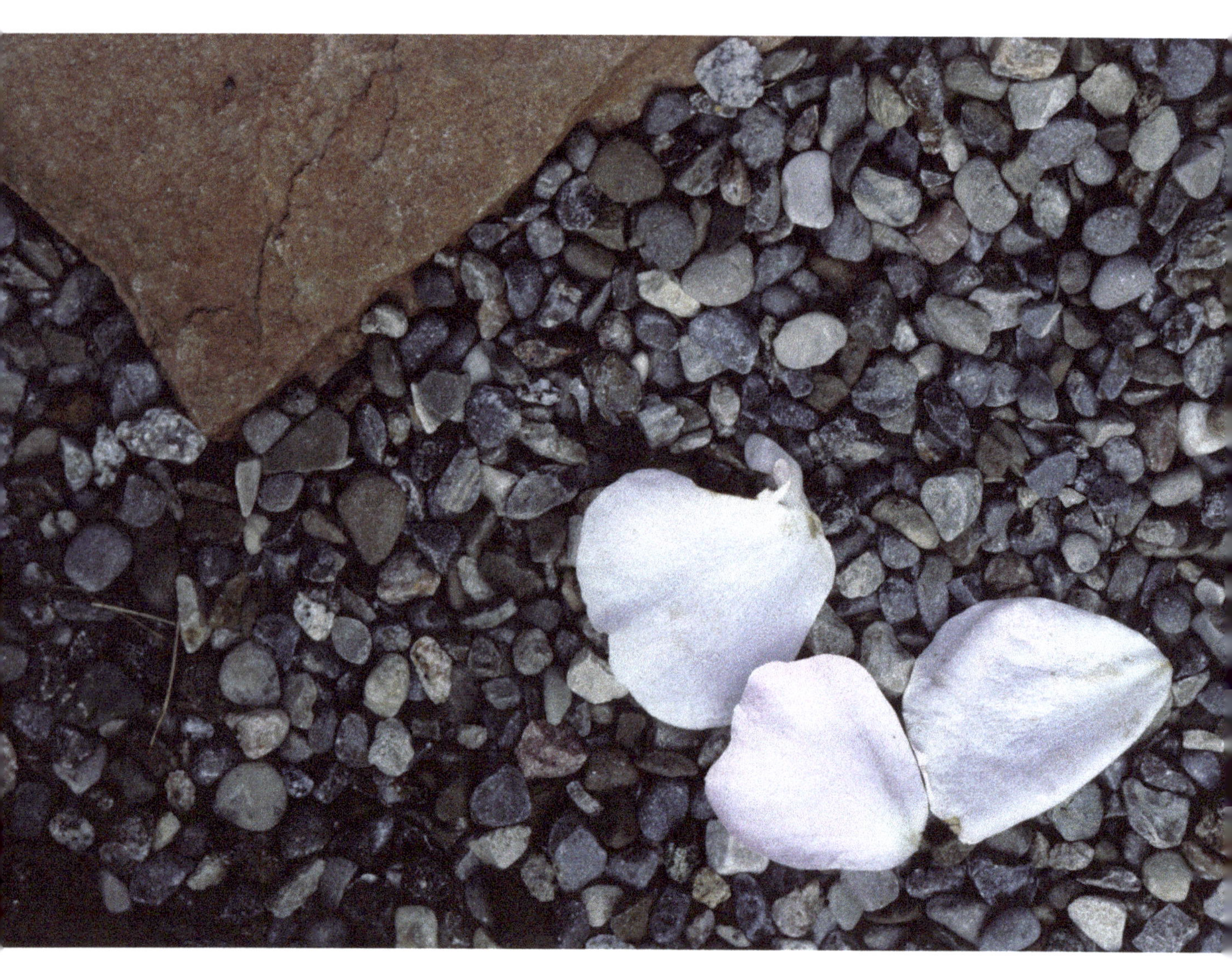

THE HEART OF CONTEMPLATIVE PHOTOGRAPHY: AN INTRODUCTION

The realm of perception is limitless, so limitless that perception itself is primordial, unthinkable, beyond thought. There are so many perceptions that they are beyond imagination. There are a vast number of sounds. There are sounds that you have never heard. There are sights and colors that you have never seen. There are feelings that you have never experienced before. There are endless fields of perception.

—Chögyam Trungpa, *Shambhala, Sacred Path of the Warrior*

The Lived World and The Paint Chip World

This is the second volume in the *Way of Seeing* series, and it presents the heart of contemplative photography, what we also refer to as Level Two, or the second program in the Nalanda Miksang/ *Way of Seeing* series. *Nalanda* refers to an early university in India which specialized in the arts, *Miksang* translates as "Good Eye" and is the lineage name of this practice. Underlying all of this volume is heart connection. The path is how this practice becomes meaningful and fulfilling for your life, and how your images become meaningful and inspiring for others.

These teachings and practices are the main and heart teachings of Nalanda Miksang contemplative photography. Entering the way of Nalanda Miksang begins in Level One, with our first volume, *Looking and Seeing*. This volume takes us to where the day-in-day-out experience of contemplative photography lives. There is a full review of the content of *Looking and Seeing*, covering the teachings of Level One, in the appendix to this book. If you have not read that volume or taken courses covering the material in that book, we recommend reviewing that material first before undertaking Level Two. The following brief review is more for people who have engaged the Level One teachings or have read the first volume in the *Way of Seeing* series.

In that first volume, *Looking and Seeing*, we worked through our basic connection with visual forms of perception—color, light, pattern, texture, space, and dot-in-space—as a way to both directly connect with the visual world and synchronize the eye, mind, and world. When we refer to Level One, or *Looking and Seeing*, this is what we are referring to. This direct contact with visual reality and the experience of harmonization of eye and mind is the first contemplative connection: to be there, with the "there," through the there. This sounds abstract, but it could not be more sensuous and direct. You actually experience *what* you experience *as* you experience it.

What you experience directly and clearly is often different from what you *think* you experience. For instance, to lean into a slogan from *Looking and Seeing*, you first experience "fire engine red" *not* "a red fire engine." Our direct experience is often not recognized until it has been filtered and distorted by a network of concepts, thoughts, interpretations, and emotional responses. With true perception, your experience is perception, and your perception is your experience. There is nothing added—we are simply recognizing direct experience before concepts, names or labels, interpretations, likes and dislikes, and so forth kick in.

Recently, John presented the following in a workshop. John asked participants to look at the wall behind the shrine in the Shambhala meditation hall of the workshop. The question was this: "What color is the wall?" The most obvious answer was "gold." Upon further exploration, though, people realized that there were many hues of gold, which depended on the many overlapping phenomenal circumstances: shadows, intensities of light, patterns and texture in the wall. In terms of experience, there were many hues of gold. At the same time, to paint the wall, someone picked a paint chip the color of a specific gold, which looked very different from the gold of the painted wall.

Try it out yourself. Find a wall illuminated by light sources and see if you can find "one color" there.

So. Which is the *real* gold? The objective paint chip gold, or the experienced, many-hued gold? They are both real in their own domains, and the point is to understand that there are different domains of reality constantly coexisting. Contemplative mind and practice orient more toward the experienced domain, the lived world, rather than the paint chip world. This is the liberation aspect of the contemplative way of seeing: seeing if your life experience consists of radiant hues of gold or a single paint chip gold.

These are the questions and practices at the start of the *Way of Seeing*. Reviewing, or reading for the first time, our first volume *Looking and Seeing* will help you a great deal with this volume, whether you are just starting out or have taken many courses or read many books. WE have also included a summary of the Level One/*Looking and Seeing* teachings in the appendix of this book.

Why Levels?

The following quote from Chögyam Trungpa, from *Mindfulness in Action*, really articulates part of the reason why Nalanda Miksang is a path with specific levels and teachings. The levels of Nalanda Miksang in fact originate from Trungpa's teachings on the three levels of perception, (found in the book *True Perception*), which we have reproduced in the appendix. It is beyond the scope of this book to break down those three levels, but this quote does a lovely job of addressing the reason for such articulations:

We might think that there is a contradiction between the two, but in fact, spontaneity and discipline go together. Spontaneity itself is possible because you are there—which is the discipline . . . When you feel delighted, resourceful, or open, you experience those spontaneous qualities because you're already being disciplined. Otherwise, you couldn't actually connect with them . . . Discipline doesn't hold you back; it actually allows you to make the connection with spontaneity . . . At the beginning, your training should involve strict discipline. Later, you should feel that you can afford to open yourself and express yourself freely. Spontaneity is possible in part because of the exertion and the discipline you have experienced. Then, spontaneity will also have a sharp eye. It will be clear seeing, which is the expression of discipline.

The Heart of Perception

Entering the heart of perception, we begin to see that perception is more than simply registering the phenomenal world: seeing red as red. That is a basic and fundamental Level One connection. But red expresses itself many ways: blood red, sunset red, the red maple leaf of the Canadian flag, red rage, red roses, ketchup red, revolution red, valentine red . . . endless reds. We can also begin to understand that eye-to-eye communication of such simple but rich color is also heart-to-heart connection. This is more where we are entering into the heart of perception, or Level Two.

Being alive is more than colors as forms, and more like color as experience. Being alive is being connected with the phenomenal world. Being connected is just that: being in touch and being touched. It means something, and that it is meaningful. We are all alive, but we often don't have the sense of being alive. This is what Nalanda Miksang offers—direct sensory contact with being alive, first at a basic eye level, and now at the heart level.

The Heart Connection

Level Two delivers us to the sensibility of perception, the heart of perception. It is the feeling of being touched and in touch, the knowing that what we see is meaningful, which reminds us at a heart level that being alive is, that our lives are, meaningful.

When you see clearly, you are there with being there; you are in touch, and you are touched. Being in touch is feeling how it feels to be alive. When we are really present, it feels good, electric, and inspiring. This is the heart of contemplative photography.

When you photograph from that heart, your images embody this sense and sensibility—*this* is the craft of contemplative photography. This is not just making images, it is more: something is communicated through the images, the heart connection. This heart connection is what radiates intrinsic beauty through the image.

These heart images touch the hearts of those who view these images, which is where we commune with each other, where we make community through contemplative photography. In Shambhala, we call this kind of connection *enlightened society* or *enlightened culture*. Unlike most of our societal structures, this is not a society of geographic, political, or cultural boundaries. It is a culture based on sharing the basic human situation and our human hearts with each other.

Even if your photographic practice and your

photography images are more personal than public to you, you can see how your images connect with something deep and heartfelt and have the potential to touch the heart of others. It is that simple, and that profound. A heartfelt image is simple. The resonance of a heartfelt image is profound.

The Contemplative Way

Why does this matter? What's the point? There is no way to give direct answers for these difficult but fair questions, since they are variations on deep and decisive questions: Why does life matter? What's the point of life? This text and practice cannot provide answers to these deep inquiries.

However, this text and practice can offer ways to engage these issues, because contemplative practices are meant to help us find ways into these big questions. Contemplative practices are little ways, like rocks in the stream, crossing from one side to the other. Rock by rock, step by step, we cross over. These little ways do not provide direct answers to these questions, but they do provide a path for us to engage them. In Nalanda Miksang Level One teachings, we start very small—with color, surface, light, and other basic visual elements. It is here, in Level Two, the heart of photography, where we begin to deepen those initially abstract explorations, going into the heart of contemplative practice through photography.

Generally, contemplatives do not ask big questions such as "What is the meaning of life?" Instead, they investigate little inquiries, such as "What is color as color?" through felt experiences that explore questions like "How does color as color feel? How does it manifest? How is our experience of color? What difference does color make to a situation?" and so forth.

These are quite ordinary questions you can ask yourself, right now:

- What difference does color make in clothes for a particular situation?

- What difference does color make in paint colors of a room?

- What difference does color make in the displays of the natural seasons: flowers, grasses, trees?

What is your heart response to symbolic color? Think of the flags of every country—just bring to mind the colors of your national flag. How do just the colors feel? For instance, the shades of red—blood red and what that evokes. Valentine's Day and its red hearts. All the colors of Christmas lights, of fireworks, of a cathedral stained glass window. All the emotions and feelings: What is the color of anger, of envy? There is so much richness in just the human symbolism of color. Then there's the use of color in art, particularly in painting. That's all without having considered nature, the primal color scene: the seasons and how they manifest through color.

Color speaks to the heart of the matter.

The fact that all of this is very ordinary and available might actually lead us to ask, "So what is the point?" The point is that this is all very ordinary and available. While being ordinary, it is also extraordinary—the gift of life. We can decide whether to just give up and say, "So what?" and move on with our lives, which actually turns us away from life itself. Or we can see life as a gift we are continually unpacking and appreciating. We can see this life as a miracle.

Much of what we experience of the world, of being alive, comes through our senses. How do you experience your world? If you are sitting in a room, how do you experience "sitting in a room"? There are visuals—space, shapes, and colors; sounds—birds chirping outside, traffic, the subtle sounds of your breathing; bodily sensations—the air temperature and the sense of being seated, tensions in the body, the rhythm of breathing, the feel of clothing on skin; the smells—morning coffee; and tastes—morning coffee. This is all your experienced world, mainly through the external senses (though we also sense thoughts, emotions, and more). It's really quite simple, yet profound.

Starting with something simple like color connects us to the contemplation of bigger topics: How are we connected to the world, or reality, for instance? How can we be the connection between reality and our experience? How can we be connected and connecting, rather than separated and separating? How can we experience our life as connection and harmony, rather than separation, struggle, and stress? The experience of connection, of living through our senses, is being connected to the phenomenal world, the experienced world.

This contemplative engagement is not religious or philosophical. It is working directly with your ordinary, everyday experience, to release you from stress and help you open to everyday appreciation. Bit by bit, on the rock path through the river, we cross over from claustrophobic habit to natural freshness, from stress to delight, from the thing world to the phenomenal world, from conventional world to ordinary magic, from confusion to insight and wisdom.

Nalanda Miksang is a photography practice, but it is a photography practice which embodies a perception practice, and a perception practice which embodies a wisdom practice. Let's break those three parts down a little more.

Photography is an available visual medium, especially today with high-quality cameras built into our phones. Traditionally, the media of contemplative arts have been simple and easily available to the public. For instance, contemplative calligraphy practice is based on what is used in everyday writing (or once was used more regularly): brush and paper and ink. Through these simple resources, calligraphy expresses the perception of the contemplative moment.

It is the same with Nalanda Miksang photography. Photography is a mass culture medium. Nalanda Miksang uses this neutral mass culture craft as a way to embody ordinary magic. By entering into contemplative practice with easy-to-access supplies, we can more easily generate a contemplative culture and enlightened society.

If your primary interest is the creation of strong, vivid, and impressive images, you have come to a good place. This book, this practice, will help you with that. Our view is that a strong first perception facilitates the manifestation of a vivid image. It is as simple as that.

In terms of Nalanda Miksang being a contemplative practice, using the same materials as everyday photography, you enter a world of ordinary magic through your visual perceptions, and you share images of that magic with others. How does that happen? Do you have to want it to happen? Magic happens through direct contact with perception.

Think of a body of water near a row of trees. What color is the water? That depends on the reflection of the trees, the sky, and so forth.

It depends on the changing conditions and circumstances and how they affect the trees, the sky, and the water—the time of day, the time of season, and the changing weather conditions. It also depends on whether you see clearly the phenomenal only-in-that-moment detail of being there. It depends on whether you are there with the there. In contemplative practice, you are there with the world as it is in that moment, and therefore you see the visual world the way it actual manifests.

This scene with the trees along the water is an ever-changing, reflective, impressionistic display. But the fact is, appearances are always this way, which you can see clearly if you are there with the there. It is just a matter of paying attention and being aware of what is happening as its happening, of appreciating the actual situation. The actual situation is always the actual situation—always fresh and free, always a live event. Your life is always a live event.

Then there is appreciation, which is being live to the alive. Being live with it all: the juice, the electricity, the harmony, the still point, the relaxation, the joy, the wonder, the fantastic, the simple and the profound. All of this is contemplative. Or at least all of this is the connection with the contemplative. It runs deeper—the other side of the stream, where the question of the meaning of life lives. We will get there in these teachings, but for now it is enough to take little steps across the rocks.

The contemplative realm is ordinary—how does that tie in with wisdom? Everyone experiences the contemplative many times throughout each day. How? We all find ourselves in moments when we are just there with the there, when, without even trying, we relax into the deeply ordinary relaxation of just being alive; there is a gap in the program. In this way, being contemplative is not different from being aware of being alive. But it is not the program we build around trying to be alive, it is a gap in that program. Through stopping our attempt to live better, we actually affirm an opening out and opening through the gap to how things really are. The opening out is liberation, and the opening through is radiance. Radiance is the experience of joy; radiance is what allows art to issue as art.

Living a contemplative life is recognizing and stabilizing that gap in the program, until it stops the program entirely. You find your freedom by refusing to be programmed. You become liberated from the conditions and circumstances of your life. You get in touch with the real situation, which is naturally fresh and free. We are presenting this as being about life, but that is because the way to be a contemplative artist is to be a contemplative human.

Sakyong Mipham, our head lineage teacher in Shambhala, expresses this need well in his book *Shambhala Principle*:

> *How do we feel? When we connect with our heart, what do we find? No matter how difficult and painful life may be, basic goodness is undiluted by conditions, for it cannot change. Obstacles and challenges may arise, but they do not reduce the enlightened qualities at our disposal. If enough of us can feel our goodness, then, in a period of difficulty, society will not break down but actually become stronger.*

A student in one of Miriam's contemplative writing classes said this about her experience: "I came to these classes to become a better writer. I realized I had to become a better human, first." Miriam would modify this to say that while becoming a better writer is definitely second after becoming a better human, instead of becoming a better human we simply need to discover that we are already good, already better, unconditionally. Ironically, however, what is simple is often not easy.

Orienting to Liberation

All dharma practices, whether contemplative or meditative, artistic or not artistic, are oriented toward liberation, which is the experience and stabilization of this gap. From this gap, a life of liberation and everyday joy can express itself. Nalanda Miksang, like other contemplative practices, is not special or extra. It is a skillful way for you to focus and intensify this natural power of ordinary magic in your life.

If this ordinary magic is always available, then why do we need to engage a practice like meditation or contemplative photography? The answer is in the question: Why are you not already engaging this ordinary magic as your everyday experience? If we are honest, most of us will acknowledge that this is not the ongoing experience of our life. If we are honest, in fact, we experience our lives as an ongoing challenge. We do the best we can to get through an average day with its many ups and downs. This is heroic, in its own way. It takes a whole human heart to engage fully with life, day in and day out. However, our birthright lives can be more than getting through an average day in an average way. Our lives are not average. They are unique.

This way of treating our lives as average, or even below average, has a lot of habitual momentum, since we've been at it a long time. To simply say we will be more present, open to the joy available at any moment, isn't enough to break the pattern of habits. We need new habits, new patterns—what we call *skillful means* in the dharma world—to break the momentum of old habitual patterns.

In your heart of hearts, you know life is good and you are unique. You know and experience situations when you see a gap in the program, when you are just there appreciating your life. Nalanda Miksang is a way of focusing on and enhancing this basic reality, insight, and experience, to encourage the connections that already exist.

Finally, it is also a way of making brilliant images. After all, this is contemplative photography, not contemplative basket weaving (a legitimate practice of its own). In this practice, teachings on how to connect with clear perception combine with teachings on how to make an equivalent image, which embodies the contemplative experience. The image composes naturally out of the way contemplative experience appears. Contemplative photography is photographing contemplative experience in a pure, direct way: art and life are not separate, and, in fact, life comes first.

The Outer And The Inner Way

In dharma teachings, we often refer to a path or set of teachings as having outer, inner, and secret elements. We talk about them as separate aspects, but really they often overlap. In Nalanda Miksang, the outer is the first connection with the visual forms of perception: color as color; light and the ways of light; the aspects of surface: texture and pattern; space; and dot-in-space. The outer is also making equivalent brilliant images of these perceptions. All of this was presented in the first volume of the Way of Seeing series: *Looking and Seeing,* and our Level One Nalanda Miksang programs.

Chögyam Trungpa Rinpoche said that in any Dharma practice, however advanced, one always includes the beginning. His analogy was combing one's hair: one always begins with the roots and combs outward. The heart of this teaching is the inner: how practice (in this case, Nalanda Miksang) can help one appreciate the ongoing way of one's life experience. Contemplative photography begins with clear perception, and the training in clear perception begins with basic training on pure visual forms: color, light, and so forth. Also included in our beginning teachings are the synchronization of eye and mind, and the connection with the flash of perception.

This basic view and these basic trainings are presented in the first text, *Looking and Seeing.* Again, if you have not worked through it, read the summary of these teachings and exercises in the Appendix in this text, or you can read about them in depth in the first volume. At a minimum we recommend that you work through the first exercises, Color as Color, Flash of Perception, and Synchronization, presented in the Appendix (Section II of The Basics of Looking and Seeing). This is also the case for those who have already engaged the Level One course and/or *Looking and Seeing,* through the text or in workshops. This comes back to Trungpa Rinpoche's admonition to begin at the beginning.

With Miksang practice we need to connect with the full process of contemplative photography because it is a template for connecting with the phenomenal world. Practicing fully helps us engage at a heart level so we can live more fully.

We start with turning the mind to intention: we intend to see clearly, usually through an assignment like color. We shift attention through intention. This sets up a self-confirming spiral dynamo: the more you see, the more you see. This is the synchronization of eye and mind internally, and of the body, world, and mind in a more whole sense.

Synchronization is harmonization, which is contemplative speak for *peace.* At a minimum there is no struggle or stress, which has two aspects.

In terms of personal experience, all worries, concerns, gossip, mundane discursive thoughts, monkey mind, and emotional turmoil have been put on hold. They are not in play, which is a release and relief, which feels light and good. But peace is not just about what we no longer feel bogged down by; we also experience this light and freeness—this buoyancy, clarity, vividness, richness, inquisitiveness, and creativity—because this is actually what it feels like to be fully alive. It feels good because it is good. When we are fully seeing, there is connection and communion. We feel touched and are in touch. It is personal, not abstract. It is you, with your life, as your life. It could not be more direct, personal, and intimate.

In conventional terms, this peace might not seem to be a big deal. This kind of shift is not usually a big revelation, rather a subtle gap in the program. That is the gap of being there, not caught up in all the distractions. Sometimes what catches us off guard, not protecting the story of our lives, is something conventionally extraordinary, say, the Northern lights. Usually it is minor, something that most of us would not notice and appreciate, such a dewdrop on the tip of a leaf.

There are two aspects of this gap: 1) it reveals something we usually deem ordinary to be an extraordinary ongoing aspect of our life experience; and 2) it is a gap in the program, which is actually revolutionary: it releases us from being programmed by various layers of conditioning and circumstances. In terms of the experience, on the spot this gap releases us from conditioning as it simultaneously opens us to what is: the phenomenal world.

This releasing to what is already fresh and free gets close to the main contemplative practice, which is seeing and identifying with the ongoing source of the fresh and the free. What is the source? We can describe it, but the point is it must be experienced. The source of the fresh and the free can be understood as the non-dualism of the perceiver and the perceived. You are not separate or incomplete from what you perceive. You are, yourself, as complete as you are completely there, with the there, through the there. Your life is always already meaningful and fulfilled.

Seeing includes insight, discernment, and appreciation. It is not only red—it is hot red or even fire engine red. The visual phenomenal world becomes articulated as meaningful. This is the golden key: it is not just connection, it is communion. Communion is both a sharing and a blessing. Communion is the transformation of the ordinary world into the ordinary magic world: the sacred world. This is the heart of Nalanda Miksang.

Already, even in Level One introductory, outer teachings, the practice and experience include a shift to the inner. We shift from relating to the world as consisting only of things to the primacy of the phenomenal world. What does that mean? We have a slogan in Level One that says it all: "Fire engine red, not a red fire engine." In other words, instead of relating to things that have aspects related to our experience, we see the experience first, before the thing. This parallels how we actually perceive, although we may not become cognitively aware of something until we name its "thingness"; before we are consciously aware of its identity, our perception has tracked many aspects, full experiences of its elements. This shift in focus helps us change our orientation to the phenomenal world as the world of experience, giving priority to direct experience over objectifying our world.

This shift toward our inner, direct experience is the heart of contemplative photography. Inner seeing is a way of touching, feeling, and being—being in touch and touched, being alive, and appreciating being alive. When we make this shift, we can connect our ongoing personal experience with the ongoing manifestation of the phenomenal world. Actually, they are not separate: our experience and the phenomenal world are the same. We are there together. Feeling this togetherness is contemplative, and through it we can touch the qualities of being fresh, fluid, and free. We drop the static sameness of the thing world, the routine habitual responses. Our fundamental life experience is always already fresh, fluid, and free.

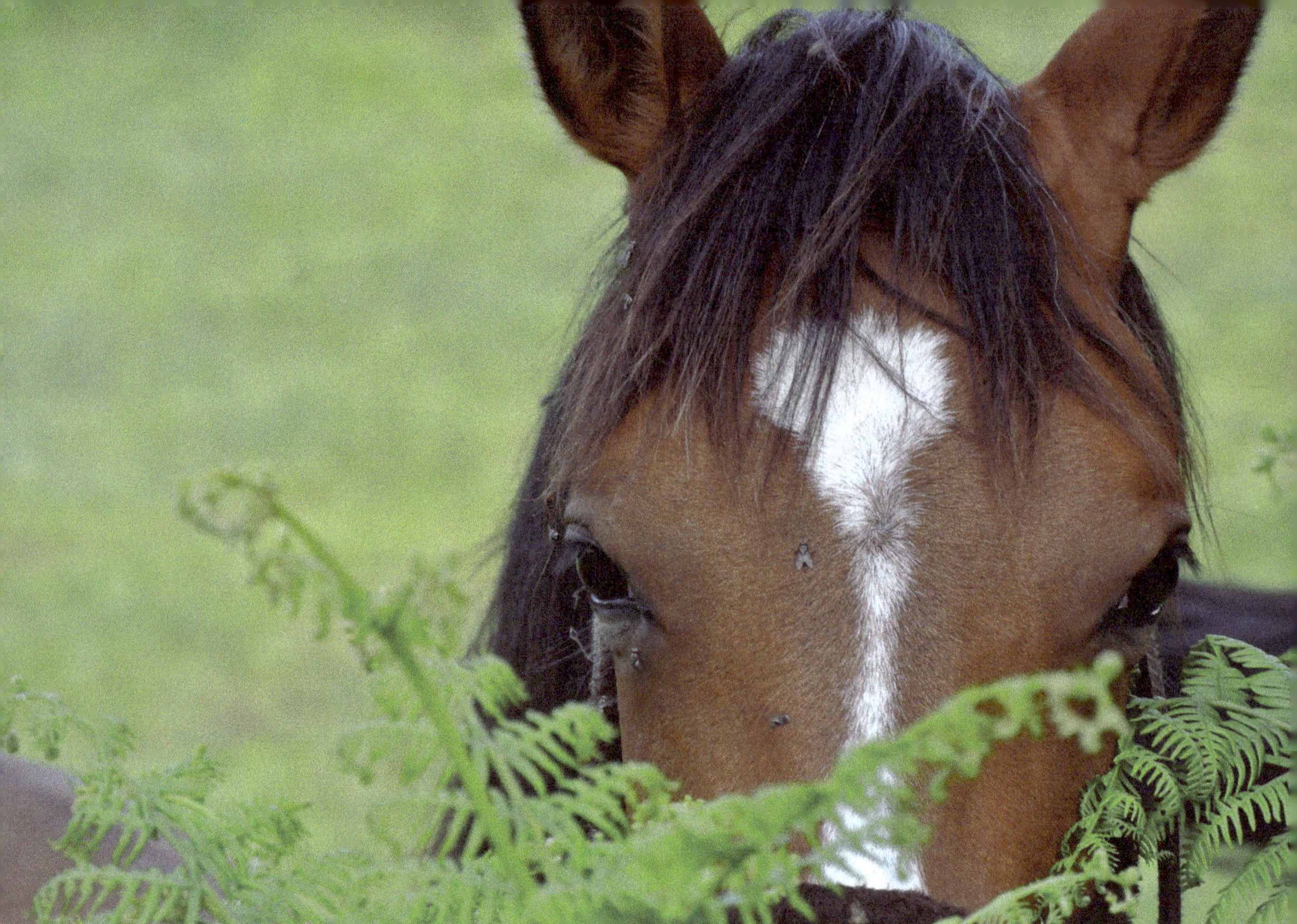

The Heart Path

In this second volume, *Heart of Photography*, we start with this inner teaching of the intersection of the phenomenal world with our ordinary lives. We approach it in two ways simultaneously. Firstly, we explore regions of the phenomenal world; based on Chögyam Trungpa's teachings, we call these regions *fields of perception*. In conventional terms, these correlate with subject or topics, but we address them with a contemplative slant that takes into account all that we practiced in Level One. Examples include names like Flowers and Weeds, and Zen Aesthetics.

You can see just by their names that these fields are not ordinary topics. The field is not called "Flowers," but "Flowers and Weeds." This points to the fact that we do not assume flowers are more beautiful or worth photographing than weeds. A field like Zen Aesthetics draws more directly on various East Asian contemplative traditions.

In this way, we explore the endless phenomenal world through specific fields of perception. We do this for practical reasons: to help us focus on one area, and because the phenomenal world does not just manifest in general, it expresses itself in its own various ways.

In this level of study, Level Two, the way of practice is more fluid and interactive than with the elements presented in *Looking and Seeing*—color, light, and so forth. These were elements of the visual as the visual. Now we are exploring the experience of the phenomenal world. This perceptual world is more holistic, including all that manifests. Because of this, there are overlaps between the fields of perception. For example, another field of perception is Ordinary/Personal World, which can overlap with the field of Impressionism. This mutual infusion is a lesson in the way of the phenomenal world, which is our lived world. Our world, and that experience, is saturated with multidimensional visual radiance.

Secondly, we explore the inner aspects of the various fields of perception, which is essential if your intention is to practice as a deep contemplative.

What does that mean? To approach this practice with the same intention as that for the meditation practices: seeking insight and liberation, in short, what the meditative traditions call an enlightenment path. If your intention is to transform your life into being there for your real life—the contemplative intention—then you have come to a good place.

In *Heart of Photography*, however, this intention is not necessary if it doesn't call to you. Not everyone has to engage Nalanda Miksang as a deep contemplative practice. You can practice with a contemplative influence and orientation. We made this text so it can work with you where you are, with your many interests and intentions.

For instance, your intention may be to make great photographic images. If that is the case, you have come to a good place. Here you can have a great experience and make great images. That is contemplative photography. These teachings and practices provide a strong perceptual foundation for photographic practice, including direct visual templates for photos. As well, if you post-process your images, with Nalanda Miksang your work will be reduced in technical terms and enhanced in artistic terms. Everyone who practices Miksang has a magic card up their sleeve: ordinary magic.

If you aren't looking for liberation but simply want to enhance your life experience, following the joy of photography as a way to the joy of life, you have also come to a good place. Here you will find this ordinary joy, and your life experience will be enriched.

The contemplative practices are ways of enhancing natural openings to being alive and lively. At a minimum, they feel good. But more importantly, they can change your life stream orientation toward a life worth living, which is not different than simply living. You go from adding complexity, to trying to make your life worthwhile, to simply living and appreciating that. It's a win–win–win situation. If your interest is in making brilliant images, this helps. If you interest is personal joy, this helps. If your interest is deep meaning, this helps. If your interest is in all three, you can have your cake, eat it, and enjoy it, too. There is no comparison or judgment between photographers, Buddhists, yogis, or ordinary Joes here. No one is ahead or behind. How could you be ahead or behind your own life?

Regardless of what brings you here, it is useful to know that this practice offers the inner teachings of the inner teachings: insight. Playing off the reality of visual practice, Miksang includes both sight and insight. We develop sight in Level One, in the *Looking and Seeing* text. Sight comes from outer practices that open to inner practices; here the basic elements of the visual—color, surface, etc.—the making of an equivalent image, open to the context of pure visual experience. How the context ties into the way light gives meaning to a visual scene.

Headed deeper into our practice, what is at stake in practices that open to inner contemplative insight practice is going from simply seeing something as a possibility (sight) to actual realization (insight). In other words, can you shift your life from habitual pattern to ongoing lively engagement? For instance, if you approach this practice mainly for the photography, at some point you will have thousands and thousands of brilliant images, most of them destined to the darkness of a digital void. The images are important, but are the images the ultimate point? The same is true for experience: practicing Nalanda Miksang, you will have many wonderful experiences—experiences come and go. That is the nature of experiences: at best they become memories. Great experiences are important and life enhancing, but are they the ultimate point?

What lasts is insight. Insight is transformation. Insight is not the same as experience; it is a deep and embodied understanding. It is not knowledge as an accumulation of information, but deeply knowing the real, leading to realization. This is a different way of knowing, and it makes a difference.

With this orientation toward insight, we can explore these teachings through each field of perception. It is good to reflect on the inner meaning of each field of perception. What does it mean to you? What is coming through your experience that is more than your experience? What wisdom is conveyed through the reality of this experience? For example, in Impressionism we ask, "Why are we drawn to this field of perception?" We suggest it resonates with the manifest truth of our experience: all of our experience is impressionistic. Until you photograph Impressionism yourself, though, this remains mainly theoretical.

Photographing Impressionism, feeling these questions deep inside, the practice of this field of perception begins to resonate as insight. We can really feel how the way of the phenomenal world is the way of our experienced world. We begin to connect with the heart truth of our fundamental, ongoing life situation. We can live the heart truth of our heart situation. This is where the inner heart of a Nalanda Miksang contemplative thrives.

As you synchronize with the phenomenal world, your realizations will help you flow with the phenomenal world, which becomes your everyday life experience. Full of actual insight, you can let go, opening to constant adventure. From this place, you make brilliant images, to share this reality with others.

Liberation Through Everyday Life

This is when Nalanda Miksang becomes a real contemplative dharma practice—an accessible, daily way to connect with insight and liberation. You just need to look and see to enter the heart of photography, and the heart of your life.

You can arrive at connection through the basics: red as red, or a red rose. You can make a heartfelt connection through the change of seasons, which mark your life seasons. You can connect through intimacy: being touched and in touch. But it is always now. The only now is now. It can be many ways, but it can only be your way through the ways of the Way.

Nalanda Miksang photography is a very minor way, but a skillful one. Photography is a perfect contemporary contemplative way. It is a public medium for the global situation. It is like how brush and ink were used in traditional Zen and Taoist ways. It is a strong, skillful means for an enlightenment intervention, which is the deep purpose of this practice. Our big intention is changing the culture for the good.

In these times and circumstances, through Nalanda Miksang photography, we can find a minor way to the Way: The Way of Seeing.

You might think that something extraordinary will happen to you when you discover magic. Something extra-ordinary does happen. You simply find yourself in the realm of utter reality, complete and thorough reality.

**—Chögyam Trungpa, *Shambhala,
Sacred Path of the Warrior***

PART ONE

HEART OF THE HEART

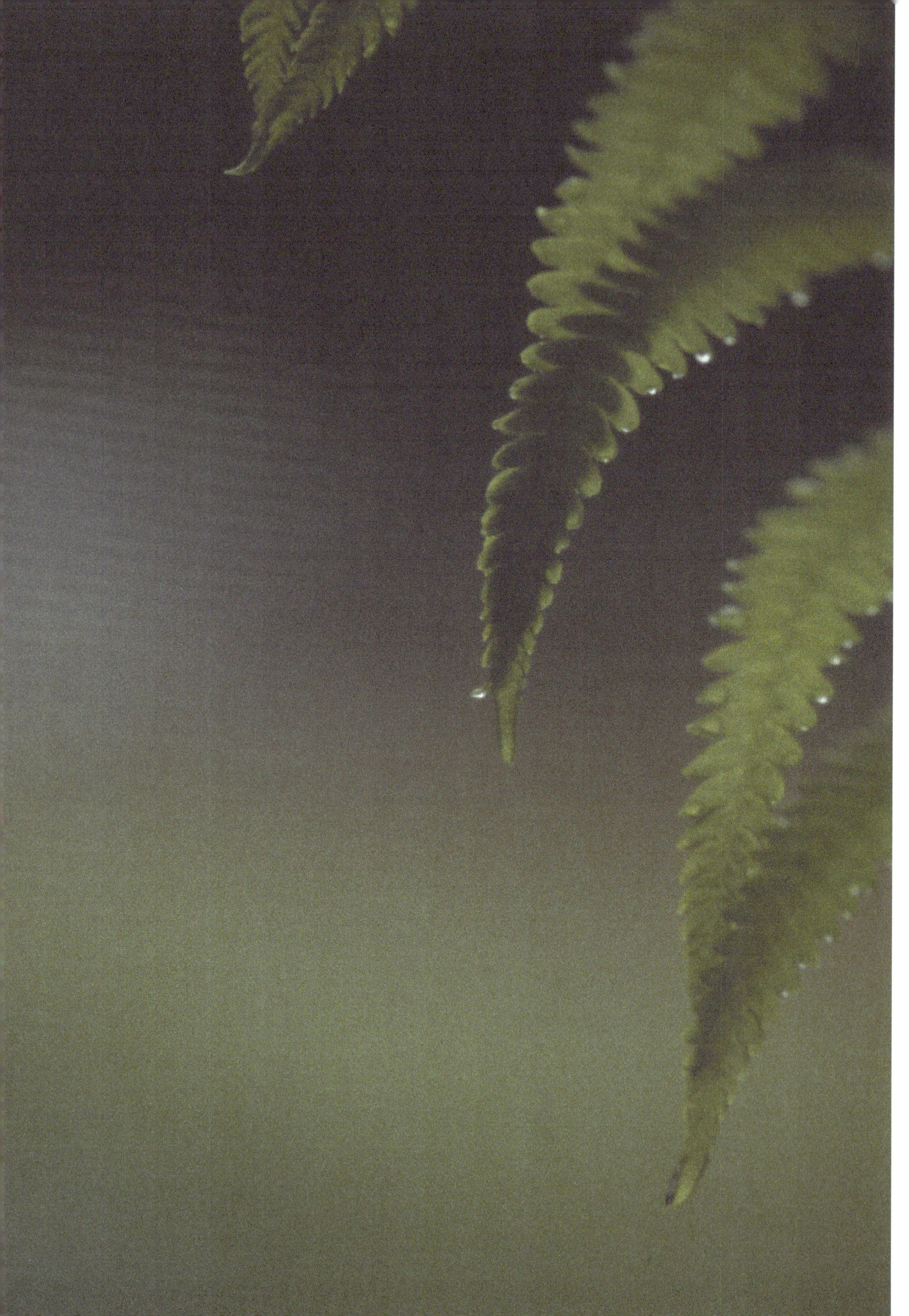

Resonance And Relationship

Contemplative view provides ground and overview. But contemplative photography is focused on practice, which combines experience and insight. Before we take on the contemplative photography assignments, let's look at experience. By experience we mean the sensibility of experience, which is the feeling of something beyond what we can get while being fully present with an immediate experience. It is an understanding of interconnectedness we have immediately and deeply in any situation, but which can be hard to articulate because it is both precise and vast at the same time.

A common analogy in Zen is to talk about the finger pointing to the moon—the idea that even to discuss it cannot quite capture being fully present. But images can communicate some of this energy. Something about a drop of water at the tip of a fern after a rainstorm is delicate beyond the fact. The simple moment of seeing a wizened old Chinese grandmother hold hands with her small and sweet-faced granddaughter signifies way beyond the fact. Seeing the sunlit red highlights in your daughter's dark hair that show both her Irish and Chinese heritage is a heart moment beyond the fact.

In an absolute sense, this heartbeat of the phenomenal world is what we call *resonance*. We often experience it in our lives on a more relative level through relationship. This is the shift from visual to vision, which is the shift to Level Two.

In Level Two, in the heart of photography, we are touched by being in touch. We relate to deeper resonance through relationship. This is what it is to be a contemplative, which is not different from simply being human.

In fact, the most obvious assignment in Level Two for seeing the resonance of relationship is in People and Other Sentient Beings. We are used to both having and acknowledging relationships with other beings. We will explore the energy of these explicit relationships more in that assignment.

However, a relationship, and the resonance inherent to relationship, can happen between a flower and a rock, between a dry riverbed and an acacia bush, between a hammock and a table. Flashes of perception in Level Two often turn out to be about two dots relating to each other in the space, making a complete dot of their relationship.

The subject of Nalanda Miksang photographs is never the topic. In other words, when someone asks Miriam what kind of photography she shoots, they mean subjects—landscape, portraits, etc. But the subject here, even with assignments oriented around more identifiable things in Level Two, is always this resonance, always the relationship at play, always the connection between, which is, in fact, not a connection but the actual co-emergence of the Miksang photographer and the situation itself.

Resonance is a momentary experience in which you feel directly, and to a great depth, how meaningful your life and all of life is; the sense that beyond ongoing life circumstances, there must be more within all this going on. In this resonance we sense that there is a beyond that is not somewhere else. We feel a connection to something inexpressible in what is expressed. We know our life is meaningful, but we may not know exactly how to express this. But we want to.

Nalanda Miksang Level Two images embody the resonance of this heartfelt expression. They are heart images. By this we do not mean sappy or sentimental but deeply resonating heart feeling. While the topic most relating to resonance through relationship is People and Other Sentient Beings, there's also an affinity between Nalanda Miksang and another traditional contemplative art, one which deeply expresses the more felt and sometimes invisible resonance we have with all of life, including rocks, water, and airplanes. That other art form is Haiku.

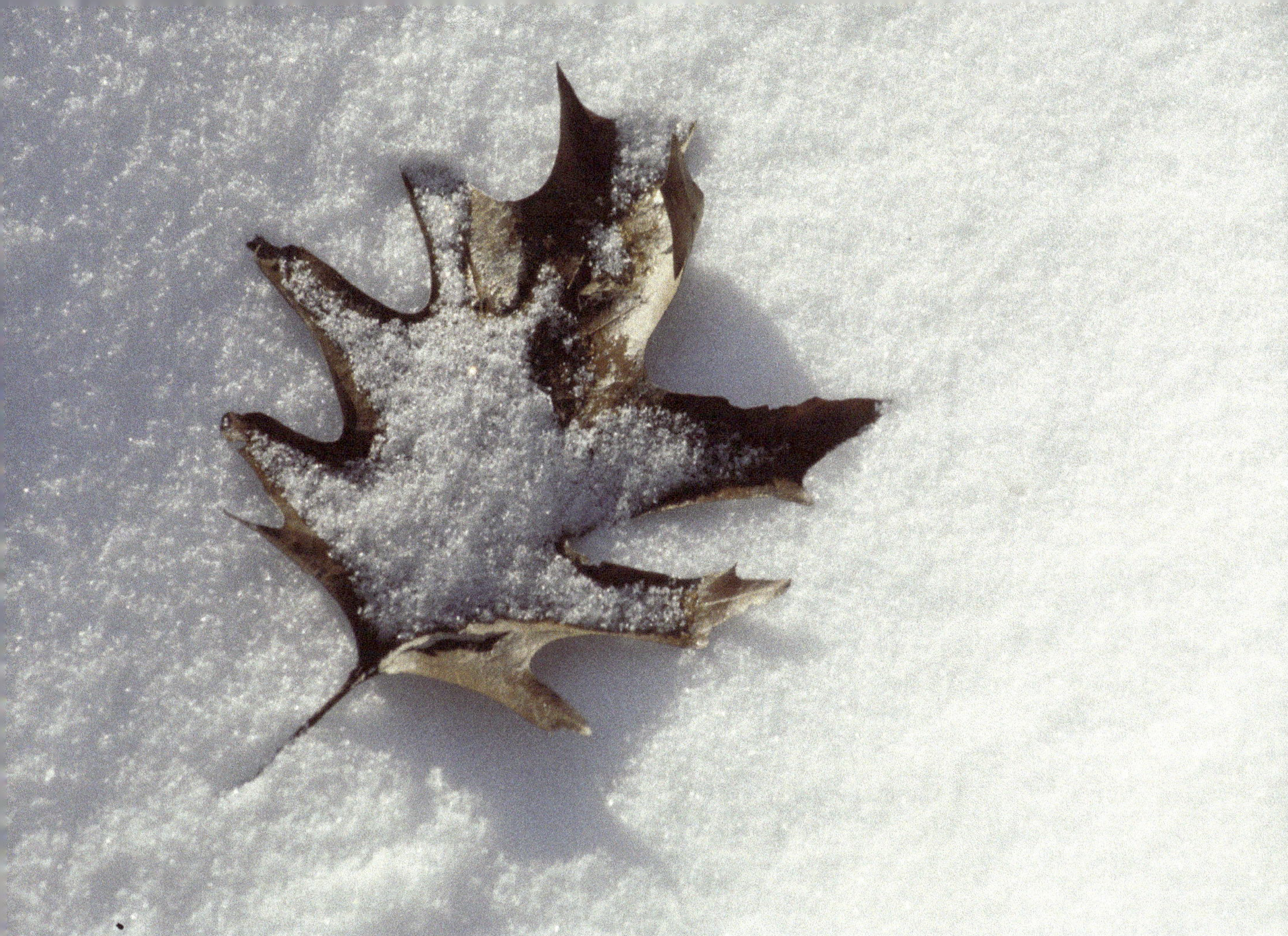

Haiku And Resonance

The art that is closest to the practice of contemplative photography is haiku. Haiku is a contemplative literary and poetic form that provides a written equivalent of a clear or true perception.

Traditionally, the pedagogical form for this practice is seventeen syllables in a five/seven/five sequence. Haiku should also include a reference to the season and nature. It is a wonderful example of the precision of resonance because it presents what seemingly cannot be said in only seventeen syllables.

The source of what we think of as haiku today is Basho. Basho was an eleventh-century Japanese haiku master who shifted haiku from a literary practice to a contemplative practice. Basho wrote what is not only one of the best known haiku but also the most decisive haiku. "Old Pond" is the haiku of haikus: the haiku that embodies the way of haiku. Translations into English of "Old Pond" are plentiful. In fact, there is a book called *One Hundred Frogs* that collects one hundred English translations.

From this collection, let's consider two:

Old Pond/ A frog jumps in/ the sound of water
An Ancient Pond/ a frog jumps in/ a deep resonance

The first translation is stronger; it leaves open the possibilities of resonance. In general, the contemplative approach is to leave some space or openness. Ironically, although the first translation is more direct and sense oriented, its lack of interpretation is part of its power. The second translation is too conceptual. It is trying to make its point, whereas true haiku only points to the point. However, for teaching purposes, the second translation is informative, particularly the lines "Ancient Pond" and "a deep resonance."

What is the difference between "the Old Pond" and "An Ancient Pond"? The Old Pond is primordial, a time before time; and fathomless, a depth that can never be plumbed. It is vast, an expanse that can never be found; and inexhaustible, a richness that can never run out.

On the other hand, An Ancient Pond resonates with the Old Pond. It is the resonance itself. This is the shift from primordial to aboriginal. It is the shift from universe to human sentience. It is the shift from the expressible to the inexpressible, through and within the expressible. It is the contemplative.

In the contemplative traditions there is an orientation toward the ancients, those who brought forth birthright human wisdom and practices. We refer to them as *perception warriors*. In this text, we will contemplate some of the perception warriors who are resources for Nalanda Miksang. As Soetsu

Yanagi notes in *The Unknown Craftsman*, "They saw; before all else, they saw. They were able to see. Ancient mysteries flew from this well-spring of seeing."

In the Shambhala tradition, we also honor those who bring forth the primordial understanding of basic goodness into the expression of the enlightened society. This is the ancient pond. Now let's explore resonance.

Consider the way the haiku is structured and how this contemplative expression manifests. Just how old is that pond? Timeless. How deep is that pond? Fathomless. This timeless fathomlessness is our ground, our basic space, the source of clear perception. Within that ground, that space, something happens. A frog jumps in. That is the specific of this haiku, but we get the point behind the point: first nothing is happening, a rich open space, then something happens. In Nalanda Miksang, we call this happening the *flash of perception*.

Then comes "a deep resonance." There are many direct and also subtle points here. A subtle point is that this is both simultaneous and in some sense retrospective. The resonance is not completely different or separated from the event of the "jumps in"—there is a simultaneous time event: a happening. Also, the resonance is deep. Again: how deep is that pond?

For a direct point, let's look at the structure of the pond. The play of surface is simultaneously the play of surface and depth: the surface of a depth and the depth of a surface. This is the structure of resonance and the possibility of appreciation: the simultaneous play of the ordinary and the profound.

The resonance is a happening that is also a trace. As it happens, it simultaneously disappears. The ripples spread out across the surface, and they simultaneously dissolve back into the surface—the surface of the depth. The sound punctuates the space of silence as it returns to silence. It simultaneously appears and disappears.

This is a trace of happening as a happening. It is a traceless trace. As Zen Master Dogen put it: "It is a traceless trace that goes on forever." This haiku hints that the whole of our phenomenal world—our experience—is a traceless trace that goes on forever. If it is traceless, how do we know it happens? Through expression, through experience. Through trusting life. Through feeling resonance.

Resonance is the way of this traceless trace, a happening that pierces the deep play, which is both the surface of a depth and a depth of a surface. Resonance is always the resonance of resonance. Resonance expresses a beyond that is not somewhere else. Resonance records expressions of the inexpressible. We cannot quite grasp or express experience—it is a slip-slide tip of the tongue—but in our heart of hearts, we experience what we experience and we know what we know.

Resonance is simply a way of saying what we know in our heart of hearts: there is more to life than the same old, same old; that our life matters and that life is an opening. Our life matters in ways we cannot quite grasp or sum up in so many words. If we cannot quite grasp it, there are ways with expression. There are many ways of expression. Just a touch is an expression. Just a look is an expression.

Nalanda Miksang is a photographic way to express deep resonance.

When we tune into resonance, we truly tune in. We realize that we are always already tuned in. We are always already in tune. We are in harmony. We are resonating. Being in tune, we can express in a harmonious way, a peaceful way. When we are in tune, we make contemplative images that are harmonious and peaceful.

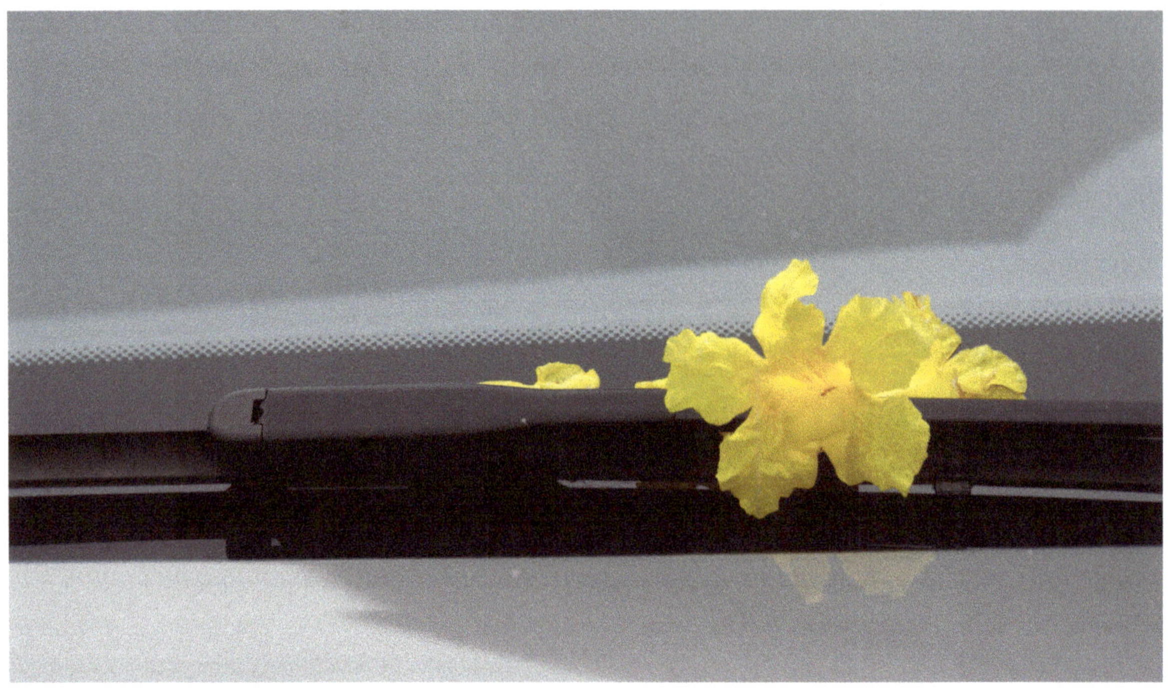

The Ordinary Magic Of Nowness

The Shambhala way of ordinary magic is more direct and pragmatic than the Chinese and Japanese contemplative aesthetic. It is more an on-the-spot enlightenment: we simply connect with ordinary magic and trust it. Here, magic is not some special power of transforming things into other things, like lead into gold. Instead, magic is seeing that the world is always already gold. The phenomenal world, our lived experience, is rich, vibrant, and intrinsically beautiful. We simply need to connect with that on the spot, which is easily said and often not so easily done. But it is, in fact, there, regardless of how much we struggle with it.

This points to a deep view of the phenomenal world. The key to both the view and practice of ordinary magic is nowness. Nalanda Miksang uses the exercises of Synchronization and the Flash of Perception to pop us into already existing nowness.

It is important to not confuse nowness with immediacy, the immediate content of the current circumstance. We especially need to not reduce nowness to something that can be measured, like clock time. This is delicate and subtle, because we only connect with nowness through current circumstances. Nowness is a constant newness; the only now is now. Nowness is the suspension of time within time. Nowness is the timeless moment. We could contemplate nowness the same way we did "Old Pond." Nowness is also a depth and dimension beyond measure. Simultaneously, this now is none other than right now. To support our contemplation, we can look to Chögyam Trungpa's presentation of nowness in *Shambhala, Sacred Path of the Warrior*:

> *To rediscover nowness you have to look back, back to where you came from, back to the original state . . . it is looking back into your own mind, to before history began, before thinking began, before thought ever occurred. When you connect with this original ground then you are never confused by the illusions of past and future. You are able to rest continuously in nowness.*

Immediate thought and all of human history are not the issue of newness. On the contrary, they issue from nowness. Nowness is an original state, before thinking began, the original ground. In the Nalanda Miksang teachings, we present this original mind state in two ways: 1) the intrinsic resource of clear seeing, and 2) the space before the flash of perception.

First of all, what Nalanda Miksang calls the intrinsic resource of clear seeing is what Shambhala calls basic goodness. Like basic goodness, Nalanda Miksang holds that clear seeing is our birthright, so all Nalanda Miksang practice and expression draw on that capacity.

At a more relative and practical level, this teaching of nowness helps us work with the momentum of our ongoing situations and states of mind. This nowness state is before and beyond our history and thoughts. It is before and beyond our storylines, interpretations, discursive thinking, past and future; our opinions of what is beautiful

or not beautiful, what is worth seeing and not worth seeing, what makes a great photographic image, and so forth. Nowness is both before and beyond the views and practices of conventional photography. Even creative and innovative approaches that break conventional rules are still ruled by the notion that there are rules. Nowness is before and beyond rules.

Nowness is before and beyond all of this, yet not somewhere else. It is a clear and free space from which we make images. Those images embody an aesthetic that is free, clear, simple, direct, and resonant. Here we see directly that Nalanda Miksang practice is a practice of nowness, with Shambhala views and principles. We find the depth of reality in nowness (what is before and beyond) through the now moment (what is happening in this present moment).

As we explore the idea of beyond, we encounter a depth that sustains resonance. This is the spontaneous space of causes and conditions. Chögyam Trungpa frequently used mirrors and reflections to describe this resonance in *Shambhala, Sacred Path of the Warrior*:

> *This original state of being can be likened to a primordial or cosmic mirror. By primordial we mean unconditioned, not caused by any circumstances . . . this unconditioned state is likened to a primordial mirror, because like a mirror, it is willing to reflect anything . . . the frame of reference of the cosmic mirror is quite vast, and it is free from any bias.*

In the practice of direct perception, we are free of bias, because the phenomenal world is free of bias. The color red does not care about your state of mind and whether or not you like it. Red is red. It is that simple, and that profound.

The key point is to find nowness, right now. It is not speculation or philosophy, so how do we find it? Shambhala teachings encourage us to contact nowness in the present moment through relaxation. Just relax and let things manifest as they manifest.

Here relaxation is not time off, or, as Chögyam Trungpa Rinpoche says, "flopping." Rather, relaxation is time on, as in the sense of good timing, being on time, being there with the there. Being there together. Then there is no separation or struggle, only relaxation and appreciation. We suddenly find there is lots of time in the now moment because the now moment is the timeless moment.

Secondly, this understanding of timeless time applies to the Flash of Perception exercise in a strong way. Often new practitioners confuse the flash of perception with conventional time. They are concerned about hanging onto or remembering the instant of the flash of perception. This causes a struggle because it is mistaken view. In fact, the flash of perception suspends conventional time in two ways: 1) it is timeless time, and 2) it is the phenomenal flow of experience.

It is timeless time, so there is lots of time. Indeed, this is the time of equanimity, duration, composure, and relaxation. There is an opening. You just stay with it, hang out with it, relax into it. This is contemplative time.

This is also equanimity time. Relaxation time is a time of composure. The composition of Nalanda Miksang images comes from the nowness composure of space and time. They are equivalents

of, isomorphic with, this nowness. The images reflect the composure of nowness and transmit the stillness and electricity of that particular, specific, now moment of nowness.

Does that feel too complex? Some of us need complexity, some of us prefer simplicity. The more direct way is to just trust the magic. Something happens. Go with that happening. The result will be a magic image.

More on the cosmic mirror from Chögyam Trungpa, *Shambhala, Sacred Path of the Warrior*:

The way to look back and experience the state of being of the cosmic mirror is simply to relax . . . you take an unbiased approach. You let things be as they are, without judgment, and in that way you yourself learn to be, to express your existence directly and nonconceptually. That is the ideal state of relaxation, which allows you to experience the nowness of the cosmic mirror. In fact, it is already the experience of the cosmic mirror.

This primordial mirror reflects the magic of the phenomenal world. Cosmic mirror relaxation shows itself as everyday perception. There is a spark to simply experiencing, and that spark is ordinary magic. The cosmic mirror is the same as its reflection and resonance. That is how it works. The just-that, just-so of salt and pepper shakers, transformed as a just-so, just-now phenomenal display, resonates. Chögyam Trungpa presents the phenomenal ordinary-ness in this passage from *Sacred Path of the Warrior*:

If you are able to relax—relax into a cloud

by looking at it, relax into a drop of rain and experience its genuineness, you can see the unconditionality of reality, which remains very simply in things as they are, very simply . . . to establish ties to your world, so that each perception becomes unique. It is to see with heart, so what is invisible to the eye becomes visible as the living magic of reality. There may be thousands and billions of perceptions, but they are still one . . . seeing one drop of water can be seeing all water . . . whether you care to communicate with it or not, the magical strength and wisdom of reality is always there . . . By relaxing the mind, you can connect with that primordial ground which is completely pure and simple. Out of that, through the medium of your perceptions, you can discover magic. "
. . . You actually can connect your own intrinsic wisdom with a sense of a greater wisdom or vision beyond you.

This is the deep and everyday practice of Nalanda Miksang. We trust the magic. The magic manifests. Therefore, the images are magic.

We will present a practical way to connect with ordinary magic later, in the Drala assignments.

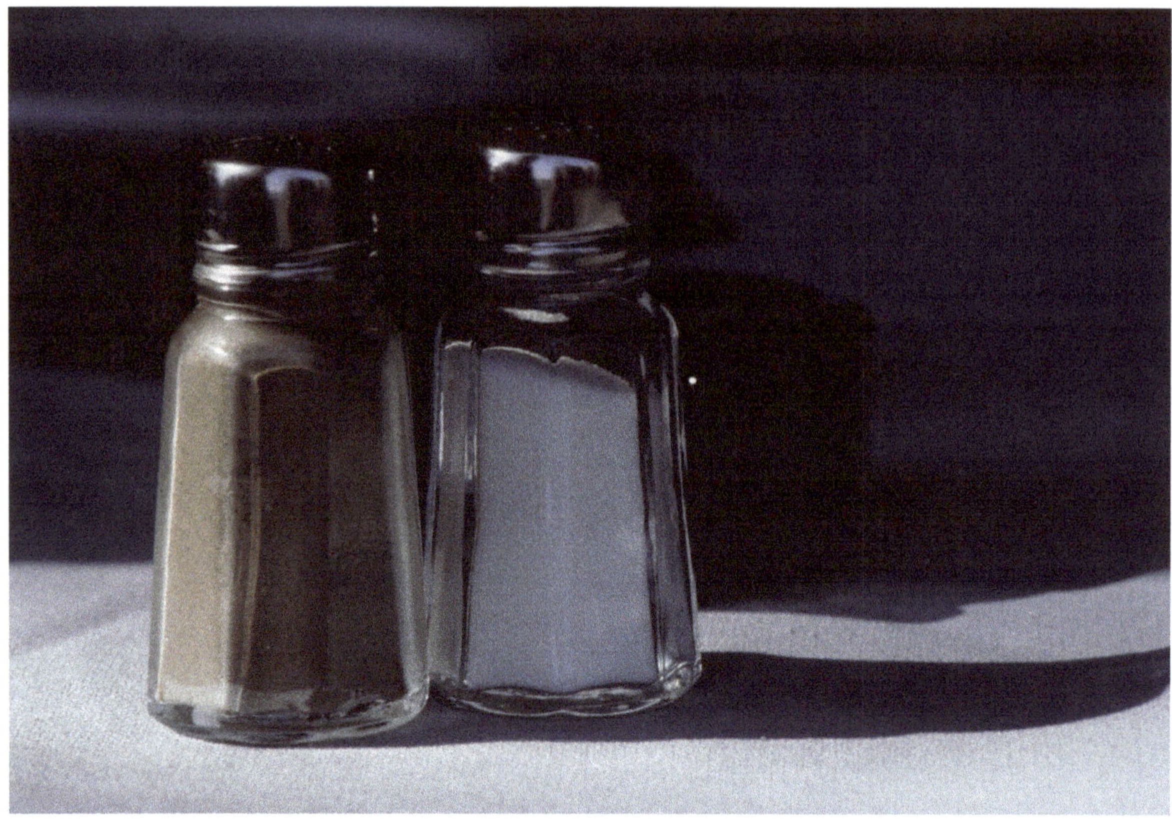

Dot-In-Space As Resonance

In our first volume, *Looking and Seeing*, we explored dot-in-space as both an assignment and a deeper contemplation. In Level Two, we go even deeper with dot-in-space, because it is perhaps the key teaching of Nalanda Miksang.

First, let's deepen our understanding of what dot-in-space really is. In Level One, it can appear to simply be a trick, a gimmick: a thing in space, something inside something else; a way to visually parrot foreground and background.

However, dot-in-space is also the form of perception itself. Perception is noticing a figure on the ground. We always see something, and that something is a something, rather than nothing, and something that is not something else. Dot-in-space also reminds us that we see something in the foreground against something which is perceived as the background. It is both unique and connected.

Going deeper, there is a co-emergence of the flash of perception and dot-in-space. A flash of perception opens perception itself, wherein perception appears out of non-perception. So there is a space or gap before, yet simultaneous with, the flash of perception. As an event, the flash of perception itself is like a dot-in-space. There is not just resonance, there is resonance of resonance.

Taking the visual form of dot-in-space further, we can also explore the contemplative aesthetic which embodies, or is an equivalent of, this dot-in-space perception form. One way to do this would be to switch senses for a moment. When you strike a tuning fork against a surface, the sound energy continues long after you cease hearing it. This is resonance, and the kind of natural resonance of an equivalent image transmitting deep resonance. Everything is constantly connected and exchanging; contemplative aesthetic recognizes the need for space to feel the energy of the dot. Resonance naturally informs contemplative aesthetic, which can be simply stated as the intersection of space, simplicity, and purity. Chögyam Trungpa presented this manifestation of dot-in-space as magic perception directly: "When we draw down the power and depth of vastness into a single perception, then we are discovering and invoking magic."

The synchronization view, motivation, intention, and orientation to the phenomenal world are what stabilize you to invest in this "draw(ing) down of the power and depth." The stabilization is just being available as there. Being there allows and invites the there to be there. The draw invites the flash of perception. And the flash of perception draws down power, depth, and vastness, aka the Old Pond. This drawing down is gathered in a single perception: a dot-in-space that finds its expression as an equivalent image.

There is something not explicitly stated in the Chögyam Trungpa quote that needs to be articulated. This drawing down of the power and depth of vastness is the primordial situation that also *includes* the draw. It is the draw before the draw. The power and depth of vastness is the primordial situation. It is a way of presenting basic goodness in which basic goodness is active, which is what draws us in.

One way we express this sense of active interconnection in Nalanda Miksang is to say we become a lightning rod for the flash of perception—an electrical, natural draw.

Our Nalanda Miksang practice is a deep resonance art. It is very ordinary and available. Something stops our mind and enters our heart response: a dewdrop on a blade of grass is a dewdrop at the center of the universe. Keep this in mind and heart as we enter the Level Two assignments, starting with Dot-in-Space, where *Looking and Seeing* left off.

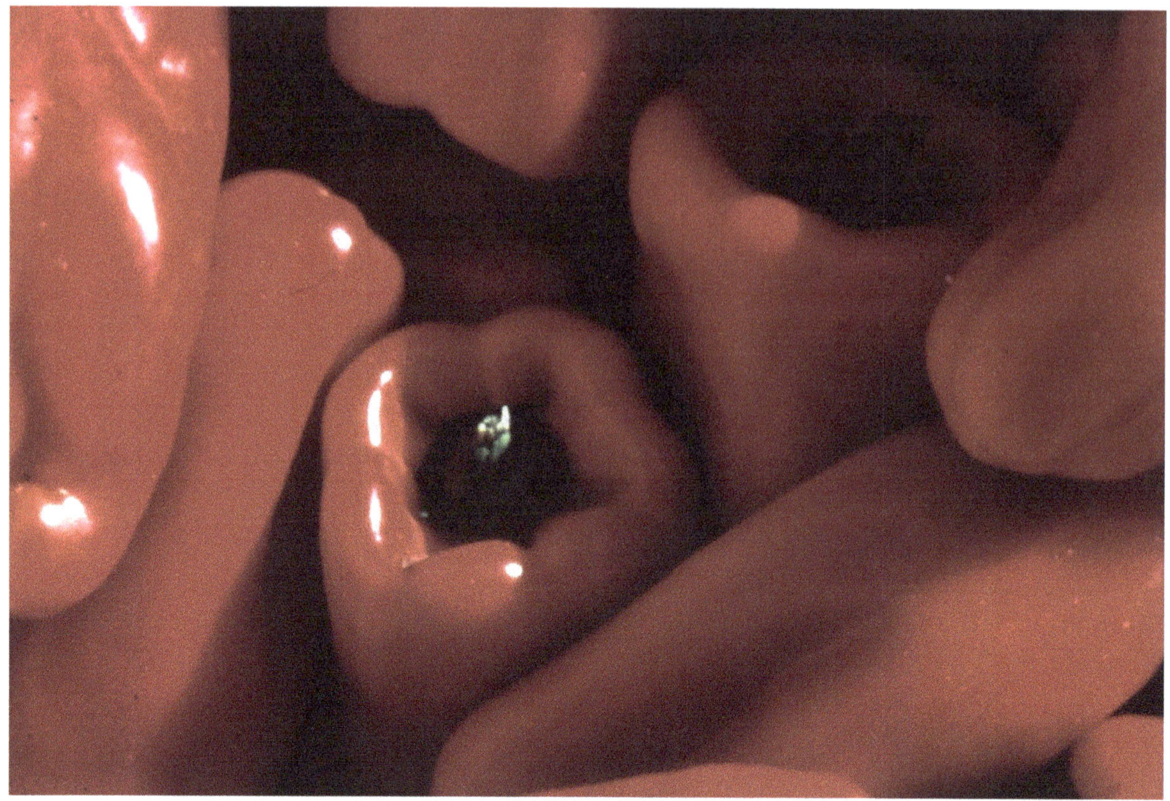

Assignment One: Bridging Level One To Level Two

In Level One, we worked with the basic visual forms: color, light, surface, space, and dot-in-space. We explored each of these visual elements on their own and made direct connections with each one. The Level One approach is somewhat formal. It can feel very static. Often our visual focus is on the foreground, with the background as a neutral visual support. Generally, we find in Level Two that every visual perception includes some or all of these visual forms of Level One. Level Two synchronizes these elements into even richer clear perceptions. The full engagement of Level Two has the sense and sensibilities of heart and magic.

For example, this image of red peppers. Here we have all the elements sustaining the perception of the red peppers: color, play of light and highlights, surface. In addition, we have the smooth skin and the contours of the form, the perceptual focus as dot-in-space, and the rest of the color and form as a space.

One of the features of Level Two is that it is contextualized. You are back into the perceived world, and you recognize what you are seeing—in this case, red peppers. In Level One we find a lot of decontextualization. When viewing Level One images, people often ask, "What is it?" Now we recognize the object, but not as an object, more as a phenomenal expression of that object. The world manifests this moment through our photos, rather than an image being a static container of things.

Those who have worked through the first book in the *Way of Seeing* series, *Looking and Seeing,* will have already encountered dot-in-space in a Level One way. We end Level One and also begin Level Two with a Dot-in-Space assignment because it is good place to transition, and also a key teaching.

These levels of perception are not static; they interfuse in diverse ways. In an absolute sense, there are no levels. We use the structure of levels to clarify perception and the path of perception into the way of seeing. In this case, we can actually do a

Level One assignment, Dot-in-Space, in a Level Two way. Let's begin by leaning on the familiarity with perceptual form of Dot-in-Space from Level One to leverage a way into the sensibility of Level Two.

The Level One way with Dot-in-Space works with formal qualities, a basic perceptual gestalt of a thing with a background. In Level Two, the content of our photos are more things, less formal or abstract: a flower, a duck, a salt and pepper shaker, a person, a hand, and so on. But we do not revert to documenting things, we still see them in a perceptual way.

For example, instead of taking a photograph of a complete sunflower, we might see the top petals of the sunflower as being more like flames. So now it is both the sunflower and something else.

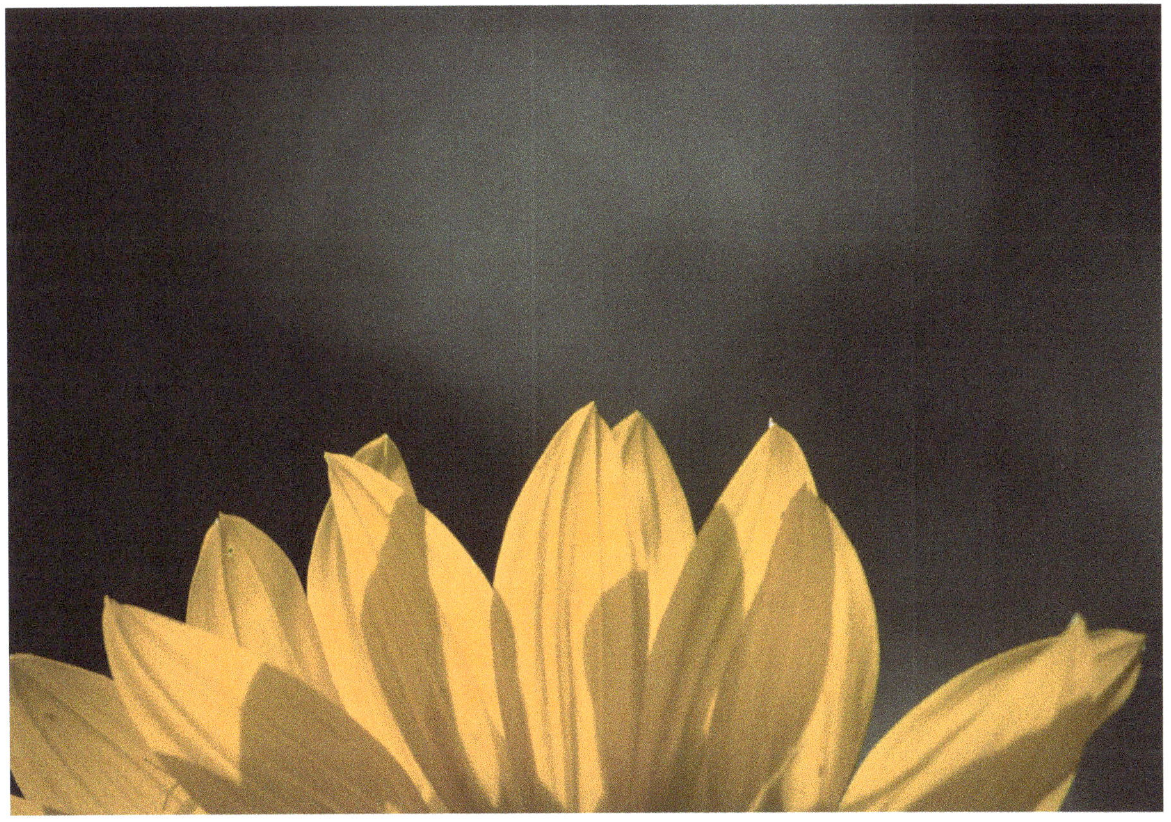

We also have a flamingo, which is more than a flamingo—the momentary manifestation of shape, color, and light in water.

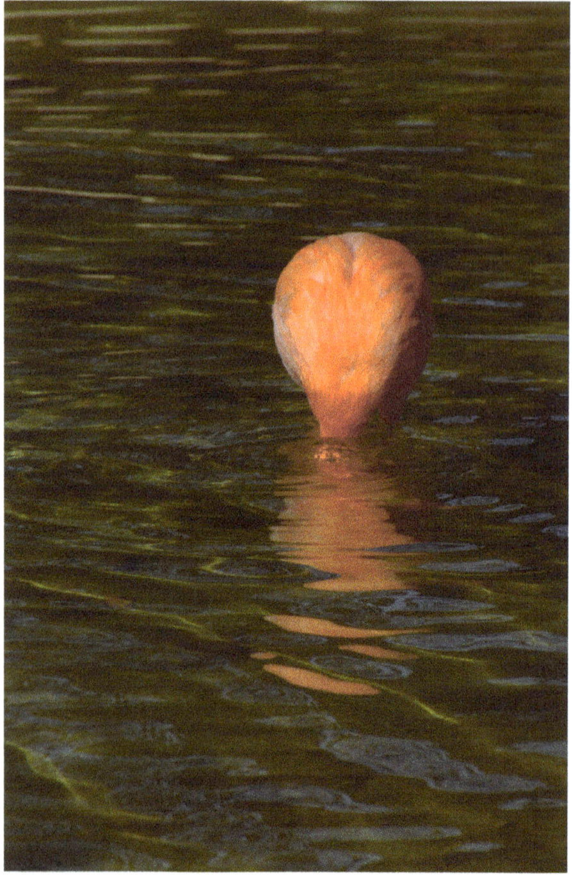

In this perceptual event, the dot (the top fringe petals of a sunflower) is more than its identity. The space, here the background, also has an aesthetic: it is an infused space. The background is not just a support; it is also a feature. In full Level Two Dot-in-Space images, both the foreground and background are expressive. There is less formal distinction between the dot and the space—they resonate.

These images express a meaningful play of surface and depth. For example, a duck is its own expression of a dot-in-space, but the background can also be impressionistic water space. A flower perception can present itself in space, but the background blur of the color space itself has its own energy. In these relationships between dot-in-space and space, there is a sense of being both complementary and complete; a hint of overallness, in which the foreground and the background are both aesthetic and pleasing. Here the foreground and background ground each other in a resonant way, in the fullness of Level Two perception and expression.

This kind of dynamic relationship between space and dot-in-space manifests throughout all the Level Two fields of perception. A flower can express itself in many ways: a formal way, a sensuous way, a Zen way, an impressionistic way, and so forth. In all of these ways, the flower anchors and also displays the field of perception. We can see how a deepening understanding of dot-in-space remains one of the fundamental teachings of Nalanda Miksang.

Your assignment now is to photograph Dot-in-Space in a Level Two way, as we have been describing. There's no particular topic; your content can run the gamut of all the assignments. Start out with that basic formal approach of noticing something (a dot) against a background (space). Then see the contemplative aesthetics of this way: simplicity, purity and space. You will see the phenomenal blend with form, and feel the heart of perception and the way of seeing.

PART ONE: HEART OF THE HEART

PART TWO:

IMPRESSIONISM

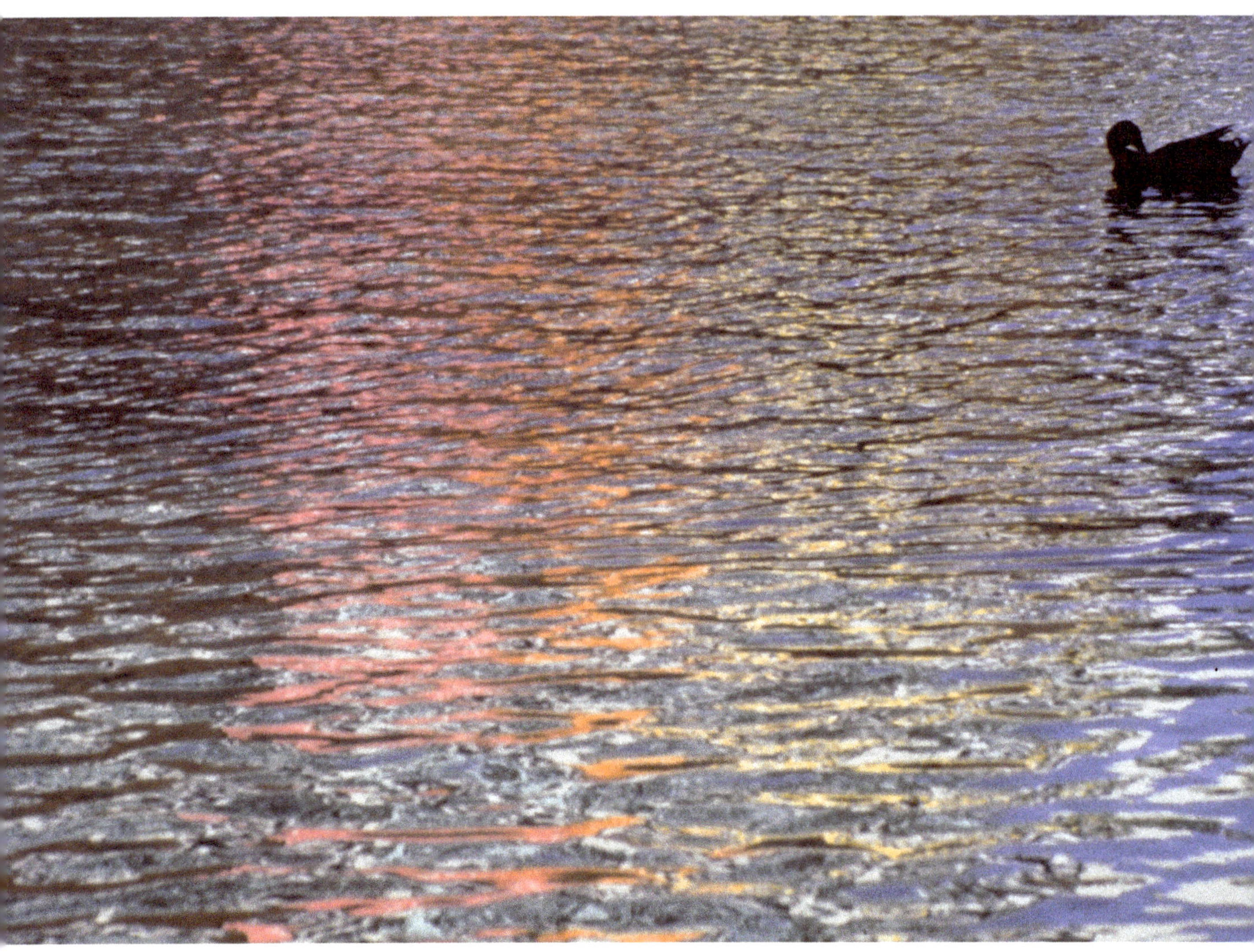

Impressionism actually consists of at least four different sub-assignments. We present those first, then offer chances for deeper contemplation and study of this rich topic.

Impressionism Assignment I: Water

The first assignment for Impressionism is reflections in water, something which held a certain heart fascination for Monet. What is it about water that both invites and lends itself to the Impressionist vision? We could start with a simple question from childhood: What color is water? Conceptually, one might answer "blue" or "clear," but Monet's paintings display an impressionistic fantasia of colors. In them, we experience water as a space reflecting everything: flowers, trees, cathedrals, water lilies, a Japanese bridge, and more. In these reflections, everything is there, but in a different manifestation than we usually see. Water manifests in a kaleidoscope of colors, a swirl of line and form, because it reflects the phenomenal world.

To begin your own personal exploration, just go to water—in your sink if you aren't near a lake— and view the many colors of it. Even puddles show us amazing impressions. This way in is an easy, available kind of ordinary magic. If you include more space, say, by going to a body of natural water, you access a fuller sense of reflection. Notice the sky and cloud reflections, and those lead you to a sense of inner depth and inner surface, the depth and surface of phenomenal display. When you get a sense of a deep shimmering—an illusion-like phenomenal world—you've found the felt heart of the assignment.

This kind of mirroring is direct experience. It's not just the things, like lilies, which are mirrored in the water; the whole phenomenal world is mirrored, revealing the fullness of that particular circumstance. This is what we mean by the phenomenal world as the world of experience.

Believe it or not, this is actually not the main point, or even the contemplative point. The world is not solid and static. Even when it is not reflected in water, the world itself is quite impressionistic. Plus, our experience of the world is also an ever-shifting manifestation. When we begin to feel the truth of this, we begin to see there is no such thing as a thing.

Finally, water is not only reflective, it is fluid. The interface of reflection and fluidity manifests as a dynamic display. Water is not just reflective, it is free-floating. The deep contemplative insight is to consider that mind is like water. It reflects and, to a degree, is the phenomenal world. The mind, too, is reflective, fluid, surface and depth, and free-flowing.

Explore reflections in water and you can't help but feel these insights.

In terms of camera craft, the further away you are from the surface of the water, the easier it is for your camera to capture the reflection and refraction of color and light. The closer you get to the water, the harder it is for the camera to understand which part of the water you want to focus on.

If your perception is of water that is softened and out of focus, then that is how your image should look. However, most of the time what really delivers a flash of perception of impressionism is for the surface to be in focus, as it is in these images. In other words, what is being reflected looks distorted and not always in focus, but the surface of the water itself is actually in focus. You can "create"

impressionism by putting your camera out of focus, or by leaving it at a longer shutter speed while moving water swishes by; but unless that is your flash of perception, that is not what we are noticing here. Notice the impressionism that naturally occurs, direct and clear, right in front of you, all the time. Once you begin noticing, it is hard to miss.

Generally, phone cameras and automatic settings on any camera will work fine, so long as you are as far away as we were for these images. But if you find your camera getting confused over the surface and depth closer up, you will need manual focus.

Also to keep in mind is the fact that what happens with these reflections is that light is being reflected. This means more light comes into your camera than usual. You may need to adjust f-stop for the focus to adjust and for the appropriate exposure. Depending on the situation and how fast the water is moving, you will need to adjust to a faster shutter speed (rapid waves need a faster shutter speed than still water) and adjust the f-stop to match. Play with this as you are photographing water to see the results.

This will be true throughout all the assignments in Impressionism—focusing on the screen, the glass, the fabric, so that the softening that comes with impressionism happens naturally, as it does with our eyes, our perceptions altered not by camera craft or idea but through direct experience with the ever-changing elements.

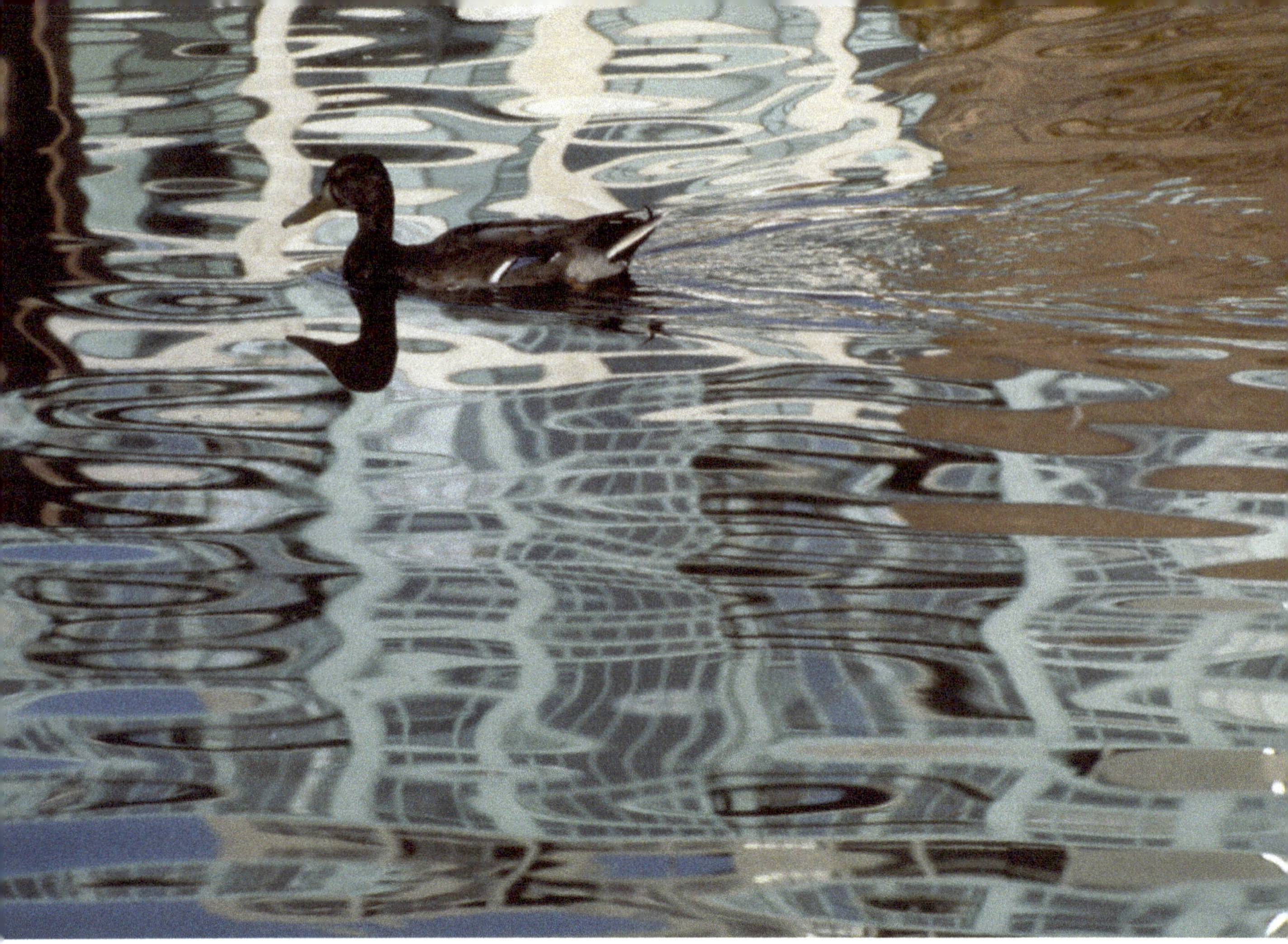

Impressionism Assignment II: Psychedelic Ducks/ Water Lilies

This is a fun assignment—let a duck or ducks into the play of perception, or anything on the surface of the water, really. This generates a more dynamic swirl of color and reflective forms. This is also an example of the overlapping fields of perception. Psychedelic duck shots merge a special water impressionism of a duck within an impressionist space. We like to think that these ducks are enjoying the fluid swirl they create as they swim through that kaleidoscope surface of colors.

Similarly, water lilies, floating flat leaves, and flowers combine two fields of perception. When you find a body of water with water lilies, you explore a space close to Monet's heart. Indeed, for this assignment, it's good to view Monet's way with water lilies. This photographing and reviewing combines the sensibility of Monet and the Zen sense of space. The water reflects the space of the sky and the clouds of the sky. Reflected clouds give depth to the surface, and water lilies reveal the surface forms of space. Paradoxically, lilies function more like clouds in the space as the actual clouds sink deeper in the reflection.

Just as in questioning the color of water, do not hold to the concept that water lily leaves are green. They, themselves, are a reflective surface. With the play of light, they appear dark green, light green, gray, silver, or gold. They are ephemeral dots in space. Water lily forms drift like ciphers between surface spaces and depth spaces.

This particular assignment shows us a more complex contemplative dot-in-space. Here there is much more phenomenal relationship between the dot and the space: the play of surface and depth with the water lilies.

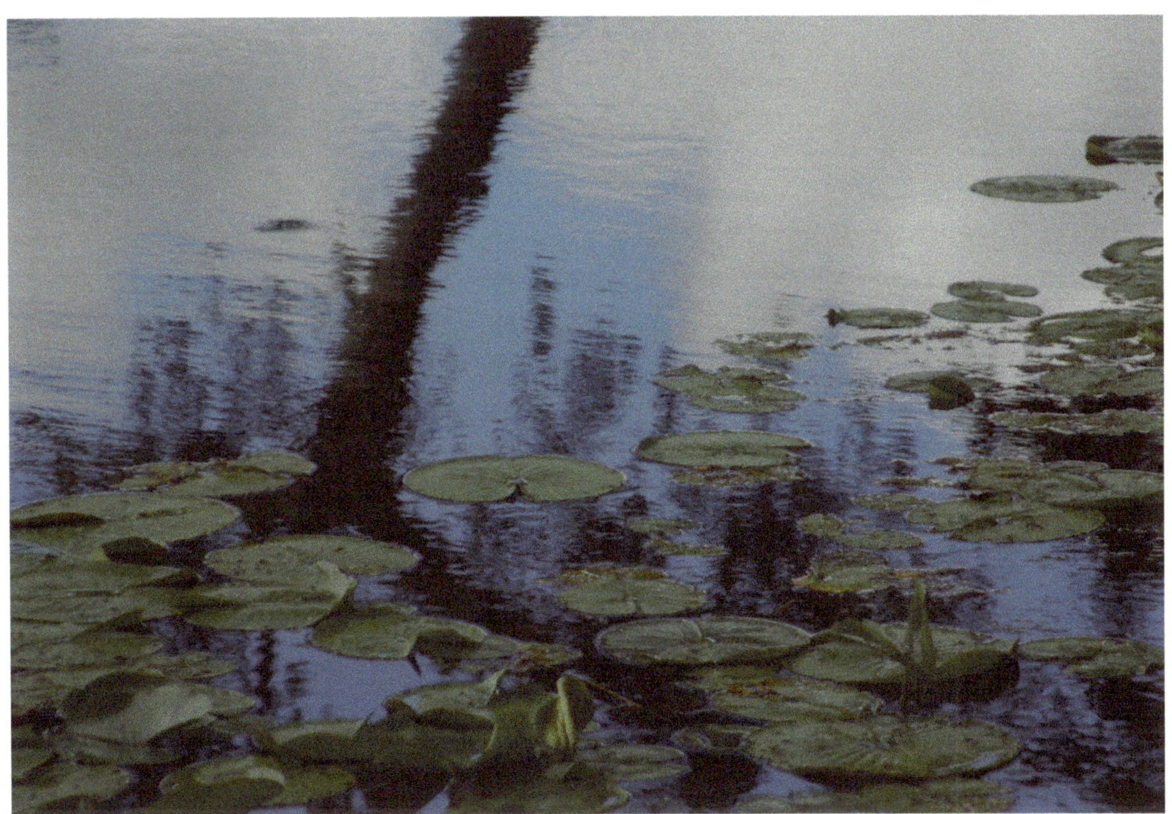

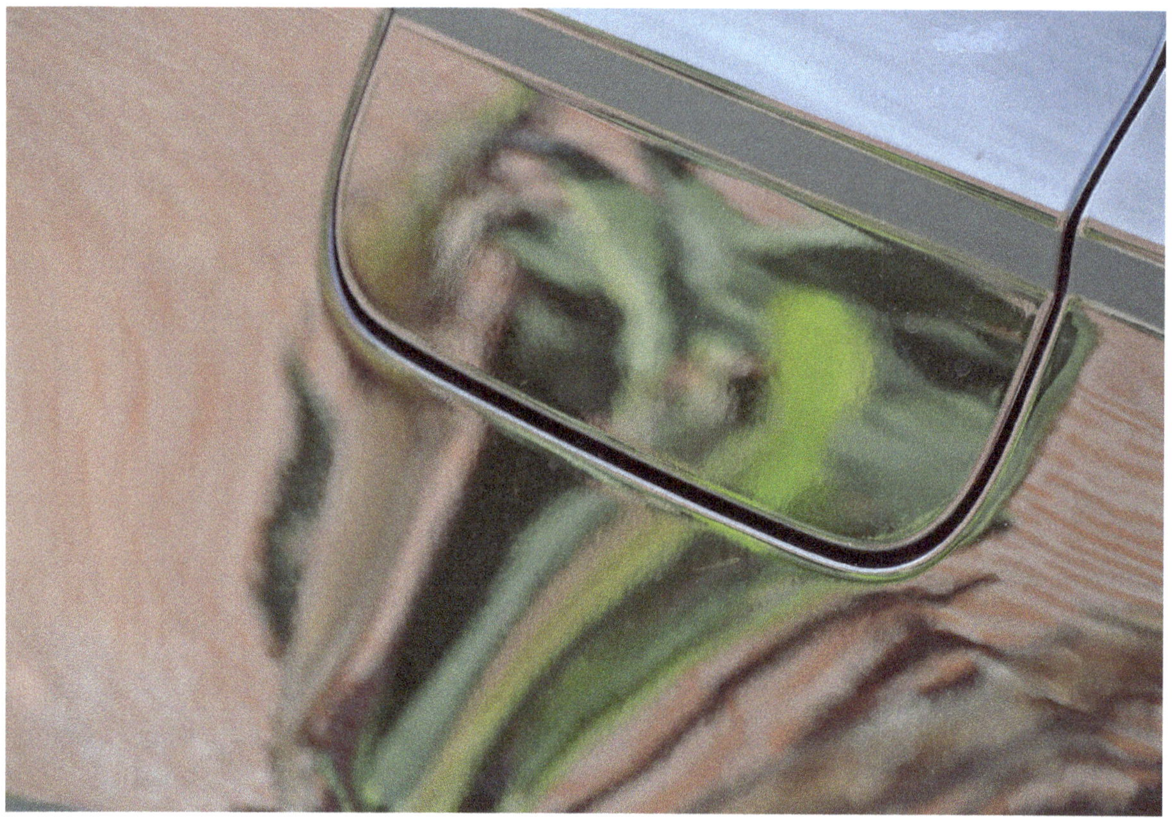

Impressionism Assignment III: Urban Impressionism

Often we associate the art movement of Impressionism with nature. But Impressionist painters, including Monet, also explored urban environments. The next feature of Impressionism is Urban Impressionism, or, reflections in large buildings.

Urban environments are filled with reflective surfaces—glass, mirrors, polished metal— which offer a perceptual fun house. Much of our urban environment, especially the commercial business core, is an envelope of reflections. As solid as these buildings seem, we can directly experience that there is no such thing as a thing, even—especially— when it is made of steel and glass. A tall office building is also a tall column of ever-changing reflection, showing us its more ephemeral side.

There is sometimes a subtle interplay between the urban reflective world and the manifestation of nature. For instance, the sky or trees will appear to be within the perception of a building surface. So there is a perceptual fusion of the natural and the urban in this kind of Impressionism.

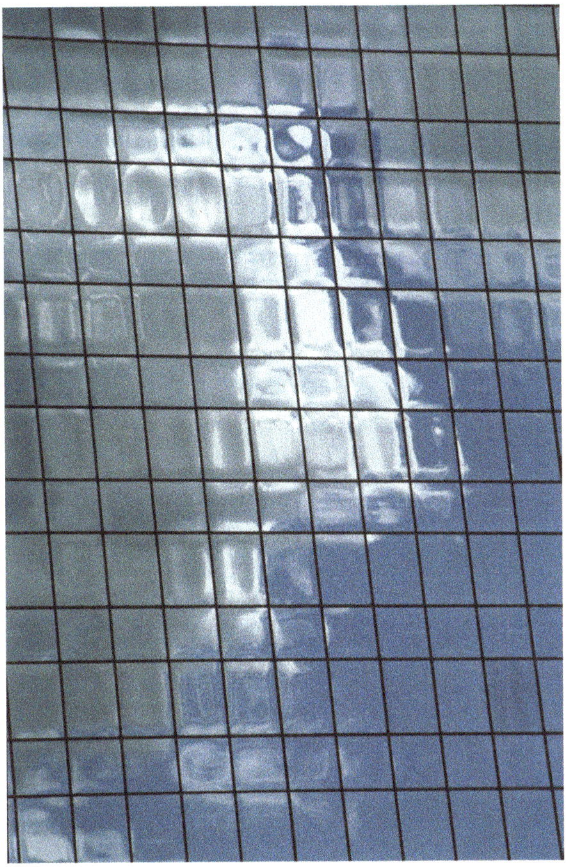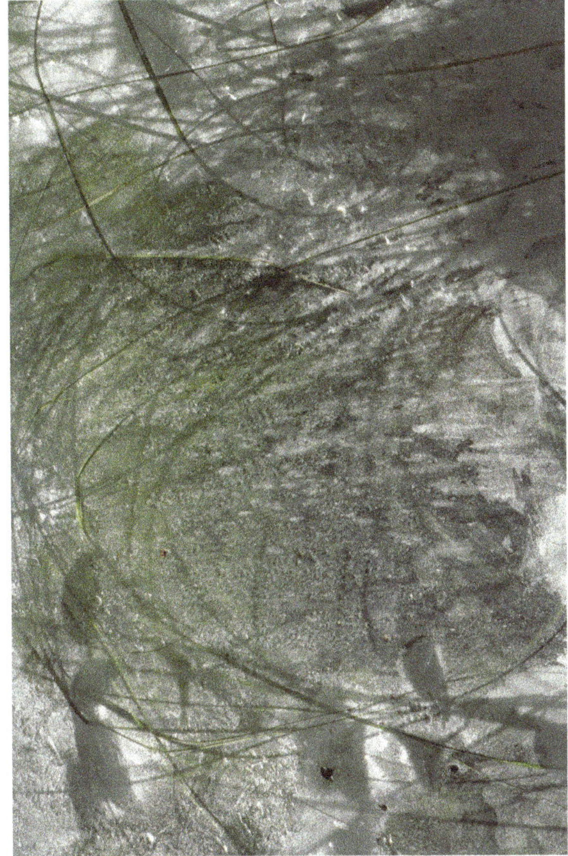

Another variation on this is more domestic—the way of water and glass. After a rainstorm or after cooking something that creates lots of steam, notice impressionistic windows with streaming droplets. Even more so in the winter, you can notice frosted windows, especially when illuminated. These are nature's stained glass windows—pure magic. Or explore a glass greenhouse for myriad impressionist envelopes—a magic wonderland.

Craft-wise, this form of Impressionism is much easier, since most city surfaces are at a distance. However, take caution with car and shop windows, as the layers of surface and depth quickly become confusing to the camera, and to our eyes and minds. We are still noticing harmony in spaciousness in Level Two. Once you notice your eyes being unable to rest, losing ground and playing in the optical-illusion quality of car windows, for instance, or of shop windows, you have gone through a slipstream of the impressionist world into a bit of chaos. First let yourself train and explore in reflections further away, which are less likely to cause confusion and more likely to let you stabilize in the water or glass space of stable, spacious magic.

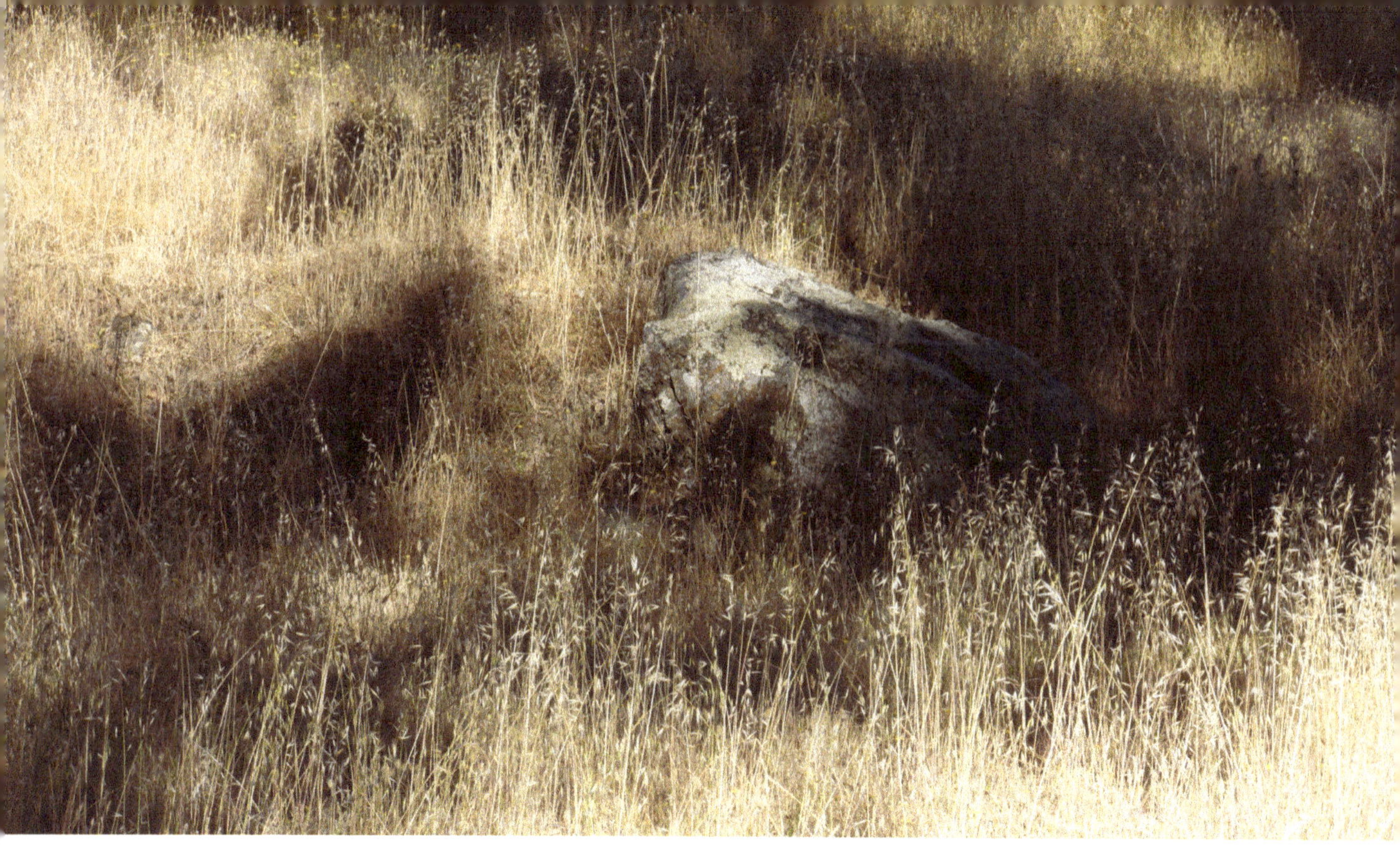

Impressionism Assignment IV: Motifs

Our next Impressionism assignment, Motifs, takes another direction, but it is still inspired by the Impressionist painters. For the Impressionists, motifs are images of the same subject, painted at different times of the year or day. Monet's haystacks are a great example. Though he worked with the same piles of hay, there is no "same old, same old" haystack. No haystack is perceptually independent of the cycles of the day, the way of the weather, the turning of the seasons. To point to another motif of Monet's, there is perceptually no such thing as a single, ever-lasting cathedral façade. In perception and the phenomenal world, there is no such thing as a thing. Monet understood and expressed this. Everything always manifests as a phenomenal form, which always mirrors the phenomenal circumstances. Like haystacks and cathedrals, our whole life experience is an everyday fresh and free encounter, ever-changing and perpetually opening. This is the everyday contemplative mindset. It is not mystical or spiritual; it is the actual, everyday way.

As an assignment, find a scene or situation or object to observe over time. Framing it is important—filling the frame with a flash of perception, then returning to it over time to explore how the same framing captures change. This is precisely the way Monet worked: he picked a haystack or cliff and returned again and again to capture the way the phenomenal world manifested as and around that haystack or cliff.

This is a deepening of the basic dot-in-space perception. Here both the dot and the space are enriched and, to a degree, dissolved. There is still the perceptual form of dot-in-space but now both the dot and the space are infused by the circumstantial phenomenal world. As conditions change perceptually, both the dot and the space change. The look of the haystack changes, and the look of the environment changes.

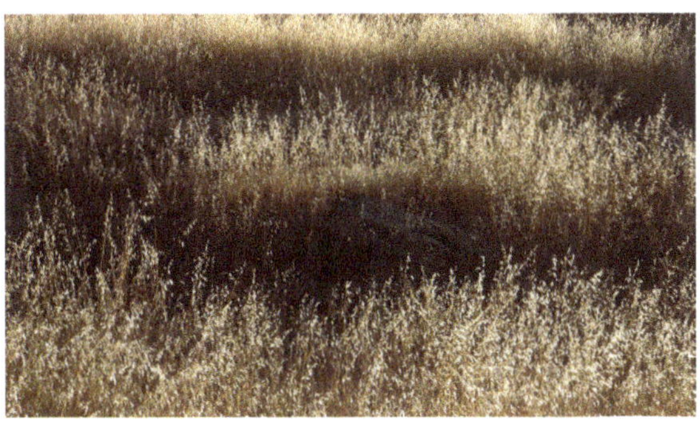

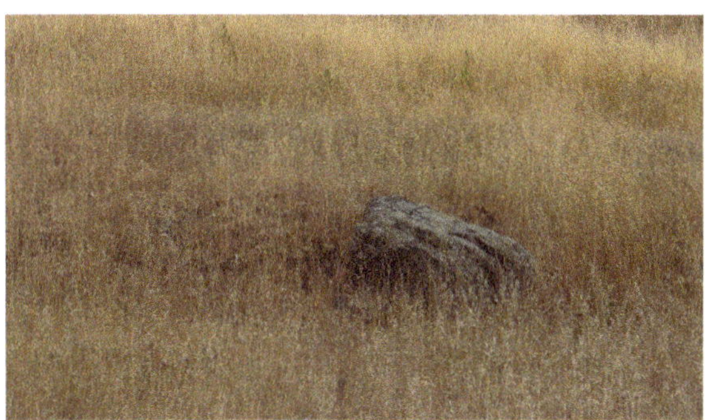

You can pick something as simple as a wooden telephone pole and wires. Or it could pick you. The photos here are from when Miriam was on retreat in California, and this rock called out to her. These images were actually taken over the course of a single day, and remind us how much changes just in the time from sunrise to sunset.

You could have a mostly sky motif—the sky through the day and the seasons—but it would include the different variations in light with the pole. Also, the weather is a factor: the telephone pole can be bone dry and pale, or wet and dark, or even plastered with snow after a storm.

In general, it is more effective if you select something fairly ordinary and nondescript rather than something complex and already beautiful. With few exceptions, this was Monet's approach. The beauty is not in the chosen frame but in the phenomenal display the frame reveals over time. That said, starting with a strong original flash of perception helps.

You can combine this assignment with the Urban Impressionism assignment. A mirrored building changes its perceptual display constantly, as the phenomenal circumstances it reflects change. Or motifs can be domestic. John's ongoing motifs include one in which he notices the way the light plays on a bedroom wall. The dot-in-space is a vase with an artificial flower on a dresser, which has different phenomenal displays; the main study is the way of the light on the wall and in the room.

Your motif can be nature or an urban or domestic situation. The situation does not matter. The point is to see how this specific situation manifests as a phenomenal display.

The point behind the point: to a degree, our whole experienced world is like this—this shifting display of appearances, the ever-changing manifestation of our lived experience of the world, as the world arrives in this manifest way.

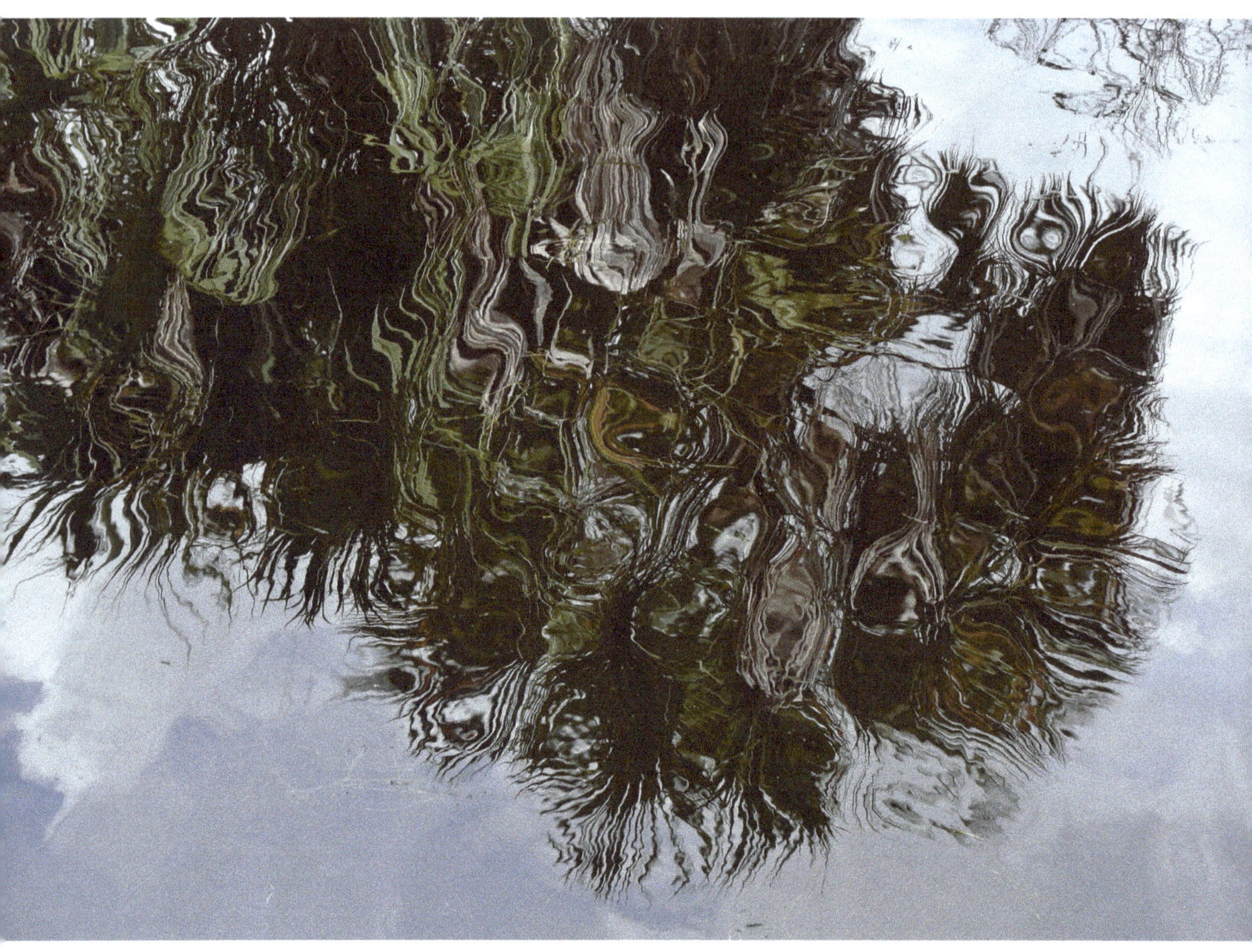

On Impressionism

It can be hard for us in the contemporary era to realize how revolutionary Impressionism was—and still is—as an art and perceptual movement. Before Nalanda Miksang, Miriam used to think of Impressionist paintings as good for mouse pads and coasters. She had very little direct experience with Impressionism, and very little understanding of how important it was as an art movement, much less as perceptual expression.

John helped her to see, through simply photographing reflections in water, how powerful a tool for perception impressionism is. Miriam began to study the Impressionists, finding out that some of them actually knew about the visual science of the times, which, thanks to the advent of photography, was beginning to indicate that shadows consisted of more than just black and showed that even "objective photographs" could change with small adjustments to light.

As her intellectual respect grew, her personal connection grew. She spent more and more time at a nearby lagoon, one she had lived close to for years but had given little attention to. Day by day, from season to season, she watched as the trees changed, as their reflections changed. A huge oak at the corner of the park closest to her house became a beacon—a witness to impermanence, shifting from light green buds to thick dark leaves to deep red waifs to empty branches.

Because Madison, WI has so much water, you don't have to look hard to find stable, spacious reflections. But you do have to look. Going out to purposefully notice what the nature of appearances are in nature itself—because, as Miriam tells her students, nature doesn't lie about impermanence like we do—you can't help but notice that appearances don't last. And, at the same time, their richness is abundant and immediately available.

While she watches some photographers playing games with perception based on reflection, her joy in photographing this natural impressionism is simple: simply seeing, directly feeling, how rich and spacious impermanence is. Nalanda Miksang is a felt-sense practice, something we learn from, and learn how to do, only by doing. Its deepest lessons come out and about while photographing and being in the experience completely.

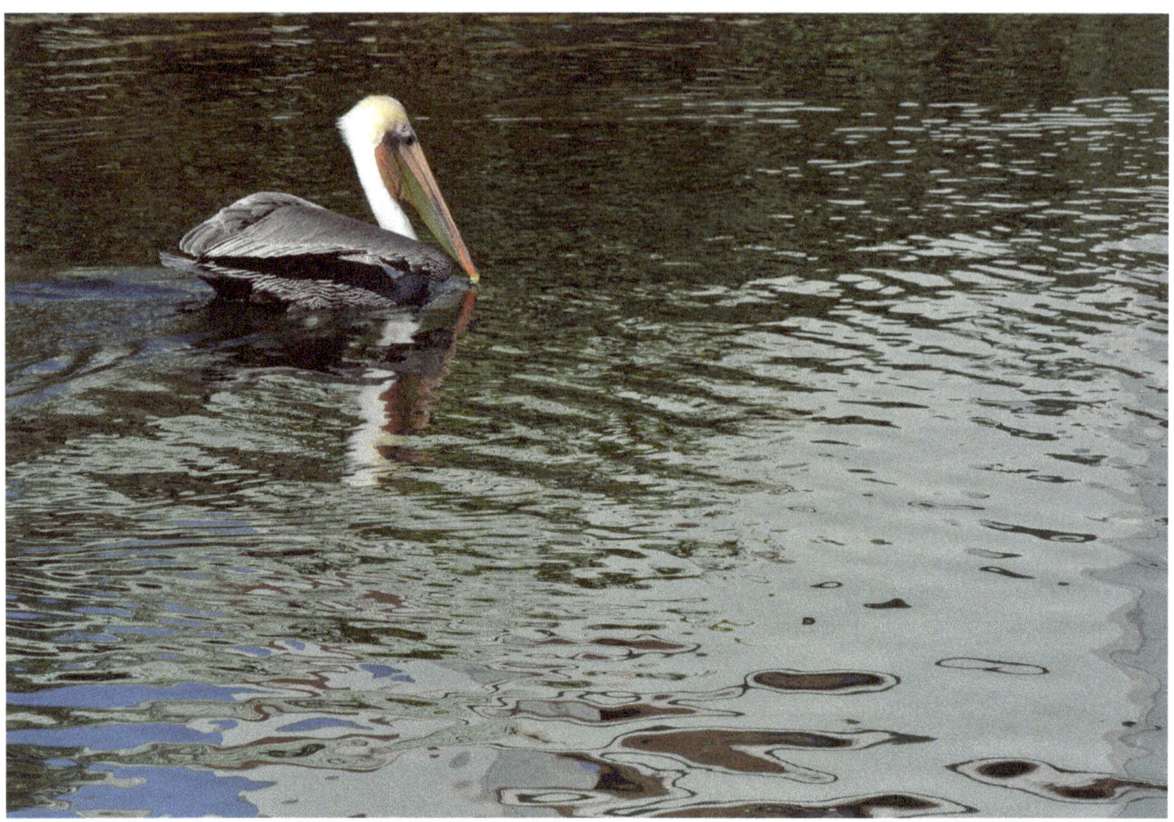

Impressionism And Resonance

With Impressionism, we really plunge into the space and resonance of the contemplative aesthetic. It is the main assignment that treats space in Level Two—in fact, for most of the time, our experience of the world appears in the underlying form of dot-in-space.

The main and deep point beneath this assignment is how the way of the contemplative mind is also the way of the phenomenal world. Like in other Level Two topics, we learn from former masters: our key Impressionist teacher is Monet. There are other great Impressionist painters, but for contemplative aesthetics, Monet is special. His explorations of light, water, and seasons lend themselves to reflection—literally in the aesthetics, and also through contemplation. Impressionism is a field of perception infused with the radiance of the phenomenal world.

The subject matter of Impressionism includes nature, urban settings, shooting through and exploring ongoing impermanence through appearances, and particular aspects of human engagement. Great Impressionist painters like Monet explored mainly nature. Monet also included urban situations in his Impressionist vision, such as cathedrals and railway stations. Other major Impressionists, like Degas and Renoir, included human beings and their environs: cafés, parks, public baths, the ballet, and so forth.

Also, there is a direct connection with Zen aesthetics. Impressionism was informed by European encounters with Japanese and Chinese art. Monet in particular was inspired by and collected Japanese prints, some of which are still on display at his residence at Giverny, France. There is not only a resonance with the aesthetics of Japanese and Chinese art but also direct inspiration from that tradition. In historical Impressionism, West met East.

Look to Monet as a contemplative. Look to Monet for the expressive power of perception. Part of the assignment is to contemplate Monet's images. Go to major cities, where you can contemplate Monet's paintings in museums. Or, peruse art books and the Internet. Don't try to analyze; just dwell with, and within, the images. In particular, contemplate Monet's later paintings, where there is no longer a horizon. For instance, in "The Water-Lily Pond," we plunge into the play of surface and depth.

The contemplation of Impressionism through observation of paintings occurs on at least two levels: viewing and insight.

Viewing is the basic exposure to paintings or reproductions of Monet's work. Just relax and view—through this, we make a heart connection. Viewing is both an ordinary and deep contemplative practice. In Japanese culture there are many ordinary contemplative viewing practices, such as watching the annual cherry blossoms fall, which may seem simple but is a deep contemplation of the poignancy of transience. So viewing can be direct and deep. Just let it sink in the way it sinks in, and let it resonate the way it resonates. This is personal surface and depth contemplation.

Insight goes a bit deeper, and concerns the contemplative mind displayed in the perception and the art. When we enter the deep mind of the painting, we go beyond thinking of the painting as being made by Monet. We can wonder what kind of mind or vision opens this way of seeing in this particular way? What is the opening behind the painting, the mind of the painting itself? What manner of seeing sees this? What is the way of this way of expression? How is the contemplative mind revealed through these paintings? This contemplation is not abstract or conceptual or intellectual. There are no answers. It is a contemplation based on your first contact, which takes this deeper, in a more reflective way.

While this kind of contemplation is a personal journey, we can give you some hints on how to proceed. Monet manifests contemplative mind. Through your contemplation, you connect with his contemplative mind, and your contemplative mind reflects his contemplative mind.

As a contemplative photographer, light is the way in to this direct visual experience. Light remains the major orientation of our practice: light through the day, and through the seasons. This, too, was Monet's focus.

Art criticism does not discuss Monet or Impressionism in terms of perception. The closest that historical analysis comes to the Miksang view is when discussing how the Impressionists painted the effects of light. Still, usually this focuses on their artistic technique: short brush strokes with innovative color combinations, generating brilliant effects. Impressionists are also noted for moving out of the studio and painting directly the countryside and cafés, *plein air*. They are described in the history of art as a transition to modern art.

For us, light and color are important in deeper ways, tied to perception. For us, Monet's work lights up contemplative sensibility: the contemplative view, contemplative aesthetic, and contemplative realization. We do not discount the Impressionist's innovative artistic techniques. In contemplative terms, these were means for fashioning their equivalent images for their impressionistic perception. Just as Nalanda Miksang photographic techniques support contemplative photography.

The name *Impressionism* came from a negative criticism of their work: it did not literally represent the world, only impressions of it. In our words, the Impressionists and in particular Monet broke from representing the world of things and entered the flow of the phenomenal world, in this case, characterized as a blend of impressions—a field of perceptions with the flavor of impressionism.

Like the word *perception*, the word *impression* implies both subjective and objective poles— the perceiver and the perceived—without being contained by either one. When we register an impression it is fleeting and fragile. It also makes its mark; it is an impression, an imprint. It is a happening of sight and insight.

In describing his approach, Monet spoke of glancing. He glanced at the subject as it displayed itself in its fluid phenomenal form. It was a dance of fluid appearances and decisive glances; a subtle and supple dancing vision that issues as impressions and impressionism. If this sounds a bit like the way a flash of perception feels to you, that's because this is the way of perception—to be constantly shifting and shimmering, glancing and glimmering.

Glimmering and radiance come from reflection, both of light and of phenomenal circumstances. If you remember back to *Looking and Seeing*, there we spoke of light, how it shows us the magic of the world as it already is.

In this field of perception, we work with Impressionism's brilliant display: the mirroring of the phenomenal world. We enter Monet's floating world of surface and depth. The space is so encompassing we could never exhaust it; the surface so vast we could never cross it; the depth so deep we could never plumb it. But we can float in the phenomenal world, and feel the full depth.

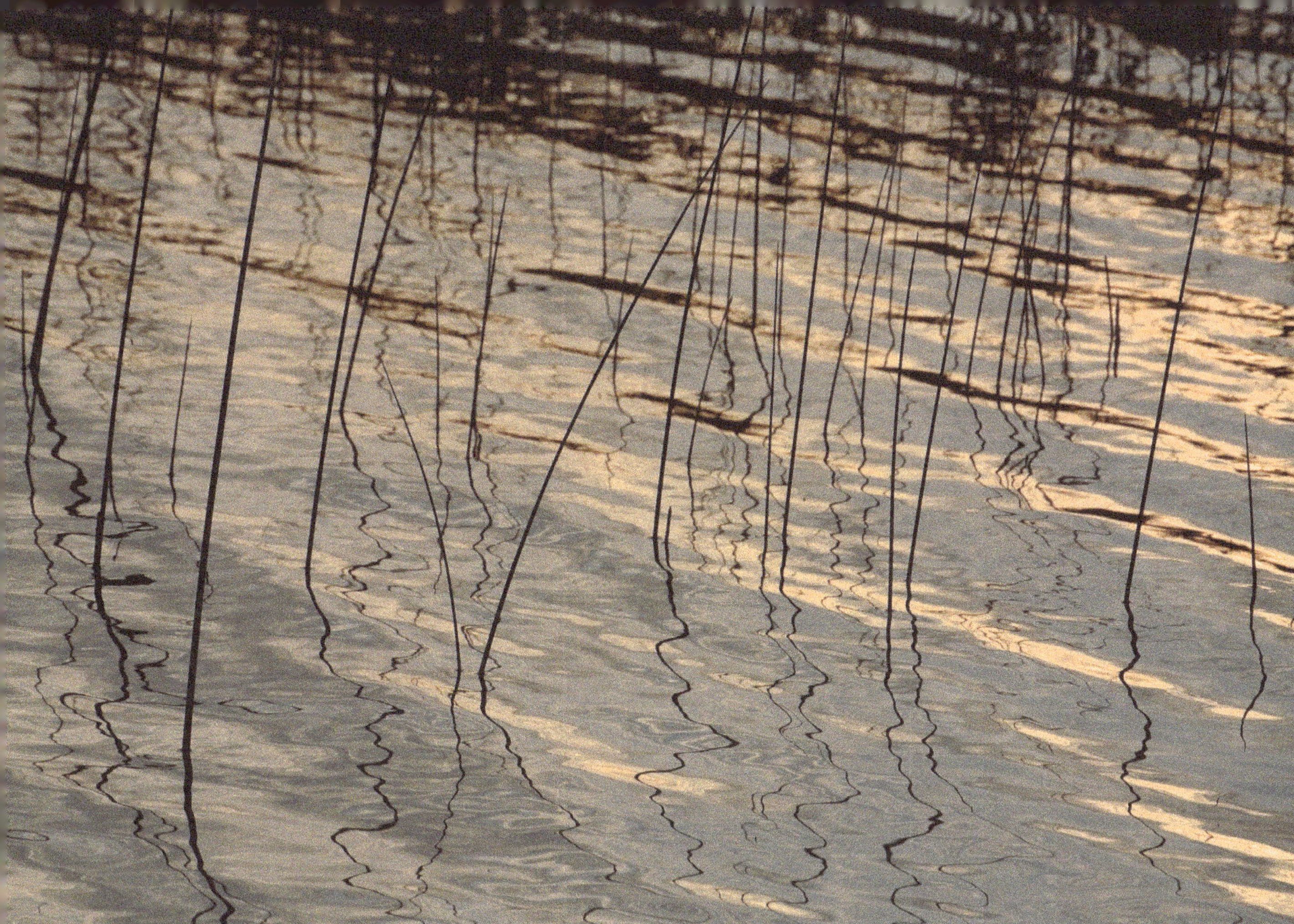

After The Shoot

As we have said, part of the contemplative practice is reflective contemplation: the insight of sight. In Monet's Impressionism, we considered the deep equivalence of the image as a contemplative icon. It is worth revisiting the deep equivalence again here, as a way of gathering the experience of the assignment.

With this assignment, you witness the magic of water and other reflective surfaces and produce beautiful images. It's fun. It takes you on a magical mystery tour, one which brightens your life. The images brighten the world. If you get that and want to stay with that, then just enjoy that—that is more than enough.

If you want to go deeper, you can ask: "What makes it a 'magical mystery tour'"? What moves us in this experience and these images? Why are we interested in water and the way of water? And what is the way of water? Why was Monet fascinated with water? And why are we fascinated with Monet's fascination with water, exemplified in his paintings?

At the visual level, the images are a basic equivalent of the clear perception of water. We connect with this perception of impressionistic water and make an equivalent impressionistic image. This is basic Nalanda Miksang practice.

But then there is the resonance. The significance comes in the echo beyond reflections in water. The images embody something essential about water that reverberates in other dimensions of perception and experience. The intuitive equivalent is to see that this way of water is resonant with the way of mind: contemplative mind.

The way of water reminds us of something other than water. Water is like a mirror. It is reflective. It is better than a mirror, because it is fluid. For contemplatives and the meditation tradition, a mirror is often a metaphor for mind and the phenomenal world. Water and mind are fluid and reflective. The phenomenal world is fluid and full of light, color, and forms. Just like the mind that reflects and flows with it.

Through iconic images of the way of water and other reflections, there is an intuitive equivalent of the way of reality. The phenomenal world is like impressionistic water. This is the contemplative, deep resonance. For all the assignments in Level Two, there is the visual equivalent and the intuitive equivalent; the sight and the insight.

Monet's work shows that, at least intuitively, he understood that the phenomenal world was not different than space. Monet sometimes spoke of the envelope of light, the envelope of impressions. From a contemplative view, this is a subtle and profound insight. This envelope is ephemeral fullness of infused phenomenal space, space infused with the rainbow display of phenomenal manifestation and the radiance of a transformative vision. Monet painted the visualization that is phenomenal space. This visualization space is neither subjective nor objective. It is perception. His equivalent paintings are sensuous, suffused with pure phenomenal world: pure light, pure colors, pure pleasure. This

is why the contemplatives are charmed by Monet.

That would be more than enough. But there is more: there is the insight of sight, the profound contemplative dimension. For Monet there was no such thing as a thing. He painted perception and the phenomenal world: the fluid revelation of things through their conditions of manifestation.

There is a famous story of Monet painting a scene late in the day as the light rapidly changed and faded. He called to his daughter to bring him canvas after canvas as he responded to this phenomenal reality. There are many such instances of Monet working with particular subject matter over several days with several canvases as he engaged the infused space of the fluid phenomenal manifestation.

It is instructive to contemplate how Monet worked with space. Sometimes, particularly in the early phase of his Impressionist journey, he worked with the basic form of perception: a foreground against a background, so in the early paintings there is a stronger sense of viewer and what is viewed. Although what is viewed has an impressionistic sensibility, there is a stable sense of a viewer of this scenic display.

For contemplatives, his later work is more decisive. The dot, or foreground, dissolves into space, the background. This merging of foreground and background builds a rich, powerful soup of suffused space, surface and depth. Frequently, in these late paintings, there is no longer a horizon— just the full space of this phenomenal presence. This space includes the reflected and the reflection, the surface and the depth, and, most decisively, the perceiver and the perceived. We do not have a sense of being outside the perception. We are plunged into the phenomenal display. With these images we are completely there, in Monet's floating world of impressionistic space.

Monet painted space almost like the dissolved contemplative aesthetics of Zen. The power and paradox of Monet's dissolving is that his images tend toward fullness rather than emptiness. Unlike the Zen aesthetic, Monet's space is not a space of restraint and implication. His space is full of color, light, and pleasure. Rather than being a space of understatement—a space of restrained passion—it is a space of release: a space of bliss. It is more Tantric than Zen. His space surges to the surface. Orgasm. Pure phenomenal manifestation.

Monet painted radiance, broaching what Chögyam Trungpa calls the third level of perception: luminosity and energy. Monet moves toward a radical non-dualism without abandoning the phenomenal world of forms. He does not use pure abstraction. The water lilies and Japanese bridge still remain.

PART THREE

ORDINARY/
PERSONAL WORLD

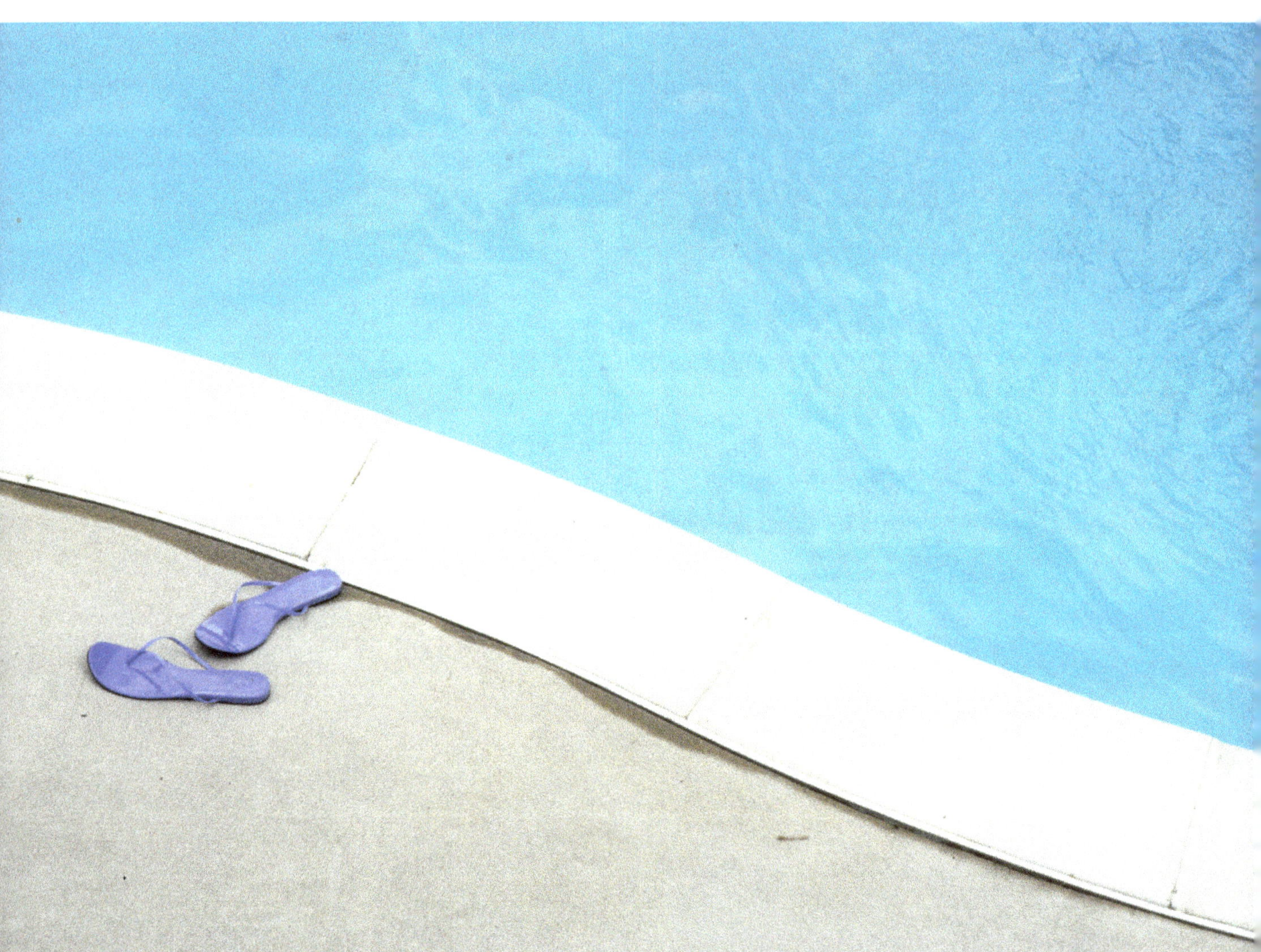

Ordinary/
Personal World

Notice everything. Appreciate everything, including the ordinary. That's how to click in with joyfulness or cheerfulness. Curiosity encourages cheering up. So does simply remembering to do something different.

—Pema Chödrön, *Start Where You Are*

Being a contemplative means wherever you go, you are there with the *there*. You start where you are. This is ordinary magic. In photography in particular, there is often the impulse to go somewhere else—find a special location to supply brilliant and beautiful images. However, as we have already discovered, beauty is everywhere, for the contemplative eye.

The great Canadian photographer Freeman Patterson has a saying we have adopted as a slogan: "One's ability to see clearly is not increased by the distance one travels." We spend much of our life in the same everyday environments: our home, our workplace, our route from home to workplace and back. We treat these environments in an ongoing habitual way, leading to us taking them for granted. Things appear to lose their luster because we are there, but not there with the *there*.

We may try to spice up our environment, renovating and redecorating, but we still wind up back in an average everyday way of being at home. What we need to understand deeply is the that dullness or brightness of our personal space does not depend only on the space itself. To a large extent, how we see our space has to do with our way of being in our space—mainly, whether we are attentive, or on autopilot, at home. As Trungpa Rinpoche says in *True Perception*:

> *. . . we are simply trying to approach reality as simply as we could. A tortoise walks and carries a heavy shell; a cow walks along and grazes by itself in a green meadow, depositing its dung; pigeons make their own noises and live on the roof. Things have their own place . . . Things are as they are, ordinary and simple. Seemingly, that is a very simple-minded approach, but actually it is extremely deep.*

The Ordinary/Personal World assignment is a deceptively simple way to address this issue of how to be at home when you are at home. It is an invitation to connect with your personal world in a direct and lively way. We can find the entire phenomenal world in our homes or personal situations. This is one of the most available ongoing assignments; it is always right in front of us. We can connect with this ordinary magic, on the spot, in our everyday settings.

Originally, in Nalanda Miksang, the ordinary, and personal aspects were two separate assignments. It is still helpful to contemplate these two apart from one another. So we will start there.

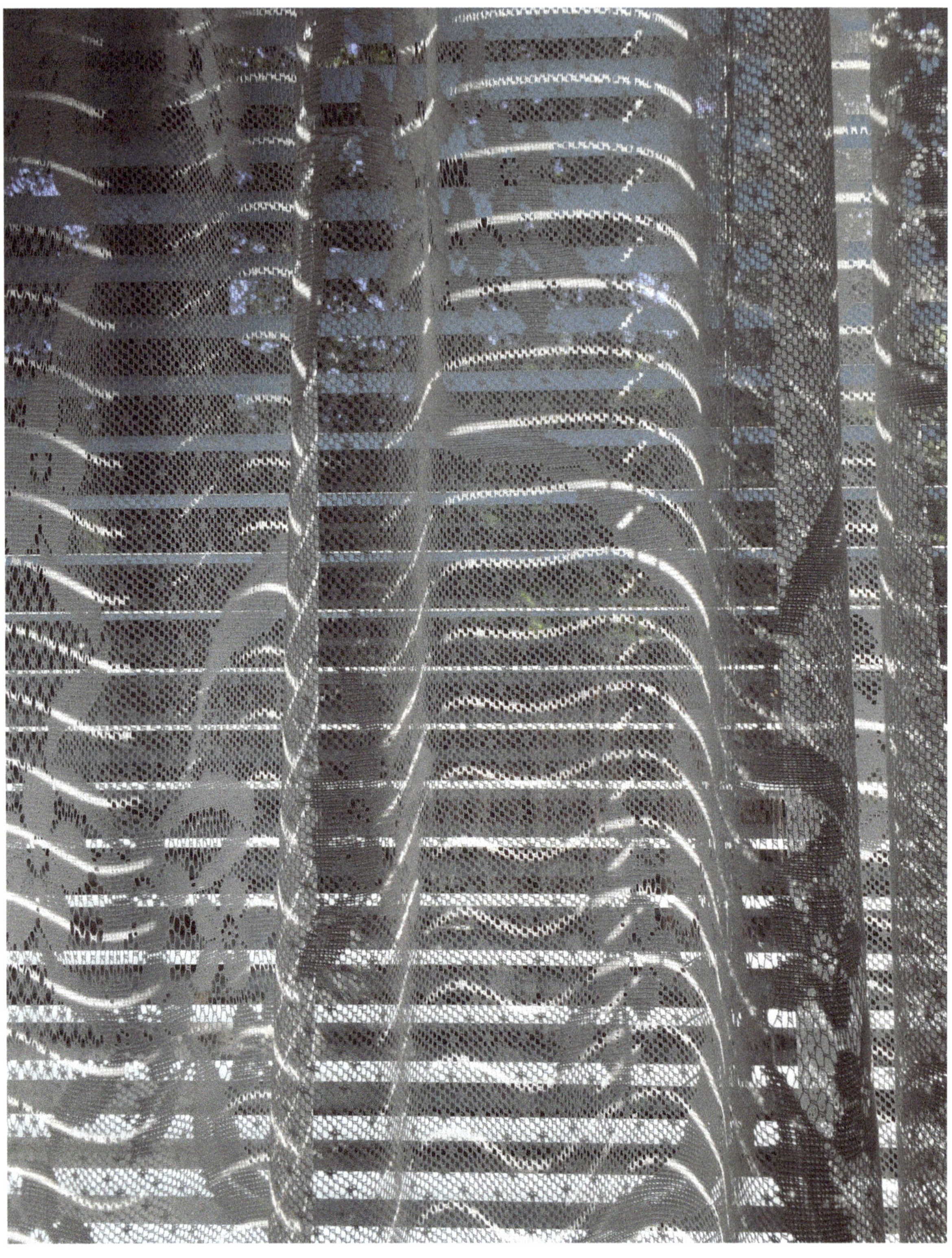

Ordinary World

Anything that excites me for any reason I will photograph; not searching for unusual subject matter but making the commonplace unusual. Through the photographic eye you will be able to look out on a new-light world; a world for the most part uncharted and unexplored; a world that lies waiting to be discovered and revealed.

—Edward Weston

In the Ordinary World exploration, we do not seek a special subject matter. Instead, anything, or any aspect of anything, is a candidate. This could include, but is not limited to, perceptions of all or part of salt and pepper shakers, a crack in the wall—everything. Even, as the saying goes, the kitchen sink! One dedicated practitioner, Susan, actually takes her phone with her to the sink every day and does what she calls "sink practice"— photographing whatever direct flashes she has of what is happening in her sink at that moment.

Basic Nalanda Miksang training and orientation really come into play in this assignment. We often find our Ordinary World perceptions through color and light. What pulls us into these flashes of perception of ordinary forms—say, oil and vinegar bottles—is the play of pattern, texture, and so forth. Ordinary environments contain many visual displays, some of which are simpler and more abstract and Level One, like light through Venetian blinds creating elegant bands of light and

shadow along the living room wall; or the pattern of the carpet broken up by the dot-in-space of a cat.

There are various obstacles to seeing this everyday magic in our regular environments. We will speak more on those later in this chapter. The main obstacle is sinking into familiarity: because we are at home when at home, we relax and take it for granted. While relaxing itself is not a problem, sometimes it gets confused with flopping. Giving up and not paying attention at all is a skill-less stress remedy, one which does not work in the long run, a way of actually hiding deeper in our cocoon in order to not engage with the world in a nourishing way. A classic example is not washing the dirty dishes until they pile up. You may think you are chilling out, just letting it go, but in the meantime the stench and avoidance actually presses down on you with the weight of procrastination. This is not relaxing. On the contrary, deep relaxation is being synchronized: being in touch and being touched. In terms of this practice, it means appreciating the visual phenomenal world, while you live your everyday life, in your everyday environment.

We are not trying to create an ideal situation. When we say pure perception, or true perception, we are not looking for any particular state of mind or situation. We are simply, though not always easily, making a direct heart connection with what is going on in the visual experience of our life right now. In this case, it is happening in the places we live in most.

Let's say our personal environment is cluttered. The point is not to get into a tizzy about clutter. Sure, maybe you need to clean up, but this practice is not an opportunity to guilt trip or worry about how you haven't dusted. In terms of everyday perception, it can all be beautiful. We have examples of children's toys being left out and morning-after party wine bottles. These are life. So it is a matter of letting things happen, noticing that they are happening, and working with what is happening. In the long run, you may find bringing this kind of open attention to your space leads to cleaning it more often, or caring for it in a way that attracts magic and attention and a desire to be present in your space. However, that is not our agenda. That must unfold naturally, out of curiosity.

In *True Perception*, Chögyam Trungpa reminds us that instead of trying to get the world to make a message to guide us, we can open to the message that *is* the world. Then something happens that is a little beyond our expectations but completely accurate. Then you are there with the there.

For instance, during the annual Nalanda Miksang intensive in 2016, one of Miriam's students, a long-haul pilot named Jenny, was struggling with the Ordinary World assignment. She prowled around her apartment, looking for special shots: poring over her favorite objects, looking closely at her pillows, patterns, pets. She made documentary photos of paintings she likes in neat light. None of it was clicking. Finally, she gave up and went to the bathroom. As she stood to flush the toilet, she flashed the shapes and spaces in and of the toilet. From these fresh perceptions, completely unexpected, she made a few beautiful Nalanda Miksang images. Edward Weston, one of the great contemplative fine art photographers, and a source of ongoing inspiration for Nalanda

Miksang, would have been very pleased; he found his way partially through perception images of toilets.

Infinite visual details and surprises unfold day in and day out, once you are there with the there. You simply need to be alive to the lively locations where you live much of your life. So this is the main assignment, and it is very simple (which we often find difficult). Pay attention to, and give attention to, the visual manifestations of your everyday environments. While you are at it, notice how this kind of curiosity affects your life experience. Does it make a difference to be so open? Are you more there with the *there*? Do you see much more? Do you connect more often with the ordinary magic and ordinary joy? After all, while Nalanda Miksang is a photographic form, the deeper teachings point to the possibility of further realization, through our simple but profound practice.

To begin with, you have to look at your ordinary domestic reality: your knives, your forks, your plates, your telephone, your dishwasher, and your towels—ordinary things. There is no thing mystical or extraordinary about them, but if there is no connection with ordinary everyday situations, if you don't examine your mundane life, then you will never find any humor or dignity or, ultimately, any reality. The way you comb your hair, the way you dress, the way you wash your dishes—all of those activities are an extension of sanity; they are a way of connection with reality. A fork is a fork, of course. It is a simple implement of eating. But at the same time, the extension of your sanity and your dignity may depend on how you use your fork. Very simply, Shambhala vision is trying to provoke you to understand how you live, your relationship with ordinary life.

—**Chögyam Trungpa,** *Shambhala, The Sacred Path of the Warrior*

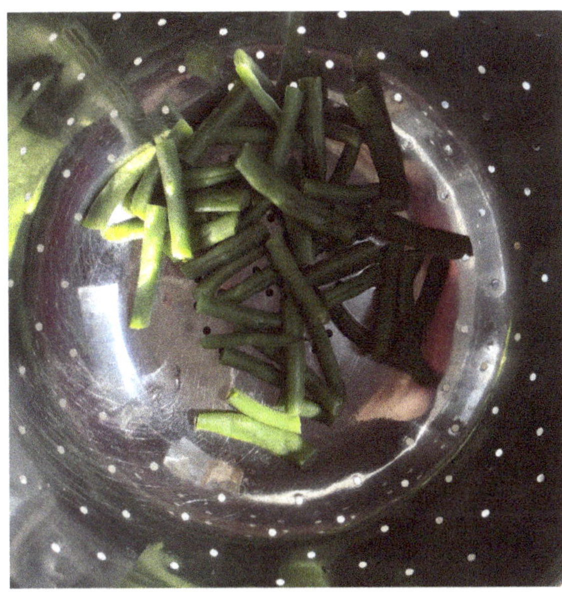

The Ordinary World assignment has two dimensions. The first, and main, practice is to be awake to your familiar environment—to see your home, work, and so forth. We live much of our life in these contexts, so they are great occasions to being awake within. We can see we are always at home with our capacity to see clearly and appreciate our life.

It is that simple and that profound. Rather than your habit in these environments being a default to a sleepy cocoon version of relaxation, you can open to engaging in a lively way of being energized. Being refreshed is one of the benefits of this assignment and practice. In one of his books, the Canadian contemplative photographer Freeman Patterson reports on his experience of coming home after being away on assignment. He notes how his familiar home seemed a little fresher: the color of the wall was more beige than the white he had remembered, and so forth.

What Patterson is pointing to is the difference between fresh perception and our blinding familiarity. As Patterson also notes, soon after he settled back into being home, he stopped seeing the already always-fresh ways of his household. This "unseeing" is the way we default to habitual comfort, but this does not have to be the way it goes. We can always come home to our real home. Our real, live, and deep experience of home is the way it actually is: an ongoing, fresh and free, flowing manifestation. You can come home every day in this way. Then your returning home is surprising, delightful, and refreshing.

As is always the case in Nalanda Miksang, there is sight, and then there is insight, the second dimension. In this assignment, sight is appreciating your lived personal environment. Insight is seeing the ordinary as a vehicle for the extraordinary. Your life can have deep meaning, and the occasion for this deep meaning is always already available. You do not need to go anywhere. You are there, now you simply need to be there with that there.

Ordinary World Perception And Contemplative Art

To me beauty appears when one feels deeply.

—Dorothea Lange

The beauty of the ordinary world is deeply appreciated in Western Art. Consider the whole tradition of still life paintings, like the simplicity and beauty of fruit in a bowl on a table. It's especially powerful to investigate the Dutch still life painters, who deeply appreciated the sublime play of light with the artifacts of domestic life.

The Zen traditions also appreciate the ordinary. Indeed, for Zen contemplatives, the ordinary became a highly valued contemplative aesthetic, in the form of what is called *wabi*. We will say more about wabi and other Zen Aesthetics in the chapter with that title, but for now, we will say this: like all Taoist, Buddhist, Zen, and Ch'an contemplative aesthetics, *wabi* has many resonances, so it cannot be summed up as a definition. In general, *wabi* is an orientation toward the ordinary (as opposed to the exceptional).

The aesthetic of *wabi* is most developed in the contemplative practice of tea ceremony, which is a way of engaging an ordinary everyday activity (making tea and drinking it together as an intimate event) in an ordinary way, while recognizing its inherent magic.

There is a sublime simplicity and ordinary communion in everyday human rituals. Tea ceremony has deep resonance with all ordinary human rituals, which are at the heart of human cosmic connection. Intimate cultural institutions are foundations of an enlightened society.

In the context of our assignment, what is key in wabi is noting the contemplative tea masters' preferences. The context of the tea ceremony is simple. Rather than the refined elegance of the court, the tea rooms are simple huts with minimalist décor. In addition, ordinary, even flawed, cups, are favored over refined china in Japanese culture. The ordinary and flawed connect directly to the reality of everyone's everyday life experience, which is always both ordinary and flawed—and magical.

This ordinary reality connection is the real realization of the way it is. Tea masters know the real sublime is the way of seeing, feeling, and being, in ordinary, contemplative ways. That is all. That is a lot. This is the inner practice, the deep teaching, and deep insight of Ordinary World.

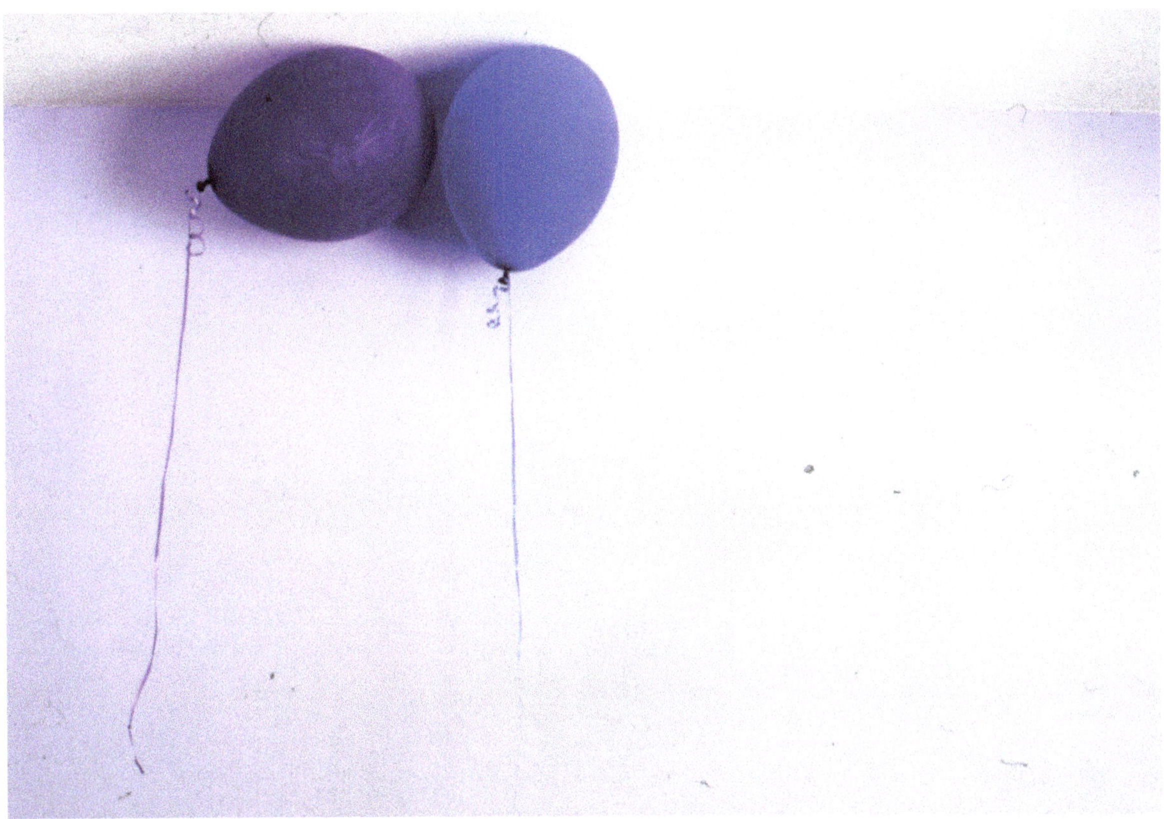

Being An Ordinary Contemplative Photographer

As Freeman Patterson, says you do not need to go to a special place where you will find occasions for great images. You *are* the special place of the great image, and your home is your everyday environment, so it is even more the special place of the great image.

For many years, John was Mr. Mom, caring for two babies, then toddlers, then young children. That meant that, in large measure, day in and day out, year in and year out, he was restricted to the household and to within stroller-restricted distance from his house.

As it turned out, these were the most decisive years of his Nalanda Miksang engagement. He found the ordinary magic in this ordinary situation, in his household and backyard, in long sessions through the streets and alleyways with a two-stroller carriage. While the children enjoyed the fresh air or were asleep, John was awake to the ordinary, everyday phenomenal world. Every day was a Miksang day.

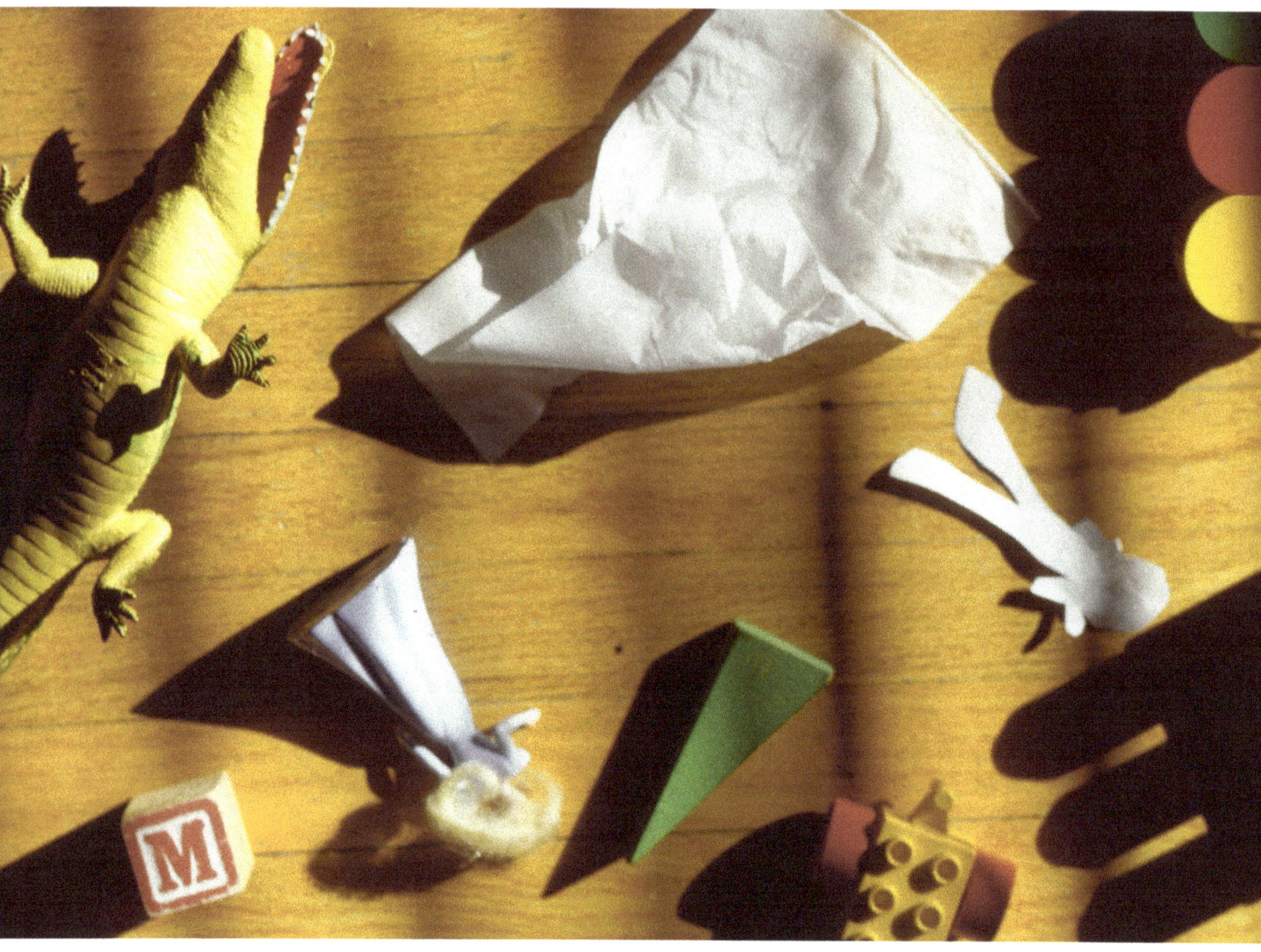

At home, the house was often a mess. One day, John found a wild arrangement of toys on the sunlit wood floor, with many little objects lying in a haphazard way. Yet it was an amazing display—blocks, paper cut-outs, dolls, and dinosaurs—a moment that became an image. Another day, after a birthday party, John noticed two balloons had floated to the ceiling, nestling with each other. That moment became an image. One morning after a big party, John noticed the empty wine bottles, and their shapes and colors, lined up on the sill of his kitchen window. That moment became an image. These perceived moments becoming images is the practice of Ordinary World contemplative photography.

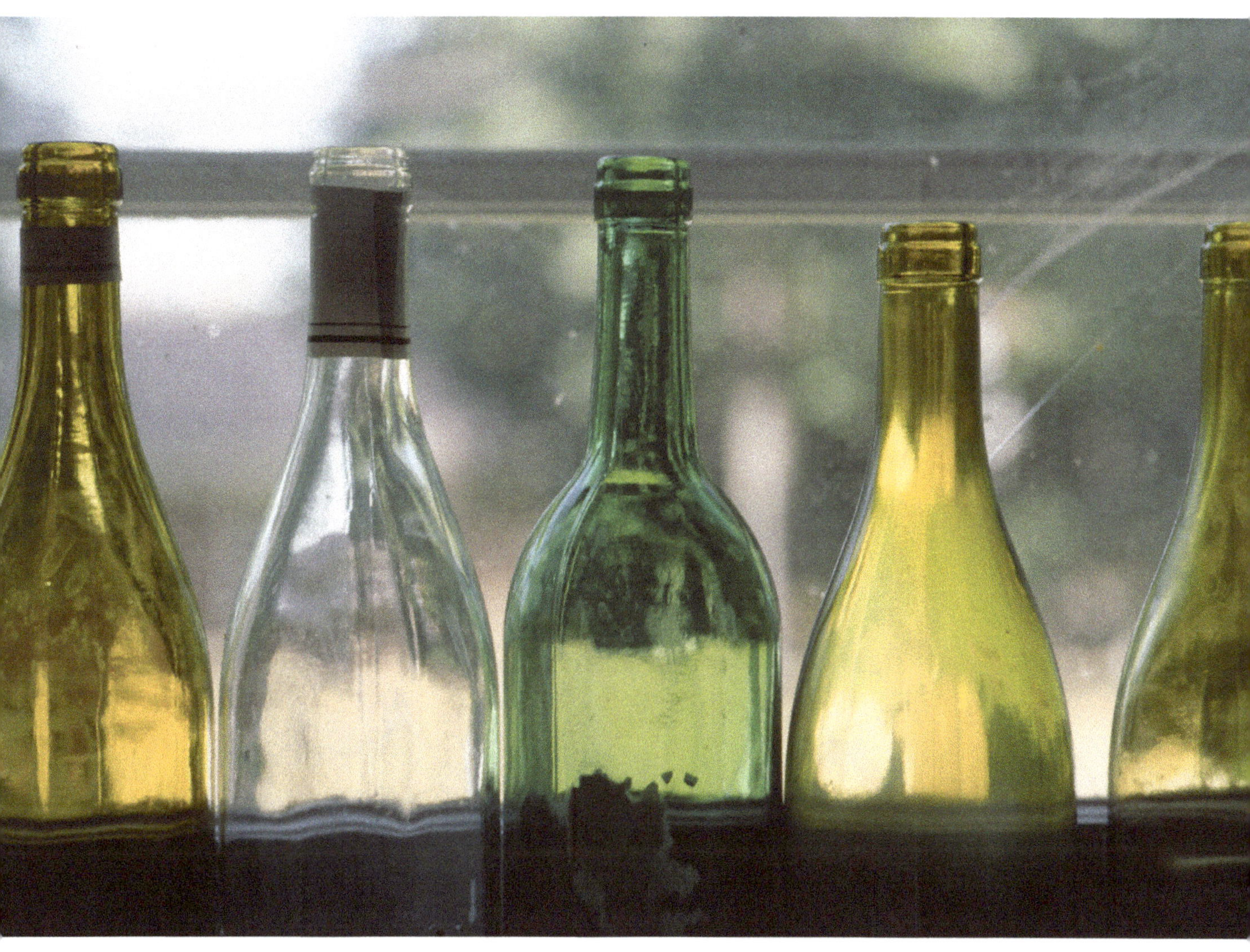

Overall, Miriam finds this to be a rich, ongoing personal practice, as many of our students do. People who do this assignment during a weekend program are at a disadvantage—we do our best to remind them that this is a deep, perpetual assignment. Day after day, light leads Miriam to old handmade afghans, power outlets, curtains, or blinds. Her cats, who are sentient beings integral to her personal world, also appear in this perceptual playground, without bias around cleanliness or tidiness. Following the trail of light around the house, like a cat, helps her to stay awake to the inside world. This trail of light is the light of the world.

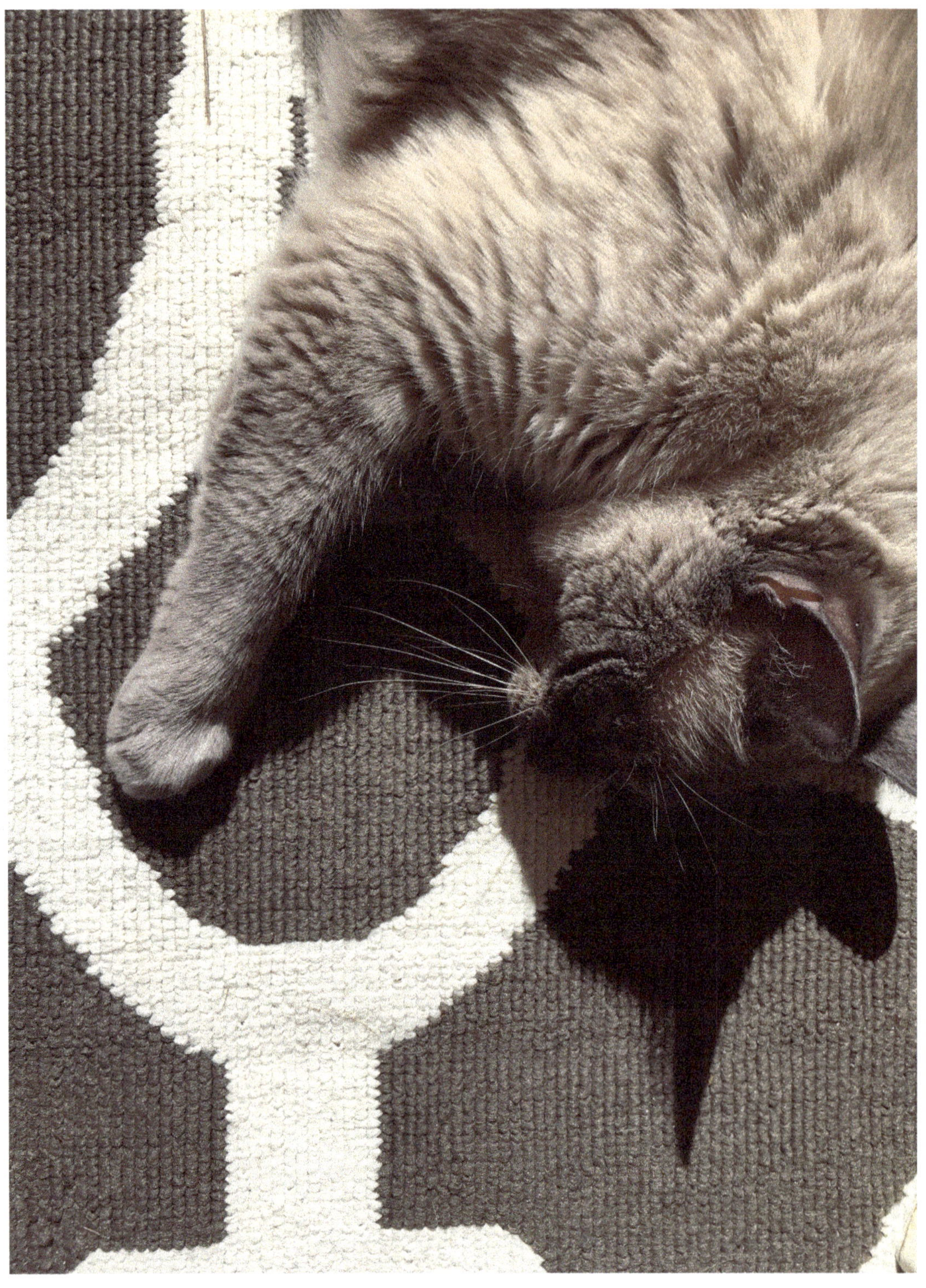

This is crucial for all of us to consider, so we do not lapse into a habitual cocoon to hide from the world. The way of falling asleep to our lives always exists, especially at home, in the familiar. But the way to be awake and lively is also always available, even at your bedside table, with the magic of dancing sunbeams.

Photography is a way to directly connect with this ordinary magic. There is the intention of the practice, the seeing, and the image equivalent. Your experience is appreciation. Your images are contemplative, beautiful, and expressive: they show the ordinary world is ordinary magic. These images have more impact than many conventional images of beautiful scenes and situations; anyone can make a beautiful image of a tropical sunset or an arctic iceberg. But to see the ordinary as extraordinary is extraordinary.

The assignment is to start paying attention to how the phenomenal world manifests in your familiar environments: home, work, dog park, wherever. You do not need to go to some special place to see clearly, appreciate the visual world, and make great images. It is actually much more powerful to do this in your everyday circumstances. This displays the visual and aesthetic power of perception.

As a contemplative photographer, your images are an expression and a teaching, a surprise, and a delight. They point to the deep point: our ordinary life is already beautiful.

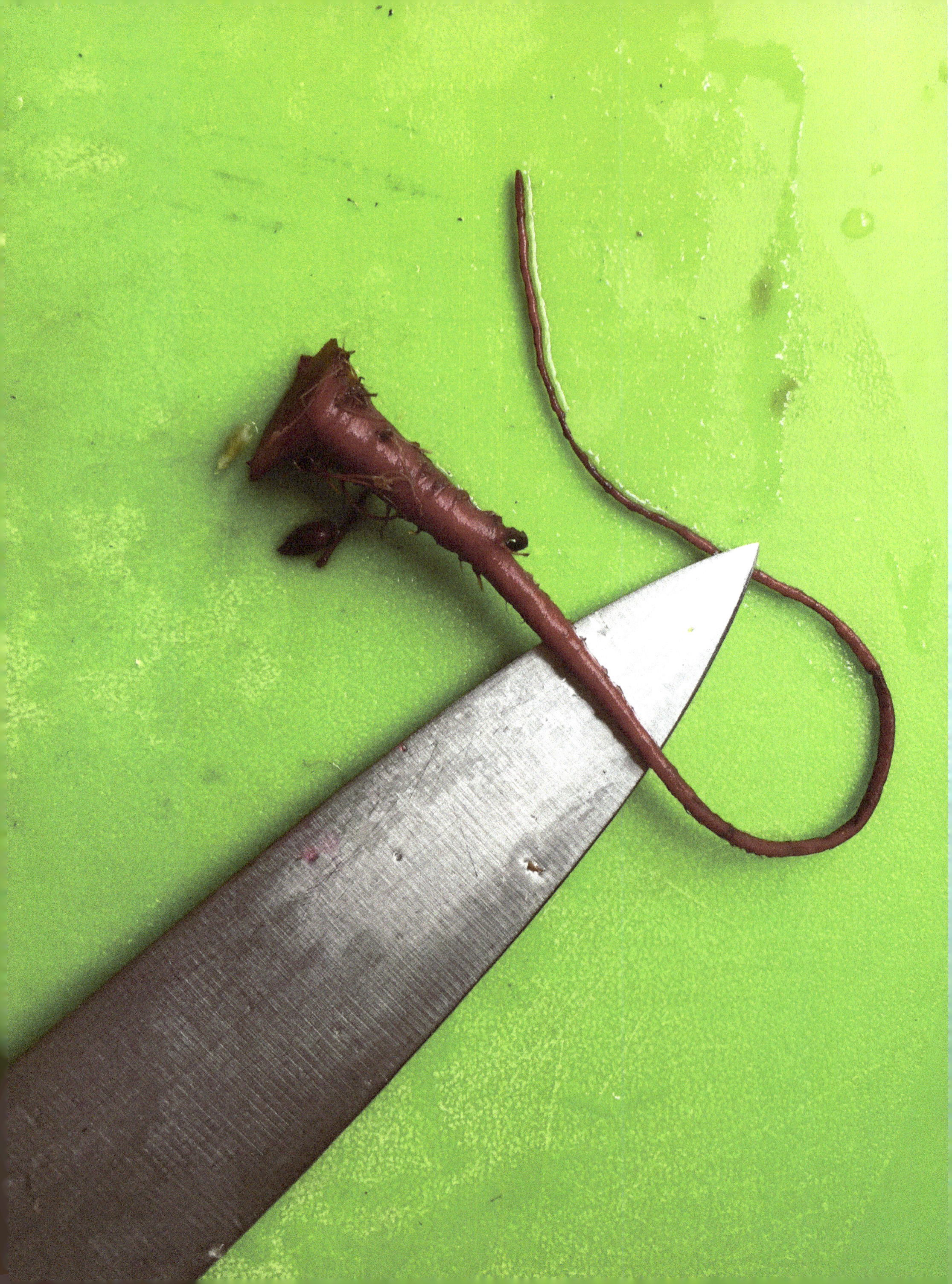

THE PERSONAL DIMENSION

The contemplation of things as they are, without error or confusion, without substitution or imposture, is itself a nobler thing than the whole harvest of invention.

—Dorothea Lange

The personal dimension is more difficult to describe *because* it is personal. The slight difference between the ordinary world and personal world is personal narrative. Seeing the abstract play of light and shadow on the wall, threaded through venetian blinds, is a personal experience, but not a personal event. Seeing the balloons after the birthday party has a deeper personal resonance. This kind of image has a deeper heart resonance: it resonates with viewers. They get something, something good out of it, even if it is inexpressible in words. These deeply personal perceptions, experiences, and images are expressions of true heart connection. They mean something, and they stay with you throughout your life.

What is truly personal is precisely that which cannot be put into words in a general way. Miriam finds when she teaches memoir that the more specific we are about personal experiences, the more others can deeply relate as intimate human beings with one another. The personal is your personal connection, personal perception,

and personal expression. Even using words, it is beyond words: we can touch something so simple and personal beyond the images or words with images or words.

Sometimes as a group assignment we collectively explore a particular visual situation—an alleyway, a park—without any assignment other than to simply see what you see in that space and deliver those perceptions. The group result is a kaleidoscope of visual images. However, these are more individual than personal. In John Daido Loori's book *The Zen of Creativity,* he describes a teacher telling how, if given the assignment to draw a line, his Japanese students will draw basically straight lines with small hints of their own human error in them. That is personal. American students, however, will get clever and draw what they feel expresses them. That is individual. An individual take is not necessarily personal.

What is personal is your heartfelt and surprise connection. There's a way in through the examples already presented: the found arrangement of children's toys, the intimate birthday balloons, the morning-after wine bottles in the window. We have also all gone to another person's house, where we can see someone else's deeply personal location in individual ways. In these explorations, everyone has their own particular visual take on someone else's intimate space.

We hope this becomes a personal practice. It is not an extra or special assignment you set aside time for. It can become part of your personal life, as a way to more deeply engage your personal life. Whatever ordinary happening moves you in a personal way is part of this practice. It could be a quiet moment after a big hullabaloo, or the ordinariness of washing the dishes and finding some space to appreciate the beauty of bubbles, space, and even leftover oil after you are done cooking.

This points to a deep inner practice of contemplative photography: intimate memory.

Documentary Versus Intimate Memory

In general, most of our personal photographs are documentary—birthdays, marriages, anniversaries, graduations, annual school photographs, prom, vacations, and so forth. They are photo album images, images taken to recollect significant events. There are plenty of studios, photography services, and even family whizzes with the camera who focus on making sure they capture these moments for posterity. This activity is quite conventional, and completely valid. Miriam once read of a woman who would actually re-stage a birthday party scene—blowing out the candles, for instance—if the original did not turn out perfectly. Though most of our documenting is not this extreme, the sentiment is the same: the image is meant to capture a memory.

But it is never what we call intimate memory, even though it may include intimate memory. Intimate memory images are more likely to includes details that stop the mind and open the heart.

These include in-between, often overlooked, subtle beyond-expression moments, which are more felt than consciously known, and can be photographed.

The examples of the toys, balloons, and wine bottles are images with a sensibility of life engaged, with intimate memory filling them. These events and images carry one's whole life of intimate memory in one moment. Intimate memory transcends conventional time; it is always happening now, as then. In it you are changed and charged at a heart level. Often these images resonate with the intimate memory of others. Your image expression may wake the viewer's intimate memory. They may wake to the ordinary detailed events and notice the subtle but powerful places where their life mattered and changed.

These are some of the deep implications of the Ordinary/Personal World practice. If it clearly means so much, why do we not see this way all the time?

OBSTACLES TO YOUR ORDINARY/PERSONAL WORLD

When we perceive an ordinary object—when we take a look at an egg or a cup of tea—there's a sense of boredom, because such a thing is so ordinary and domestic. We already know what an egg is like, and we know what a cup of tea is like. But when we are presented with something extraordinary, we begin to feel we are being treated to a special show. So in either the ordinary or the excited state of mind, whether we find the world extremely boring or extraordinarily entertaining, there's always a sense of confusion and aggression. Such aggression is an obstacle to . . . sense perceptions, and to understanding reality in its fullest sense. So some kind of fundamental discipline seems to be absolutely important and necessary. Without any actual practice . . . nothing can be heard or seen to its fullest extent; nothing can be perceived as we would like to perceive it.

—**Chögyam Trungpa,** *True Perception*

Mental challenge arises out of our connections with our ordinary and personal spaces. These include emotional connotations ("My mom gave that to me,"), mental jargon ("I really should sweep,") and the difficulty some of us have in finding "space" at home. Sometimes the default for this environment is to "document"; one can clearly feel the lack of "feeling tone" in photographs that are documentary in style—this is my fridge and look how little food is in it.

The Shambhala Art teachings have deep resonance with the understanding of what gets communicated and what is simply projection. For instance, Miriam has a small felted doll she keeps near her computer. She got it for herself, and it has a spiral on it, which is a big personal symbol for her. She keeps it around to remind her of something. She likes not just the object but also what it represents. If she were to take a photograph of it, just documenting the object, it wouldn't communicate the experience she feels when she looks at the doll. To the viewer it would be more like, "Here's this doll Miriam keeps around." That's just documenting its existence, with the anticipation that you're going to project the same things onto it that she projects. In order to photograph her experience, she needs to open to finding a visual experience that communicates the felt sense of the doll, and see through her own projections about the doll's meaning to what really happens when she simply sees it.

What this all speaks to is a tricky area, but one which is possible to explore with this assignment: "Are we having the experience right now, in this moment, that's visual and also energetic but, at the same time, is not a construct? Or are we sharing something that actually isn't in direct perception?"

Stories about our personal spaces and objects quickly become about clutter. You can have a direct flash of perception about your dirty laundry, no matter how chaotic it is. You can photograph a cluttered home in a mindful way, one that honors the situation for what it is, rather than attempting to explain or justify it. The frustration in this assignment arises because the mind of the photographer is cluttered. A clear sign of this is when you trade ordinary/personal worlds with someone else and they are able to see your situation clearly: the situation is not the chaos; it is in the mind trying to work. The photograph of the flash of perception of the environment mirrors the mind.

Documentary photos lack a heart connection because there's a feeling of flatness, a distance between the viewer and the thing that's being viewed, so there's a sense of inflated subject–object, which happens in a lot of traditional photography. We're taking a picture of some*thing*, and when we take a picture of some*thing*, as opposed to the flash of perception, the connection, then we get a documentary photograph. When we don't photograph the connection, when we photograph a *thing*, then we already have a sense of distance, so sometimes the distance arises there. Sometimes the distance arises because we can tell that this object or this situation has a lot of meaning but we can't feel it. We can tell that it means something, but we're being *told* it means something, which is this definition of documentary. We're being told that something has meaning, and we have to be careful about that. You can't tell someone to care or to feel the way you do; you need to share the experience and let that person connect.

An Allergy To Yourself

Chögyam Trungpa Rinpoche refers to our tendency to be allergic to ourselves. Some of us literally are: allergic to the dust mites who live off our dead skin, or allergic to our own systems (auto-immune disorders). But he is speaking of a much more psychological state, one in which we are afraid to go into our own minds (lack of trust of our own sanity and basic goodness) and even our own self-created environments (shame about how our home looks). This self-allergy creates a block to directly observing and appreciating a great deal of our situation.

Even if you travel a great deal, the fact is you are with yourself—and your tendencies, habits, and preferences—constantly. Some kind of friendly familiarity with your own self and your current manifestation is good for you and good for the world. And it is a helpful basis for your perceptions. This does not mean favoring what you think is best—you judge that lace is the best for doilies, and therefore reject any other materials. This means noticing that favoring through perceiving, photographing, and being curious.

Often people find when doing this assignment that their first level of emotional experience is embarrassment. This is not an uncommon response to our living environments, and it is also a common layer of protection around our minds and psyches. Can you imagine what life would be like without that thin veil?

All of Nalanda Miksang is about direct experience and perception. Underneath our positive or negative assessments, which seem to arise most quickly in our intimate lives, there are direct perceptual experiences we are having that are valid, powerful, and vivid in their own right. Slipping off that itchy tulle fabric can be scary at first, but it is an important part of connecting with direct perception. There's no better place to master it than in your already-known spaces.

Ordinary/Personal World And Photography Craft

Camera craft can also be an obstacle of sorts in this assignment. Please read our craft suggestions, but also know that you need to really let go and trust, let yourself feel the ordinariness of your life, regardless of whether it's your personal life or someone else's, and just be really curious about that. Have as much curiosity as you can, do whatever you can do to inspire curiosity. The Flash of Perception and Synchronization exercises are there to help jump-start those flashes. Watch out for stories about how ordinary your gear is as well. If you start telling yourself a story about craft, something like, "I just have an iPhone. I don't have the kind of craft that Joe and Jane have with a large lens," really see if you can drop that. Let yourself work with the ordinariness of where you are with your camera right now, as opposed to some escapist idea: "If I had $1,000 and could get this particular kit, I could get the best flashes of perception."

The basic Nalanda Miksang orientation is the way of perception, so photographs are equivalents of direct perceptions. In Level One, *Looking and Seeing*, at the beginning of the Nalanda Miksang exploration, there is little need for photographic sophisticated craft and technique. Since what is primary is the perception, it is enough to connect with the direct perception of color as color, for instance, and make an image. As we proceed on the Nalanda Miksang path exploration we need to engage more with craft. As we discover subtler perceptions, we need subtler camera skills. There is no better place to see this than with light.

In Ordinary/Personal World, as always, we recommend that you work with natural light whenever possible. Work with the light from outside illuminating the interior of your home. Why do we suggest this? On a practical level, you don't have to interfere with settings as much with natural light. White balance, for instance, is calibrated to outdoor natural light. Outdoor sunshine is usually brighter than indoor light.

This does mean, however, that camera settings are not as reliable for indoor lighting—florescent, incandescent lamps, and so forth. So if you do work with artificial light, you may need to change your white balance. Regardless of what kind of light you have indoors—and using artificial light is absolutely fine if that is all that is available—indoor light also tends to be less strong than outdoor light, even if it is the sun coming in through your blinds. Though generally we don't use tripods outdoors in Nalanda Miksang, as they can encourage a "setting-up" quality to making photographs, you may find you need a tripod to keep your images from getting blurry. Or you may need to lean on something to keep your hands from shaking in low light, to make clearer images when indoors. For example, John used a tripod to make the image of the nesting balloons. If your circumstance includes only artificial light, go into a room you wish to explore and turn on all the light sources, then step away for a bit. When you re-enter, you will find you'll be able to see freshly again in this new/old space and have some light to make your images with.

Miriam and John have seen students do amazing things in hospital rooms during long-term stays and in dorm rooms during college versions of this course. Again, it is important to remember that this practice is about appreciating what is there, rather than wishing you had something else, including a different environment.

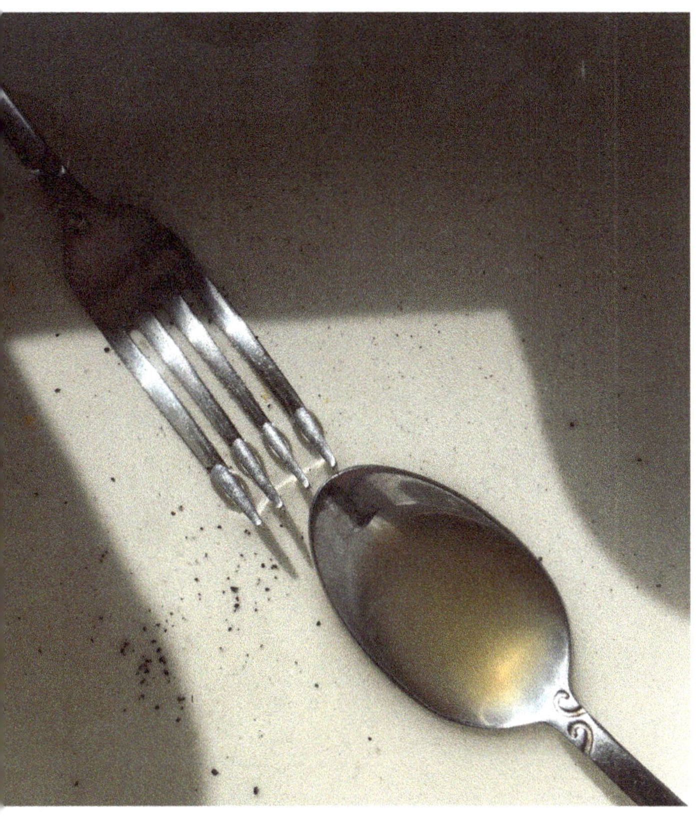

Natural Light And The Contemplative

There is also a contemplative aspect to natural light. Natural light has its own power and magic. We currently live in a world that exudes artificial light in endless myriad ways, from street lights to the screen light. But for millennia, and still currently, the main light is the natural light of the sun and the moon. This is magic light. It is the light through the day and the light through the seasons. Fundamentally, these various kinds of light communicate to us the rhythms of impermanence. The sun and moon dictate our moods, our cycles, and our connections. Shambhala teachings refer to the Great Eastern Sun as a metaphor for enlightenment, and Miriam likes to joke that we don't call it "Great Eastern Halogen Lamp" for a reason.

Natural light is what illuminates your personal situation in high detail. Day in and day out, season in and season out, natural light is the ordinary magic—or *drala*—manifestation. It helps the magic already inherent in so much of life to become visible. It reveals the subtle differences between ordinary and ordinary magic. It is the way the light catches the eye, the way the light softens the eye, the way the light highlights the ordinary.

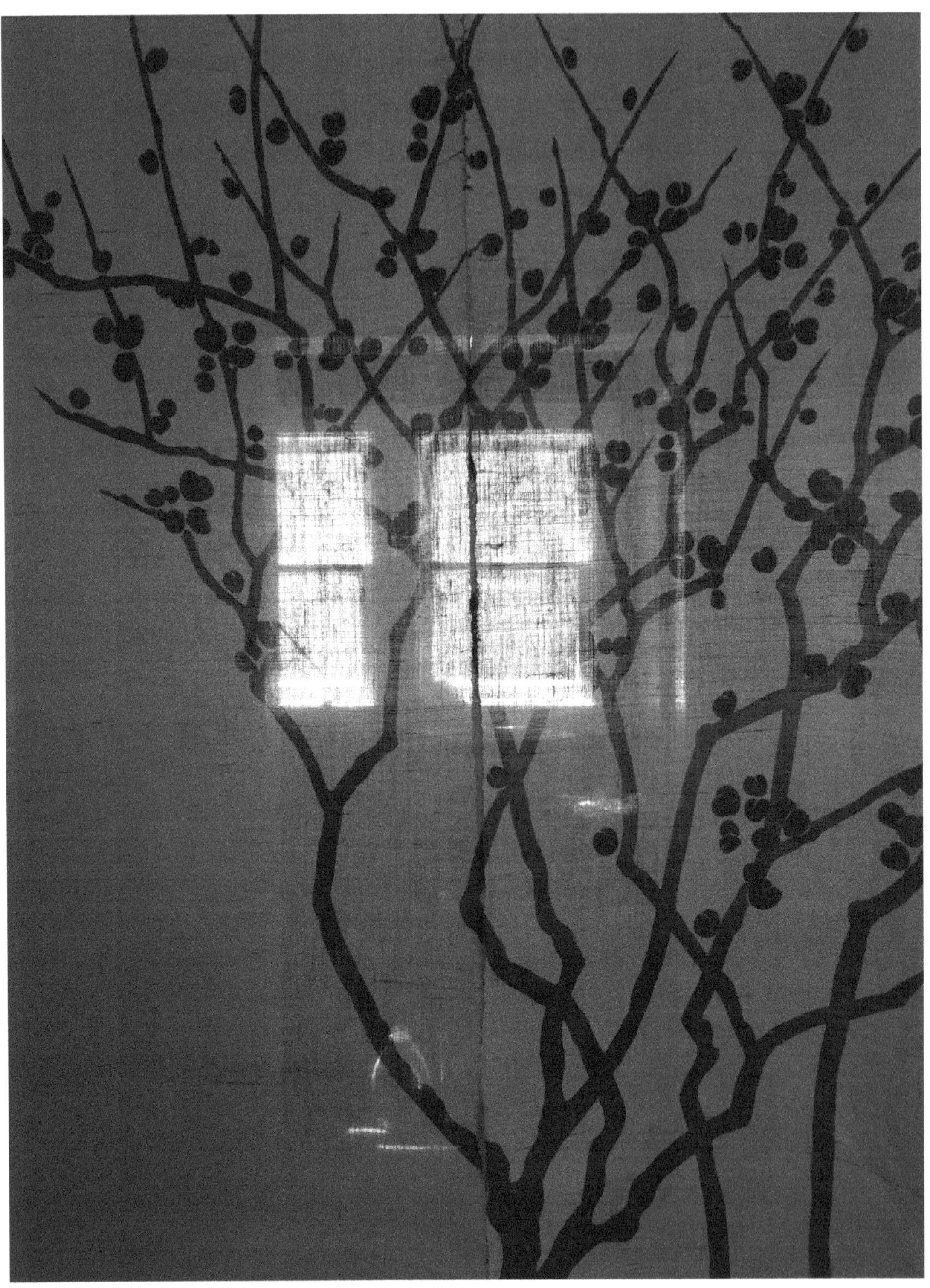

Ordinary Life And
Ordinary Magic

Despite all our emphasis on light, of course light is not the only magic. Ordinary magic can be anything and everything, just that occasion in just that way. The soap suds with their rainbow bubbles in the kitchen sink, too, are ordinary magic.

This assignment goes beyond the appreciation of familiar circumstances, such as home or work. Sometimes we live in places where the "ordinary world" is considered quite extraordinary by others. Miriam has been teaching online quite a bit the last couple of years, and often has students in classes who are from disparately different places—like Niagara Falls and Cape Town—in the same class at the same time. For instance, recently a student who lives near Niagara Falls spoke of photographing things like dandelions, shoes, and sidewalk cracks while at the Falls, when normally they, too, would be fixated on the "specialness" of the falls. An American ex-pat in the same class, now living in South Africa, made a trip to Rwanda. This person noticed how Nalanda Miksang practice adjusted their perceptual lens in this still new-to-them place, so that more of what is ordinary to the locals stood out to them in a way they hadn't noticed on a previous trip. This juxtaposition reminds us not to overlook the ordinary, even in "extra special" places.

When you tune into how your personal ordinary world manifests in magical ways, you can extend that understanding in a larger way. You can see the whole world as the ordinary magic world, like seeing how light illuminates a sugar, salt-and-pepper, found arrangement on a table in a city street café.

Everything is ordinary, and at the same time, *ordinary* is a kind of special word in Shambhala teachings, because it's often followed by the word *magic*. When we say, "Everything is ordinary," behind that is the understanding "Everything has ordinary magic." By being ordinary, by being exactly what it is, at that moment manifesting in that moment, it is magical.

The inner teaching and practice says we are doing more than making magic images. By doing this practice, we are engaging more of an ordinary magic life, inviting it in. The practice shifts our momentum, focus, orientation. Instead of the day-in–day-out job of washing the dishes, it is a magical daily sink practice. It is not just being in a room but being alive to the lively play of light in the room. It is not just walking to the corner store to get some milk, but a walk through the phenomenal world, with its never-ending kaleidoscope of ordinary magic.

As Pema Chödrön said in the quote at the beginning of this chapter, "Curiosity encourages cheering up." With a practice like this, which consists of pure curiosity and exploration, it is possible to profoundly cheer up on the spot. This helps you get through the challenges of an average day with a smile on your face and glow in your heart. So much of our life is ordinary. The contemplative way is to see the ordinary as ordinary magic. Then we access natural resources for ongoing awakening, appreciation, and deep life meaning.

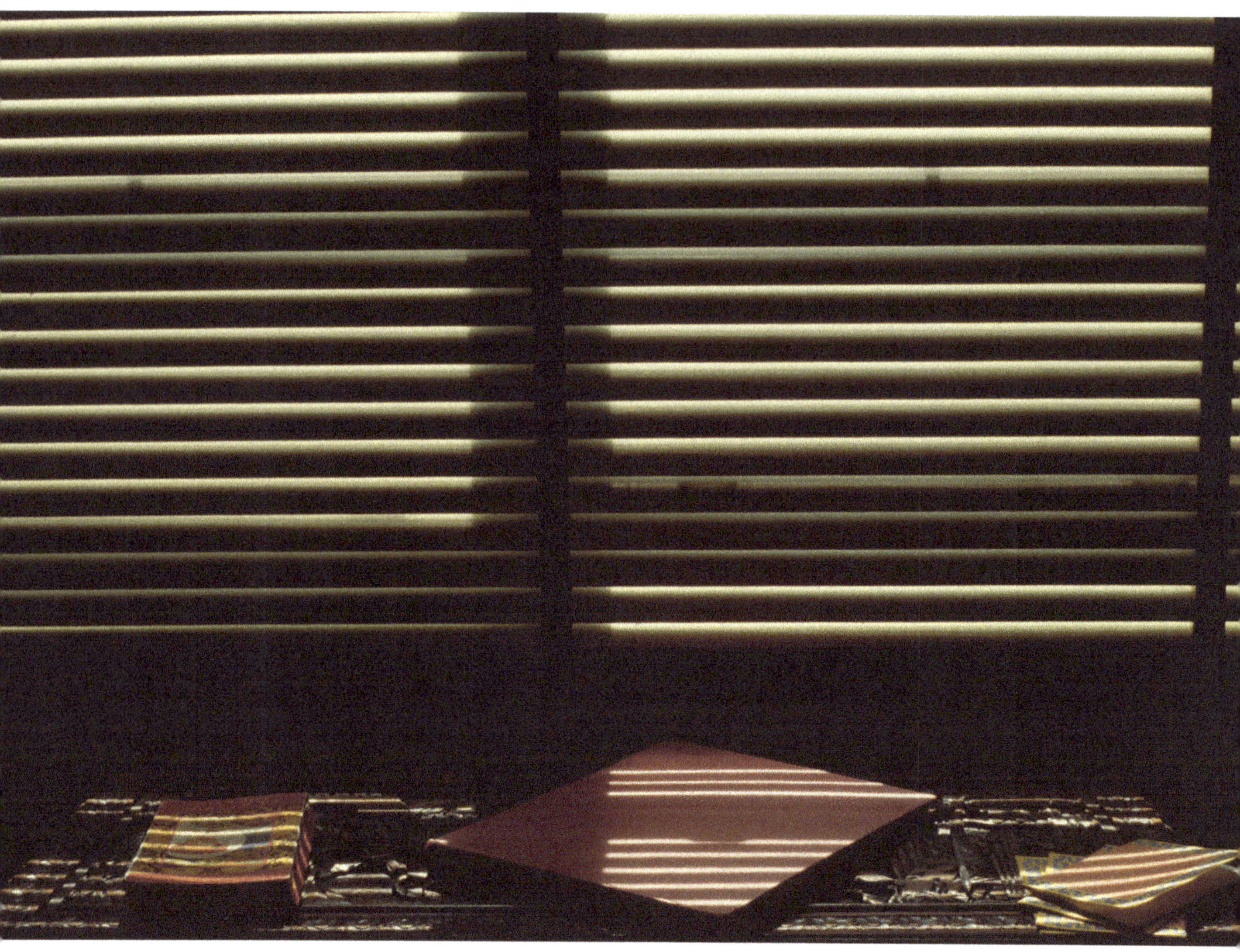

Assignment Three:
Ordinary/Personal World

Practically, it is very simple and straightforward: just explore and appreciate your ordinary and/or personal world. This connection can happen at different levels of intention and view. It is all contemplative. It all starts with a simple perception and an equivalent image. Remember, you don't have to look for ordinary magic; it will simply appear in your ordinary and personal environments.

You can approach the assignment one of two ways. The first is to see and photograph the ordinary as ordinary magic: bathrooms, kitchens, backyard. Explore specific environments. Another way in is through the more personal and intimate realms. You find them around the edges of personal moments, and through them, you share your heart with the heart of the world. This is more spot-shooting, based on a felt sense of a moment.

The first time you approach the assignment of Ordinary/Personal World, it's good to frame the time, set aside your other life engagements, and focus on doing it. Tune into this radio station only, and don't mix it with your life or explicitly with other assignments. However, Ordinary/Personal World is a very rich, ongoing, long-term practice. Most people find it unfolds over time, and not just during one shoot. You're washing the dishes and all of a sudden the clouds part and the sun comes out and it comes through the glass in a particular way: ordinary magic.

PART FOUR:
FLOWERS AND WEEDS

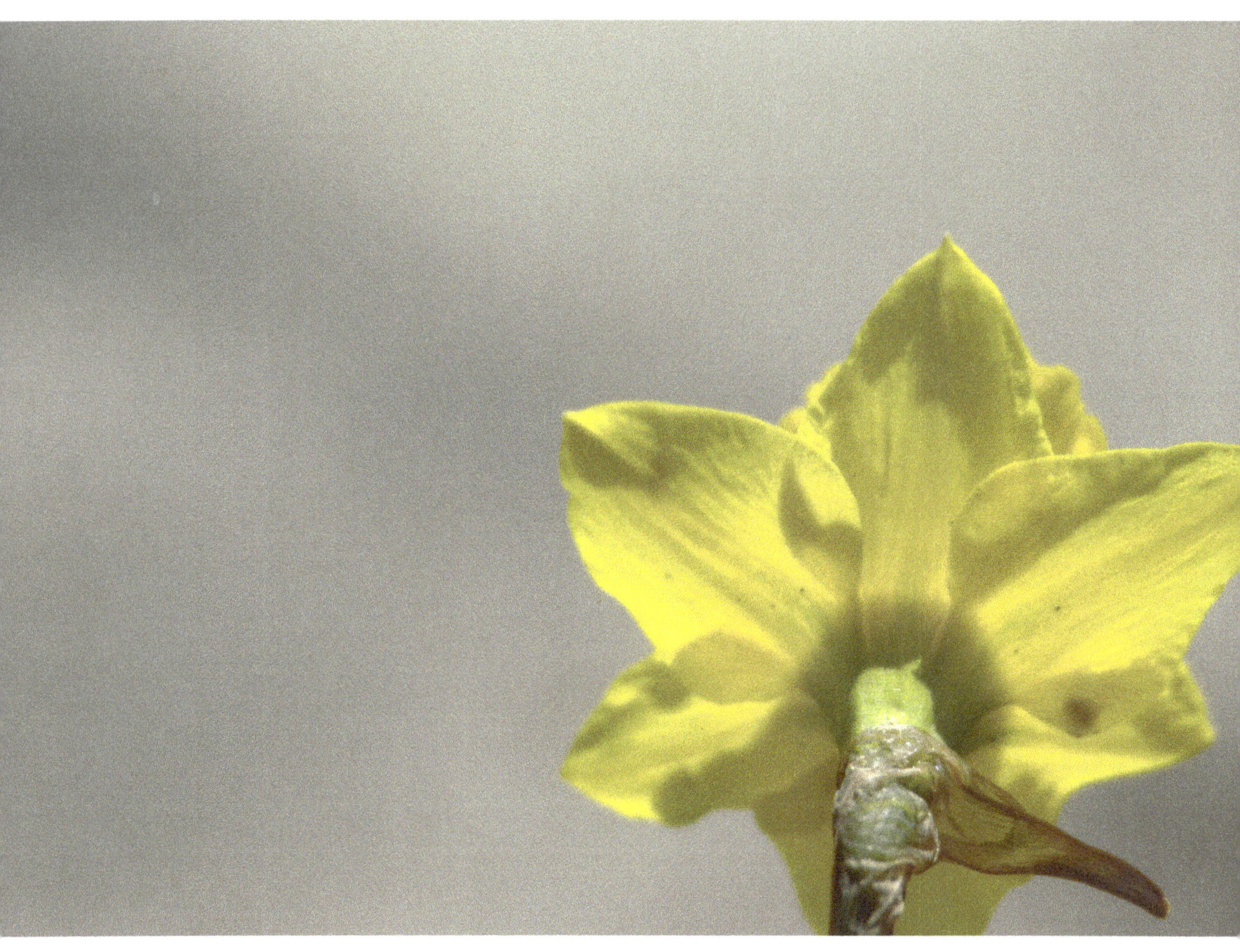

Assignment Four:
Flowers And Weeds

Flowers have always been a popular subject matter for photography (from botanical studies to macroscopic abstractions) and painting (from still life to Impressionism). Because of this, flowers, whether just cut or still growing, seem like an easy and available topic. However, for contemplative photography, flowers are considered a difficult subject. In fact, we suggested in Level One to avoid photographing flowers for the Color assignment. It's more likely the perception or photograph will appear as a flower with color in it, rather than just color.

There are at least two reasons for this.

First, flowers are intrinsically attractive; they say, "Look at me!" They evolved to attract pollinating insects, and they attract humans, too.

Sometimes they attract us so much we cannot see them as simply flowers in their phenomenal manifestation. For instance, for a few summers in a row, Miriam presented a Nalanda Miksang Level Two workshop at the London Shambhala Center. During a workshop, in order to photograph Flowers and Weeds, the participants went to a huge rose garden at a park easily accessible by public transit. As soon as they walked into the park, Miriam knew they were in trouble. The garden was huge and filled with dozens of varieties of roses. She had already warned the students that flowers can be difficult to photograph, specifically because they

are so beautiful. Roses are the ultimate flower in this sense: our concepts get ahead of us and we can't see clearly, more so than with other flowers.

The students gathered, already stunned by the beauty of the roses, not to mention scent, before they took one photograph. Miriam encouraged them to go slowly, to get down at ground level and crawl around or lie down. She reminded them to return to their perceptions, being inquisitive to find out what the flash was underneath their idea of what was going on.

The normally somewhat reserved Brits and their European guests did a good job of exploring: they squinted at the scene from the benches surrounding the garden, lay on the ground under the edges of the bushes, looked further into the branches and thorns, not just the blooms and buds. Just about everyone captured many images of expected conceptual abstract macros, or casual snapshots, of roses. Yet every single participant also got beyond the surface level of being overwhelmed and went deep into direct experience of nowness: that rose, in that moment. We could feel it in the resulting images, which captured our eye immediately. The variety was endless and rich.

This leads to the second obstacle in photographing flowers. We associate a lot of memories, ritual, and symbolism with flowers. For example, think of weddings, funerals, romantic offerings (Valentine's Day, anniversary, apologies), and hospital visits. There are specific flowers for certain occasions, like the poppy for Remembrance Day. As well, flower arrangements (whether secular or sacred) often appear in one's home or on a shrine or altar. So there is a cultural overlay when we engage the subject matter of flowers in a contemplative way. How do we get past that?

Don't see flowers as flowers.

See the way the just-so, just-that flower presents itself as this just-so, just-that perception. The point isn't to record the flower as a flower but to open to its display as a perception. It could be the top of the petals. It could be stems. Or the dew on the hairs of the stems. Or a dewdrop at the fern tip. It could be from behind the flower. It could be the way the back light illuminates as magic. It could be any way, but it will always be just that way. That is the contemplative and the resonance.

Remember, our subjects in Nalanda Miksang are never objects—never a flower, for instance. The subject of our photograph is always the flash of perception or the easing into the synchronization of perception—this moment with you, the flower, the camera, and the world gathered together; you as you always already are, plus the world as it is, all embodied in an image.

For example, rather than taking in a whole sunflower, you might perceive the flame-like yellow forms in space that are the top petals in a general background (see Dot-in-Space as Resonance, in Part One). That is just one way they can manifest, in parts. You can also find a whole flower, but as a contemplative display: a pink cosmos blossom seen as dot-in-space. There are no formulas. Watch out for your ideas about what is contemplative and what isn't, and try to go beyond them. Flowers are

never the same, so be open to any way the flower opens as manifestation.

Again, the flash of perception is in play. Here it may be subtler. Rather than a "hit" it may be more of an opening, even a soft opening. Something attracts and comes into play and into perceptual focus. The flower or weed or whatever living form attracts us. Try to relax and "hang out" in an open, attentive-gaze way and let the flower make the first move. It usually will not be "Look at Me!" but a subtler seduction: these delicate petals, the grace curve of these vines, the sunlight with leaves, stems, dandelion puffs, petals.

Let the flowers make the first move and then enter their world, which will be fields of perception within fields of perception.

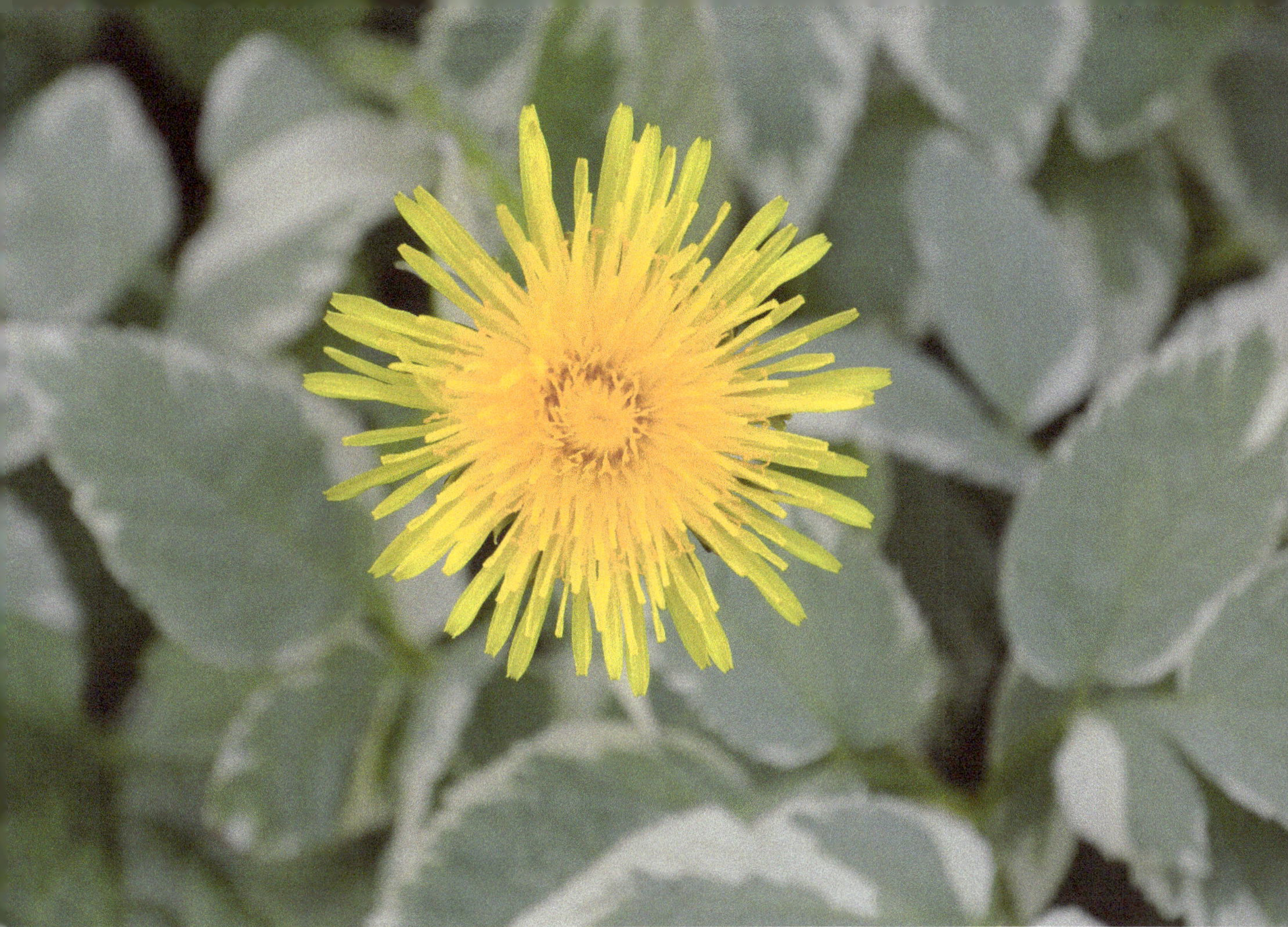

Why Flowers And Weeds?

This exploration is not just limited to flowers. To highlight this approach, we title this assignment "Flowers and Weeds." In our everyday life, we separate flowers as special and distinct from weeds. Here, our approach is to appreciate the beauty of any of these living forms—really, all plant life, including dandelions, trees, and weeds.

Why do we call some things weeds? Because they grow where we don't want them to grow, or because they are not native. For a moment, can we suspend these biases and enjoy the visual display of all plant life? Is a dandelion really less beautiful than a rose? Is a blade of grass less aesthetic or less worthy of contemplation than a rose? No. We live in a beautiful contemplative universe, and the displays of nature are one of the great expressions of that contemplative universe.

Say "yes" to weeds and to blades of grass. Say "yes" to the whole display of nature's life forms. Here there is the contemplative mind aspect: we can be open and free of bias, concept, and self-confirming interpretation. Don't see flowers as flowers. Don't see weeds as weeds. We can just relax and see what we see in the way that we see. That seeing will be free and fresh. Now we are free and fresh.

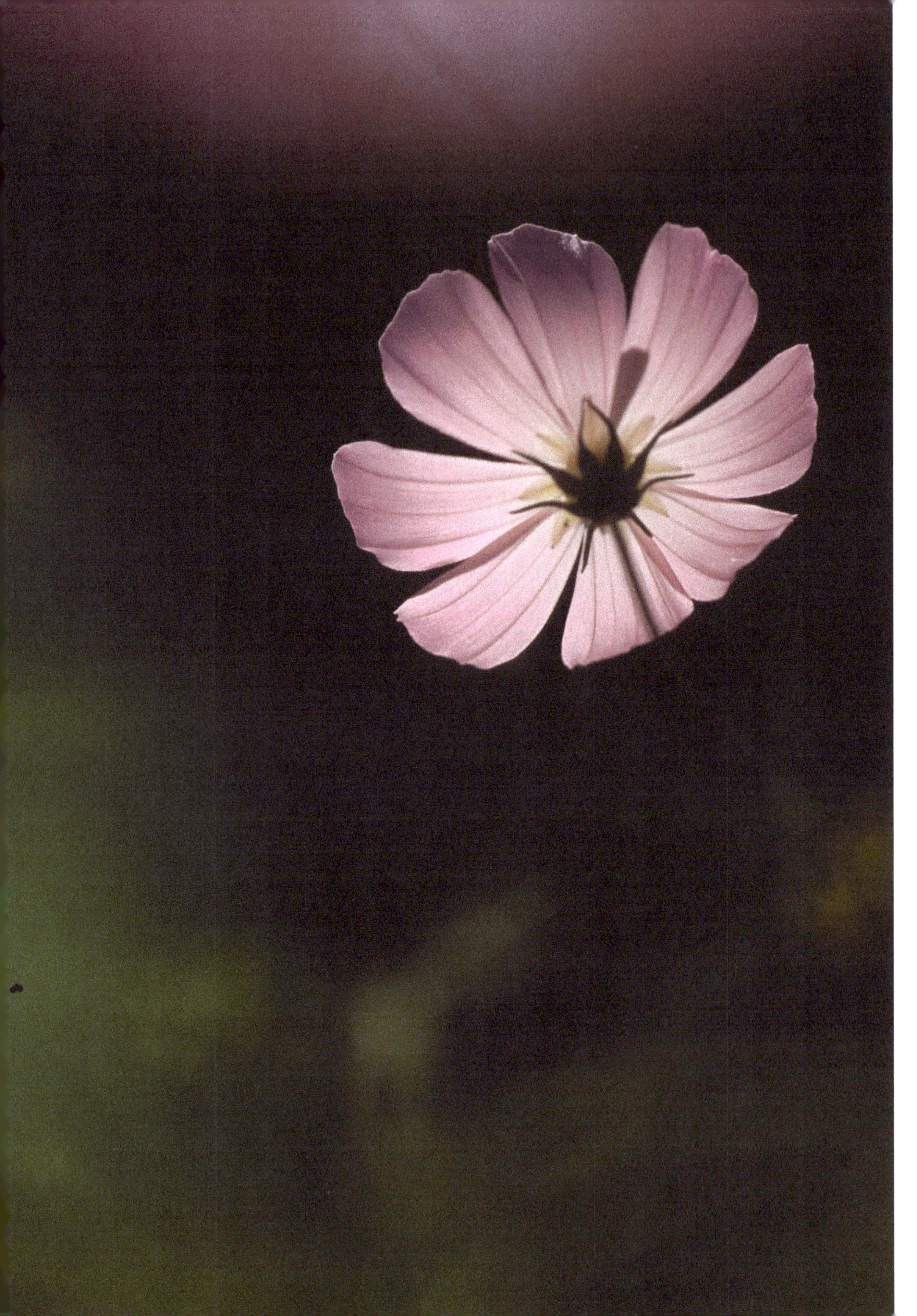

Flowers And Weeds As Dot-In-Space

A good way in to this assignment is through the form of dot-in-space. Flowers grab our attention because their dominant forms and colors jump out of the background of green. They are a natural formation of a form on a background, aka, a dot-in-space. Again, it does not have to be the whole "real flower"; your perception and image could be aspects. These aspects are also perception and, as such, in the dot-in-space formation.

Another way in is through the form of space—within flowers, within leaves, or fields of flowers or grass. Remember, at this point, every photograph is either space or dot-in-space, whether it is Level One or Level Two. Keeping this in mind can help you relax into exploring the flower and weeds realm.

We can work with a subtle way with the fields of perception. When we break with the concept and interpretation of the thing "flower" or the thing "leaf," and so forth, we enter the perception world of the flower, leaf, and other natural forms. There is an unfolding perception world of a flower, an unfolding perception world of leaves. A leaf may open to the color and pattern of its form. Or it may open to a dewdrop at its tip. Or it may open to how in autumn it fell and got caught in a wire fence.

There are many fields of perception for each natural phenomenal being. There are fields of perception within fields of perception for each phenomenal appearance through which we enter the deep and intimate contemplative universe. From ordinary flowers, ordinary leaves, and just natural beings, we find all this magic. Ordinary magic is always ordinary.

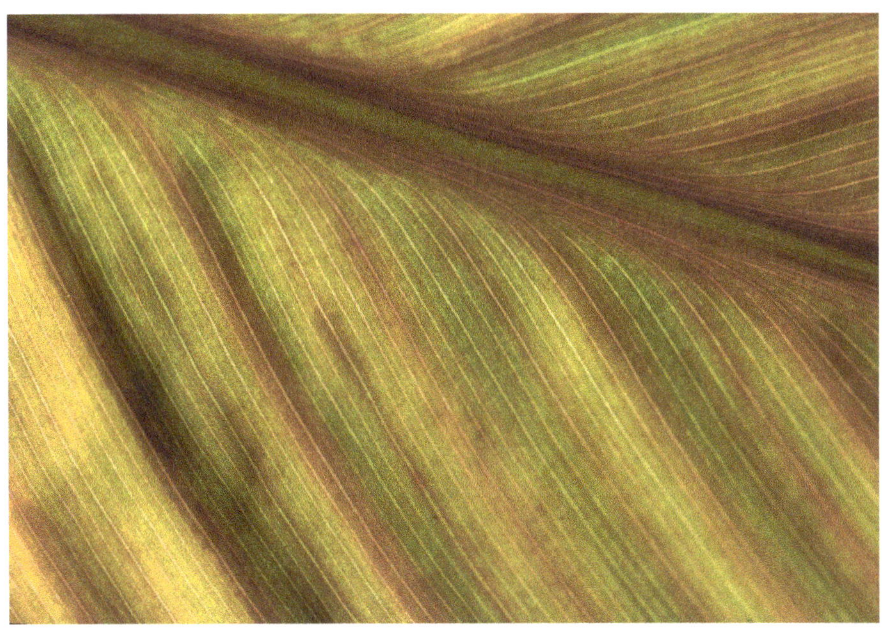

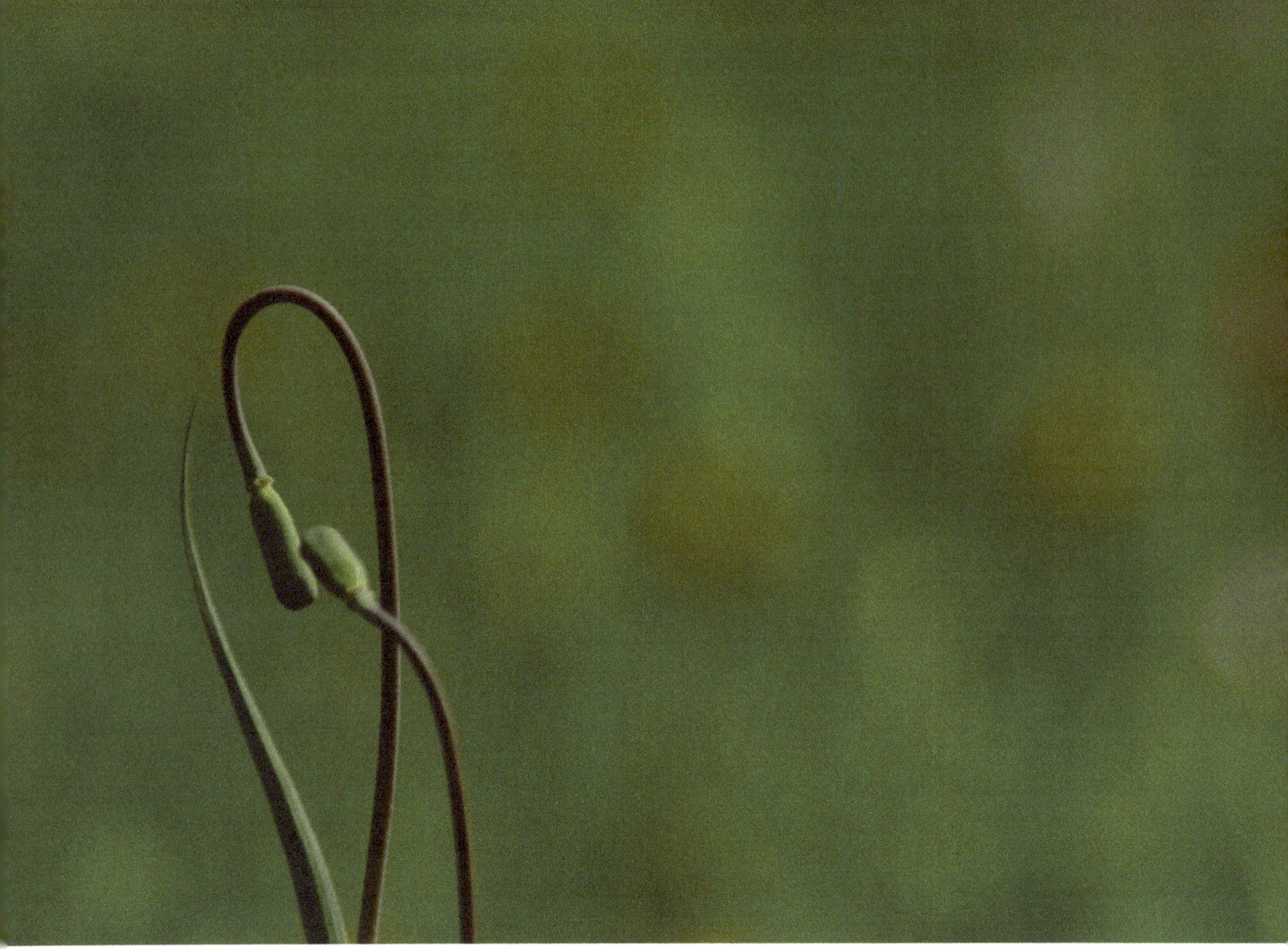

Photographic Craft And The Way Of Flowers And Weeds

In terms of camera skill, in order to photograph the expression of flowers and weeds, we need a little more technical ability than we have needed so far. Not a lot more, but a little more. Basically, you need to know how to work with depth of field and exposure, which means your camera or phone needs manual controls, which almost all do have to some degree.

As always in contemplative photography, our way is to find perception and make an equivalent image of that perception. In the Flowers and Weeds assignment, your perceptions may be subtler and so require settings to deliver subtler perceptions.

Depth of field refers to the part of the image that is in focus. On a fully manual camera, this is controlled by f-stop settings, which go from small to large. Ironically, aperture (which is what f-stop measures) is actually inverse to its numbers: larger numbers like $f/22$ actually represent a smaller aperture opening; smaller numbers like $f/1.8$

represent a larger aperture opening. A simple way to remember this is to think of the number of things in focus: a larger number means more things in focus, a smaller number means fewer things in focus. A large f-stop setting— $f/8$, $f/11$, or beyond to $f/22$—puts anywhere from most to everything in focus, from where you stand to the horizon. This is called a deep depth of field, and it is good for the likes of landscape photography.

In Flowers and Weeds, often the perception is a detail, a local focal point: the tops of petals, or just the stems, or just the dot-in-space flower. For these image equivalents, you need to know how to use shallow depth of field, which helps bring out the foreground—your flash of perception—from the background, which becomes bokeh, or blurred. If your perception was just this specific detail, the rest of the visual information needs to be diffused. In other words, we use shallow depth of field not for cool effect but to reproduce the perception as accurately as possible. Shallow depth of field begins at f-stop settings of $f/5.6$ down to as low as $f/1.8$ (depending on your lens and shutter speed). When you are working with a point-and-shoot camera or phone camera, usually putting the focus on (or finger on) what you want in focus in the foreground helps the camera "know" to bring it out from the background. Using portrait setting can help in this regard when using a semi-manual or point-and-shoot camera. The result is an image that is an equivalent of outer and inner perception: a subtle image, with a subtle and poignant sensibility.

The other camera craft area is working with light. Overall, this is one of the major areas of camera craft, which we covered, technically and perceptually, in great depth in *Looking and Seeing*. The main point of this assignment, is

to explore the way light and forms of the world interact, providing the way the world looks and is perceived. A stucco wall illuminated by front or side lighting looks very different: front light on a wall seems to flatten it, while side light brings out the texture. It is the same wall, but a different experience and another perception reality. This is what is called the phenomenal world. In *Looking and Seeing,* we explored the ways of front, side, and back light and how these ways of light inform our perception of the phenomenal world. If this all feels a bit intimidating, please take time to explore it outside your Nalanda Miksang practice. How you expose for directional light also affects how many things can be in focus (aperture affects focus and the amount of light getting in). Consider taking a local entry-level camera class or simply playing with the camera to learn through experience. We give some pointers for this assignment below.

Finally, we need to know how to work with light and shadow. In many of John's Flowers and Weeds images, the perception is highlighted against a dark or black background. Sometimes people think he uses a black background board, which is an old-school trick. But in Nalanda Miksang, we do not set up shots, nor externally manipulate them, or use filters or digital tweaks in the camera, and we try to minimize post-production digital imaging. What you see is what you get.

John simply makes an equivalent image using basic camera craft. When the perception is a highlighted flower against a shadow area, he needs to highlight this in the image, and automatic settings will not tolerate that kind of difference in light. On automatic settings cameras are programmed to even out the contrast between light and dark, among other things, so you have

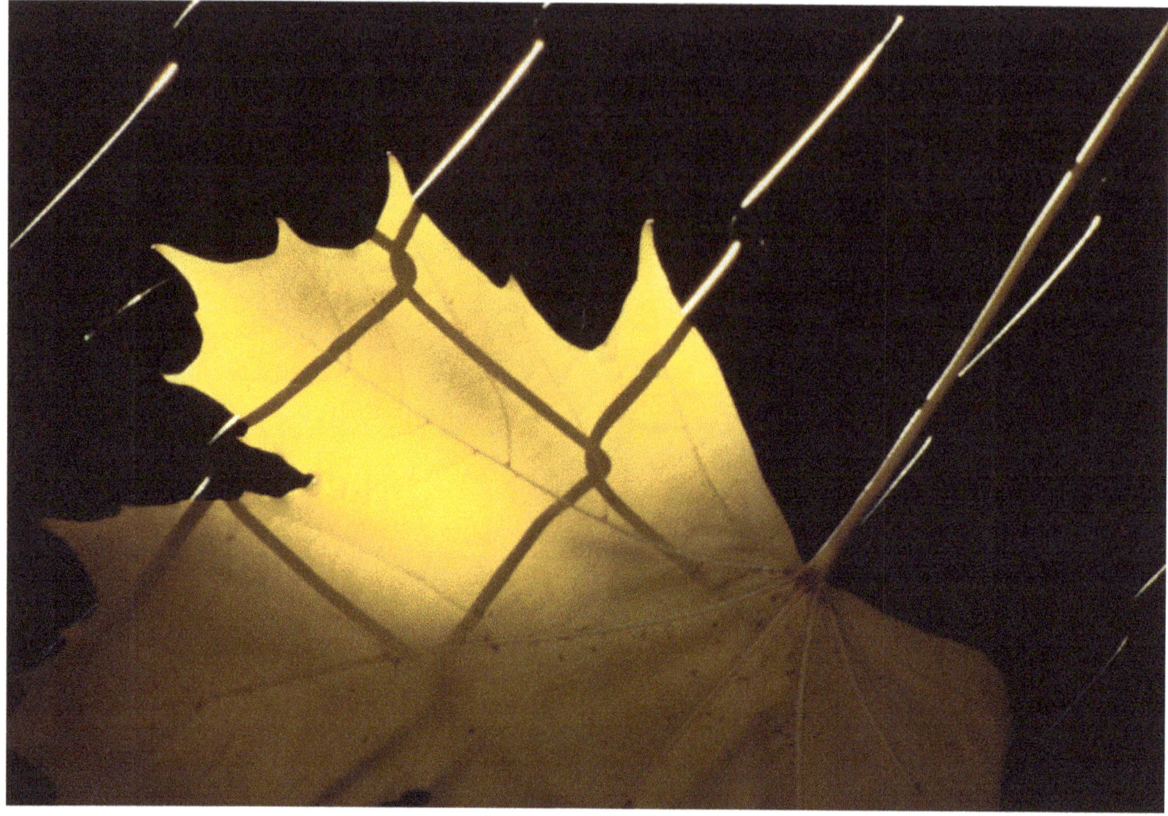

to manually (or semi-manually) force the camera to adjust for your perception. Hold the lens to the light you are exposing for, adjust your settings until they match, then depress the shutter half-way to lock in that exposure. Still pressing the shutter half-way, return to the flower and frame the perception. Ignore the camera and make the image. This deepens the shadow area into a darker tonal value while highlighting the highlight, making a vivid equivalent image.

If you are using a point-and-shoot camera, try using macro mode (small flower, for up-close details) or portrait mode (head and shoulders, to help your dot stand out from the background). With a phone, simply place your finger on what you want in focus and exposed—part of the flower or the whole flower. The fact is, automatic settings of most point-and-shoot cameras or phones will not be able to handle the deep difference between the lit-up foreground and dark, more distant background. Keep in mind that not all perceptions appear as this dot-in-space manifestation. If your camera or phone simply cannot capture a flash with such high contrast, learn to recognize that, enjoy the perception, and move on to what your camera or phone can do. Not all dots-in-space are this dramatic or hard to expose for. Eventually, it is probably best to invest in a camera with manual capacities. It does not have to be an expensive camera; many point-and-shoot cameras have manual options. There is also something quite special about having a device just for photography, especially as people's personal devices become more and more multifunctional.

Please keep in mind that even though this is more advanced camera work, we are still engaging in contemplative photography. We are not resorting to documentary or conventional forms of photography, in which the subject, for instance, would be "this beautiful flower," "this rare species of flower," or whatever other reason for photographing the flower. We use the camera settings to help highlight being touched and in touch, to deliver a heart connection through a pure perception. The further along we go into the heart of photography, the more important camera craft becomes to transmit genuine connection through an equivalent image.

As always, the key point here is to see the flower or weed as a phenomenal display and to deliver an equivalent of that display. Note how it shows itself through the details of its manifestation, which are the subject matter of your perception—just-that detailed flower part or weed aspect, just now. It is a delicate and intimate space.

PART FIVE:
ZEN AESTHETICS,
VISUAL HAIKU, DRALA

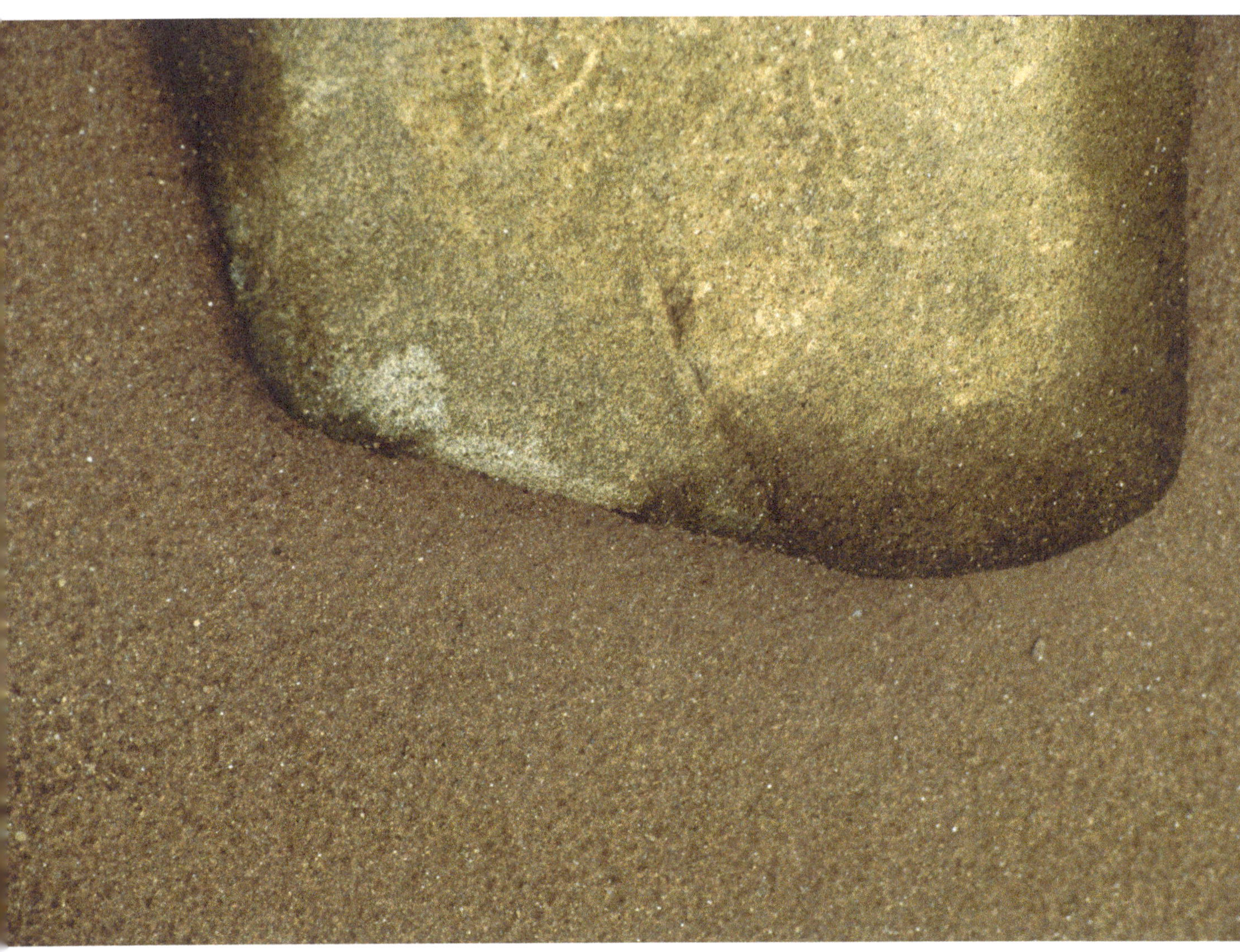

This collection of inter-related assignments gives a chance to explore some classical contemplative teachings through our eyes.

Assignment Five: Zen Aesthetics

This then: to photograph a rock, have it look like a rock, but be more than rock.

—Edward Weston

So far, we have engaged the four main assignments of Level Two, which open particular fields of the phenomenal world for contemplation. The next few assignments are a little stronger on view and aesthetic, but not specific content.

Zen Aesthetics does not have a focus like Impressionism, Flowers and Weeds, or Ordinary/Personal World. Its focus is more on the contemplative aesthetic itself. More precisely, it is a particular expression of the contemplative aesthetic: the one embodied in the contemplative arts of predominately China and Japan and associated with Zen (C'han), such as brush paintings, tea ceremony, haiku, Ikebana (flower arrangement), rock gardens, and calligraphy.

Nalanda Miksang does not hold the franchise on contemplative mind, aesthetics, and practice. Purified perception has been articulated through many contemplative arts and traditions. In particular, the artistic traditions that resonate with the spiritual traditions of Taoism, Buddhadharma, and Shinto are an exemplary manifestation of this contemplative mind and aesthetic.

In Level Two exploration, we include study and contemplation of the arts and traditions of contemplative mind. We recommend that you spend some time with examples and displays of these aesthetics. We mention many sources in the appendix to this book, and there is much you can find online.

The assignment here is to explore the phenomenal world through Zen aesthetics. In Level One, you engaged this aesthetic in general, as the baseline of Space, Simplicity, and Purity. Here is a brief review, as we take it beyond the abstraction of dot-in-space as form and into the full in-world experience of Zen aesthetics.

Space is the existence of accommodation, which is sustaining and all-pervasive; the *that* of just-that. Simplicity is being there; the *just-so* of just-that. Purity is existing without stain, nothing added, nothing taken away; the *just-that* of just-that.

Modern American Zen Master Daido Loori Roshi articulates features of this aesthetic in his classic, *Zen of Creativity*:

The characteristics . . . are essentially palpable qualities. Still point, no mind, simplicity, ordinariness, mystery, playfulness are traits that can be seen in a picture, heard in a poem, or perceived in a subject. There is, however, another aspect of the Zen arts that is less obvious. We must rely on our intuitive faculties to become aware of it. It is suchness.

Suchness (or thusness) is used in Zen literature to suggest the ungraspable there—a truth, reality, or experience that is impossible to express in words. It refers to the *that* in "it: that is self-evident . . . "

In *The Shambhala Principle*, Sakyong Mipham links this nowness with basic goodness and being present:

If we can feel, then we can simply be. Basic goodness is not abstract; it is alive and runs throughout our whole being . . . The Zen tradition addresses this notion of nowness, as did the ancient Greeks and Marcus Aurelius, the philosopher emperor of Rome. Each of these cultures understood that nowness has tremendous power . . . The Taoist sages called it the Way. Whatever we call it, there is, within the continuum of time and space, a clear and perfect ever-present moment that is whole and singular. Now is humanity coming into contact with its beating heart. In the Great Perfection this is known as heart essence . . . The present, the singular, the now, is not a fleeting moment. Rather, in that moment, the absolute and relative, the micro and the macro, are completely held . . . when we see stars and galaxies or embrace each other, we are touching the beginning of the Big Bang. The Tibetan word for basic goodness refers to this sense of timelessness, for it literally means

"primordial goodness." . . . Primordial means "beginningless." However, the beginning is not some long ago time when our goodness was born; it refers to this very moment: Our goodness is being born now.

Across the millennia, contemplative artists have articulated a subtle contemplative sensibility and aesthetic. Three key dimensions of contemplative aesthetic are *wabi*, *sabi*, and *yugen*, translated as "simple/ordinary," "loneliness/heartbreak," and "suchness/beyond."

One way to understand these three is by encountering transience and the ungraspable. There are meanings that cannot be summed up in so many words or images. There are inexpressibles which can only be sensed through being expressed. However, what is expressed can never exhaust or contain the inexpressible. This is the contemplative way, which is just an intensification of the human way.

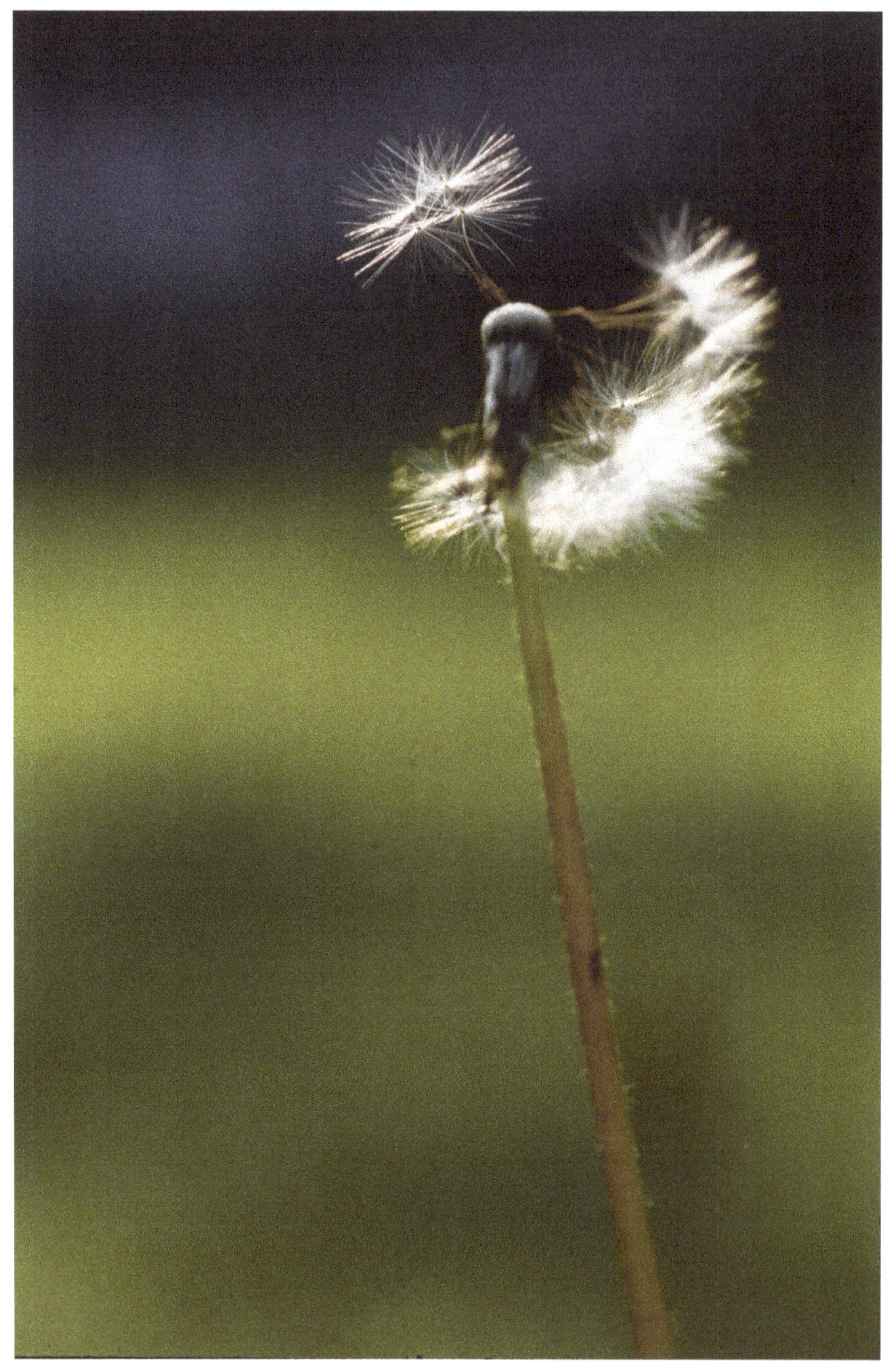

Wabi: Simple/Ordinary

We already encountered wabi as we explored ordinary world. Here, wabi gathers a sense of being seasoned through the realities of impermanence and imperfection.

The aesthetics of space, simplicity, and purity can be misleading. One can envision a pure realm, purified of worldly characteristics. This is wrong view. The presentation of space, simplicity, and purity articulates that worldly characteristics are, in fact, these perceptual aesthetics. It is the transformation of the ordinary into ordinary magic.

Wabi is helpful in this regard. It is the frank recognition that the way of the world is transience—nothing lasts and everything falls apart. We can see the wear and tear of time. Nothing is ever 100% put together, and we will never get it together. Everything is filled with flaws, which would seem to say we never have the ideal situation. On the contrary, this is real life, the only life we have. It is the only life we *can* have. So it cannot be otherwise. As such, it is as such; it is suchness.

In traditional contemplative arts, the sensibility of wabi is embodied in Cha-do, the Way of Tea, or the contemplative tea ceremony. For example, in the tea ceremony, rather than using fine china, the Japanese use ordinary, hand-crafted tea cups; those cups with distinctive flaws are favored and cherished.

Wabi says experience makes you experienced; you become seasoned. To be seasoned is to be in tune with the seasons, to gather the time flow, the time turn, the time-tide of the seasons. The seasons are the day-in, day-out, year-in, year-out turning of your life. To be seasoned is to gather the insights of experience. We call this wisdom.

So wabi, as an aesthetic, sets in play a poignant, heartfelt, ordinary world wisdom. In contemplative photography terms there is a general orientation to the ordinary world as the contemplative world.

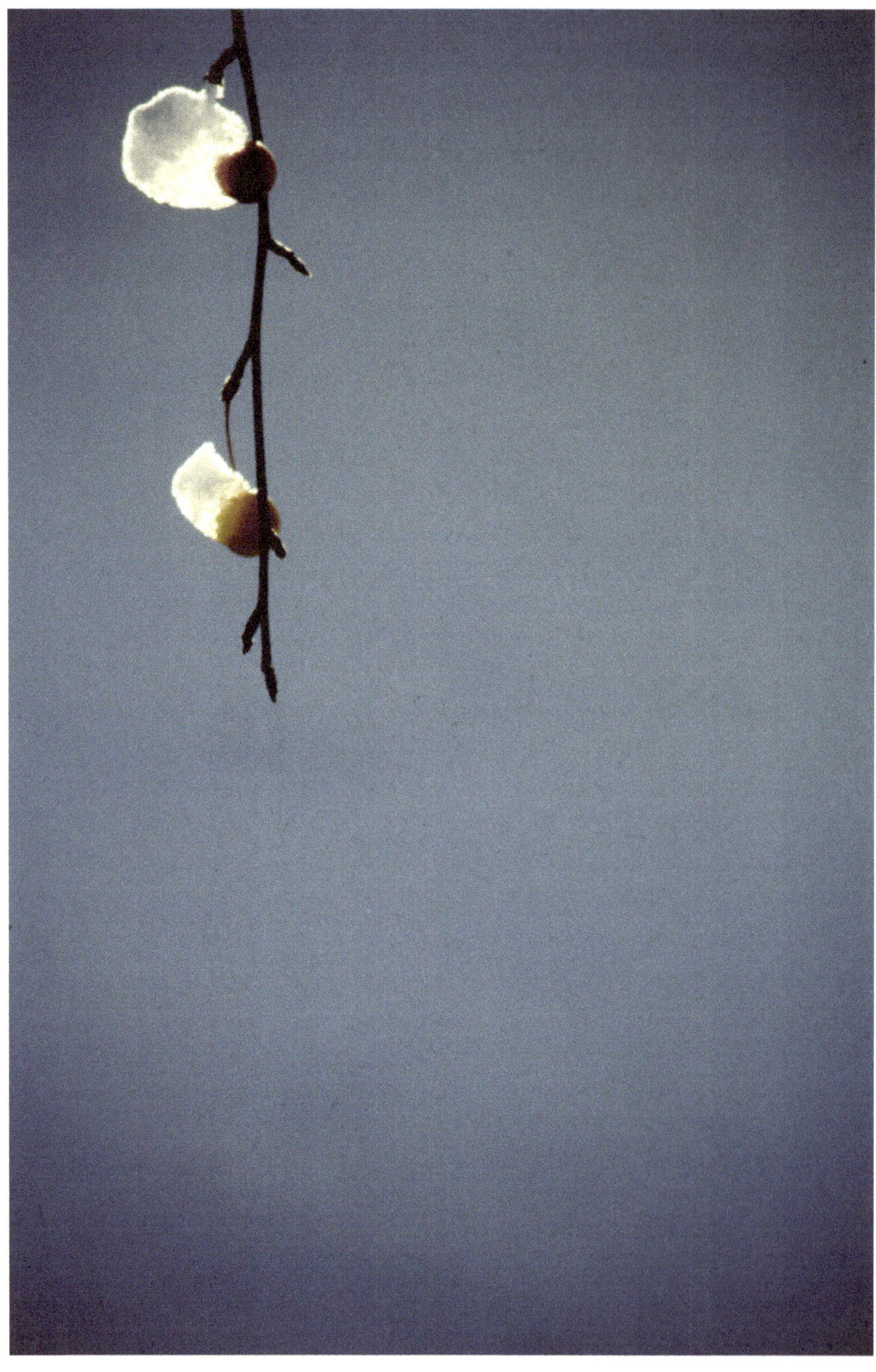

Sabi: Loneliness/ Heartbreak

Sabi is the heartbreak of the heartfelt.

Chögyam Trungpa Rinpoche says to be a contemplative is to live life as an unrequited lover. Sometimes he speaks of the genuine heart of sadness: the genuine recognition of impermanence delivering both amazing, real-time experience, and also a tinge of sadness in knowing loss. This is counterculture. We are already stressed, if not distressed. We seek happiness and fulfillment, not heartbreak and sadness. We want to be actual lovers, not unrequited lovers. It's not a great selling point, but it is the point—and in fact, an inspiring point.

Here we come to a decisive point, the contemplative point: the happiness and fulfillment you seek will not be attained by the ways you may be seeking them. You are already missing them, precisely by seeking them. They are already there, in the way they are there (which you may be overlooking in hopes of them arriving the way you want them to).

Sabi is one of the ways happiness (as sad joy) is already here. Sabi can be expressed a few ways, but let's consider loneliness, and the unrequited lover feeling first.

Loneliness exists in part because you are you and everyone else is everyone else. However intimate we get, we can never ever be each other. It is that simple and that profound: we are fundamentally alone. Sabi is realizing *we are alone together*. This is real intimacy. This is longing and passion and even, sometimes, ecstasy. The heartbreak is the heart connection. This is what makes us friends, lovers, family, even society.

What about on a larger scale? We have already broached this when considering Impressionism and haiku: the ancient pond is so deep it can never be plumbed, so vast it can never be crossed, so full it could never be emptied. The manifestation of the phenomenal world is inexhaustible. It can never be completely expressed. It remains an eternal, inexhaustible, inexpressible richness. This is also sabi.

In terms of contemplative photography, it is the same. You will never get that one perfect, final image; it does not exist. You will not get it. Realizing this is the case is what makes the practice worth continuing—knowing you will never, and never can, get it. That *is* the ultimate getting it. Do you get it?

Then there is the deep aspect of loneliness: loneliness as being alone with the alone. Why will you never get that final image? Because of this paradox: what sustains expression, by principle, cannot be expressed; yet what sustains expression can only be shown by expression. We must express. This is what it is to be human, and, in this case, a contemplative photographer.

The good news is, the more you try to express what cannot be expressed, rather than your idea of what would be a good expression or photograph, the more powerful and beautiful the image. Now you are a contemplative photographer. Now you can bring together your photography practice with your life experience. Now you understand that your life is an unrequited love affair, and that's the most beautiful thing it can be.

Yugen: Suchness/ Beyond

Finally, there is yugen. This is translated in various ways as the mysterious or ineffable. Yugen is the most elusive concept precisely because it is the most available. To a degree, yugen is understood in Zen to mean suchness. But contemplatives present this in a slightly different inflection.

As usual, contemplatives take a more pragmatic approach, risking a theistic approach, by working with a sense of the beyond. The beyond is very simple and ordinary. Often we have a sense of something *beyond the current situation*. There is something more than can be said in so many words or expressed in so many images. In contemplative photography, a strong image is one that resonates something more than just the subject matter. What is the *something more*? And from where does that *something more* come? The *something more* and *something where* is yugen.

This has at least two layers or dimensions: the why and the how. The first dimension is that the image resonates beyond the subject matter, because it expresses what cannot be expressed. It manifests as resonance rather than as matter-of-fact. That is yugen, and it is deeply contemplative.

Secondly, how does yugen happen? There is something that sustains this possibility of expression that is not somewhere else. It is not outside the expression. But it is not exhausted by the expression. Yugen is the elusive inexhaustible. Deep contemplative practices, including deep contemplative photography, orient from yugen.

In closing, these three contemplative aesthetic templates—wabi, sabi, yugen—often manifest simultaneously in a contemplative image because they embody a contemplative perception, and because contemplative perceptions embody these qualities.

Beyond these basic templates of contemplative sensibility, there are other values and orientations that inform the Zen aesthetic. For instance, much of what we have called Eastern art is presented in shades of black, white, and gray. Often an image progressively dissolves from shadings of black, to gray, to white, making monochromes with subtly different tonal values. This aesthetic expresses the sublime identity of the phenomenal world with space. The phenomenal world, even when understated, shimmers and dissolves in a vast depth and expanse. In fact, our whole life and world is a shimmering and dissolving in a vast depth and expanse.

Chinese contemplative arts embody this well, in particular through brush painting and contemplative poetry. Here is one example from the contemplative poet Wang Wei:

Deer Park

No one seen. Among the empty mountains

Hints of drifting voice, faint, no more

Entering these deep woods, late sunlight

Flares on green moss again, and rises

Here we can really feel transience. Often Zen aesthetics favor fading life, like the festival of cherry blossoms as they fall and drift, where they bump into Visual Haiku, our next assignment. The poignancy of transience makes for powerful experience and, therefore, poetry.

In North American and European aesthetics, we often value a flower at is its peak, in full bloom. In Zen aesthetics, the heart nature of a flower displays as it begins to fade, say, a petal drooping. The fading displays its fragility, which in turn displays the fragility of life and beyond.

The Zen Aesthetics assignment is to keep this orientation in mind. Notice phenomenal expressions of this aesthetic, and reproduce equivalent images.

In Level Two explorations, these are pointing out instructions. This is not necessarily an assignment you go out and accomplish. You do not need to go out with the intention of finding examples of these qualities. Rather, you gather your mind to an open perception of nature, noting Zen aesthetics where they already manifest.

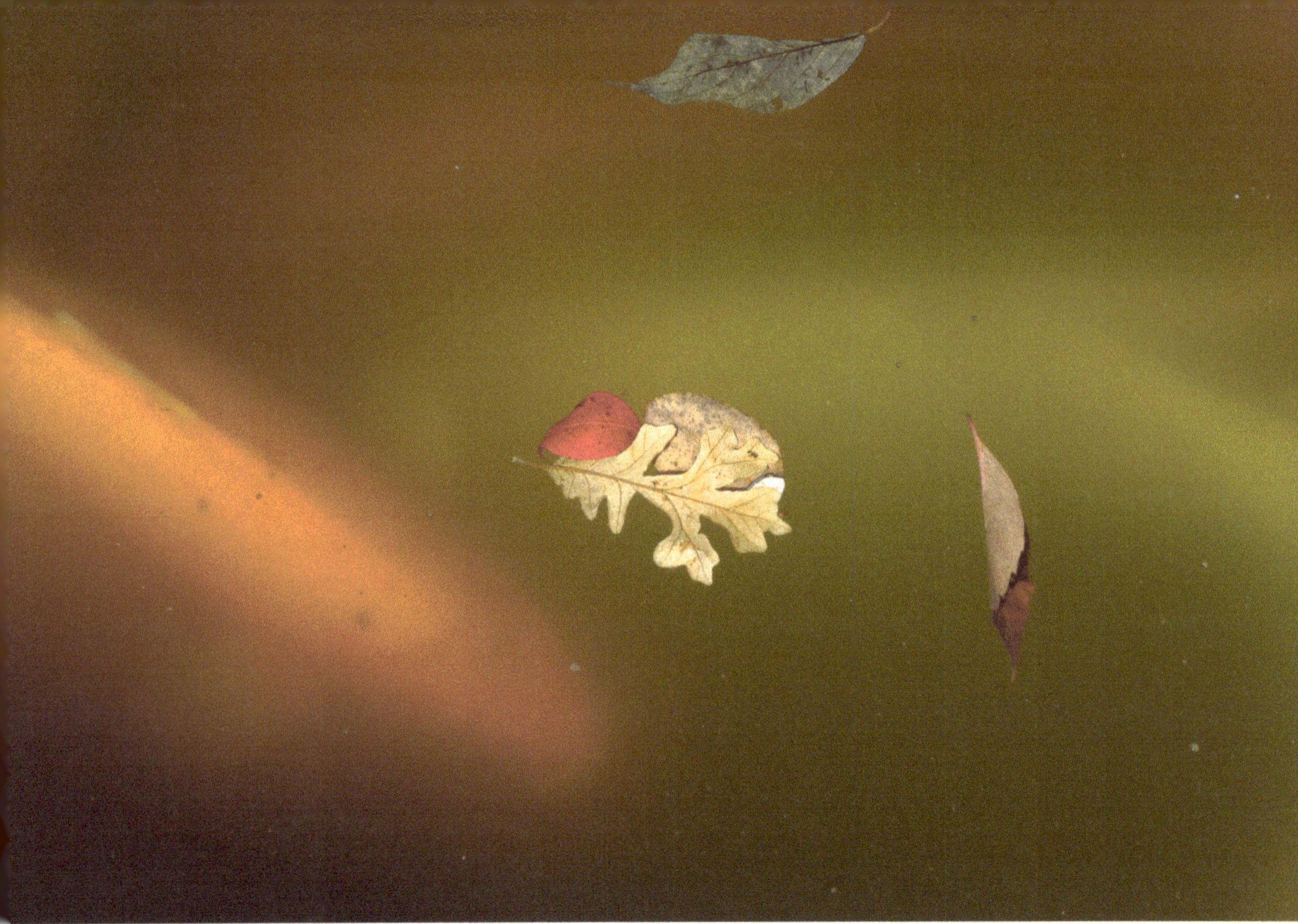

Assignment Six:
Visual Haiku

Of all the traditional contemplative art disciplines, written haiku is closest to our contemplative photography practice. Haiku is a brief literary form expressing a clear perception or insight. In English, traditionally haiku is written in seventeen syllables, divided into three lines of five/seven/five syllables, including a break highlighting a contrast of two parts of the haiku.

Haiku also includes a season word. This could be something as straightforward as stating the season—autumn—or something subtler, like a phenomenal feature of the season—red maple leaves representing autumn. That is the formal structure, the surface of haiku. But there's depth beneath this, revealed by some of its history.

As stated earlier in the book, haiku as a contemplative practice was initiated by Basho in eleventh-century Japan. He wrote one of the most famous haiku, "Old Pond" (discussed in depth in Part One):

Old Pond –
a frog jumps in
the sound of water.

This translation does not carry the structure we outlined. That is because, while the original Japanese carries a seventeen-syllable form, translations often fail to keep the feeling when they keep the form intact. It also points out to us the communication, the something ineffable being expressed, is fundamentally more important than the surface form of syllables. Here, the seasonal reference is the frog, associated with spring. There are also the two parts juxtaposed with each other: Old Pond is the ground upon which there is a foreground happening: a frog jumps in/the sound of water.

So what is visual haiku? Since visual haiku is not a literary form it does not retain the literary structures of haiku. Rather, it works with deeper contemplative features of direct perception, sensibility, insight, and season, as exist in written haiku.

Working with direct perception and insight are already a part of our practice. But in visual haiku, we tune in to the tension of impermanence and poignancy. We pay attention to the trace of something happening within that perception—a frog jumps in, which acts as a little narrative element. These tiny natural narratives are the manifestation of the haiku moment: there is a situation in which something happens. Often this appears as a trace, a hint that something occurred or will occur soon, because frequently this is when we perceive it, at the edges of it coming or going.

For example, an out-of-season oak leaf still clings to the branch, then blows off and lands on the snow. Then there is a light snowfall, and some snow gathers in the leaf. The perception and the equivalent image is the brown leaf on the snow, with more snow cupped in the leaf. In this particular example of visual haiku, the contrast is autumn meeting winter. It is enough to have one seasonal reference, but to include two is subtler and is very prized in haiku aesthetics, both visual and written.

If we are paying attention, we can trace back through the occurrence, feeling the resonance of what it took to arrive at this moment over time. It is a little contemplative time capsule. Visual haiku, therefore, is quite simple: an image of a clear perception that contains a little narrative, a seasonal reference, and a hint of tension.

Our recommendation is this: like Zen Aesthetics and Drala, do not go out looking for Visual Haiku. That will yank you out of the contemplative mindset and plop you into a hunting mindset. This balance is always tricky in Nalanda Miksang, but especially with Visual Haiku. It is better to simply head out and explore nature. You will recognize a visual haiku when you see it, if you tune into these sensibilities, but not by looking for it.

Parallel to this assignment, there is much for us to gain from reading haiku masters and practitioners. Originators of haiku discerned the way of the contemplative mind and aesthetics, which can inform our contemplative photography practice. For instance, here is an instruction from Basho:

Go to the pine if you want to learn about the pine, or to the bamboo if you want to learn about the bamboo. And in doing so, you must leave your subjective preoccupation with yourself. Otherwise you impose yourself on the object and do not learn. Your poetry issues of its own accord when you and the object have become one—when you have plunged deep enough into the object to see something like a hidden glimmering there. However well phrased your poetry may be, if your feeling is not natural—if the object and yourself are separate—then your poetry is not true poetry but merely your subjective counterfeit.

There is much here for us to contemplate. He shifts our approach from subjective and conceptual to perceptual. He points to the notion of equivalence rather than construction. He encourages us to let the phenomenal world take the lead. These are aspects already presented in the way of Nalanda Miksang contemplative photography. We enter the same contemplative way as the haiku way. They are both Ways of Seeing.

Haiku poets work with all the senses, including visual, so some written haiku are other kinds of visual haiku. Basho has the best intention and view as a haiku master; he wrote some visual haiku, but his orientation was more toward contemplative sensibility and insight. So we turn to another master for some visual haiku examples in written form, Buson.

Buson was also a visual artist; during his lifetime, he was more renowned for his visual art than his haiku. As a visual artist, he had a visual sensibility, and because of that, many of his haiku express visual perceptions. Here are some examples of his visual haiku:

White dew-
one drop
on each thorn;

Evening wind:
water laps
the heron's legs.

A gust of wind-
whitens
the water birds

Not quite dark yet—
and the stars shining
above the winter fields.

Summer shower—
a flock of sparrows
hanging on to the grass

On the mountain crests
a line of wild geese
and the moon seal

Peony petals fall—
piling on one another
in twos and threes.

The assignment, inspired by this writing and these examples, is to explore nature, noticing when visual haiku in photographic form arise.

Often, people go out to photograph all of these assignments together—Zen Aesthetics, Visual Haiku, and Drala, including even Found Calligraphy (which is forthcoming). Because they are rooted in sensibility and tone, which often overlap with one another, looking for one often leads to another. Immersing yourself in all these tonal assignments (in contrast to subject assignments like Flowers and Weeds or Ordinary/Personal World), let yourself find all the subtle layers and profundity they have to offer.

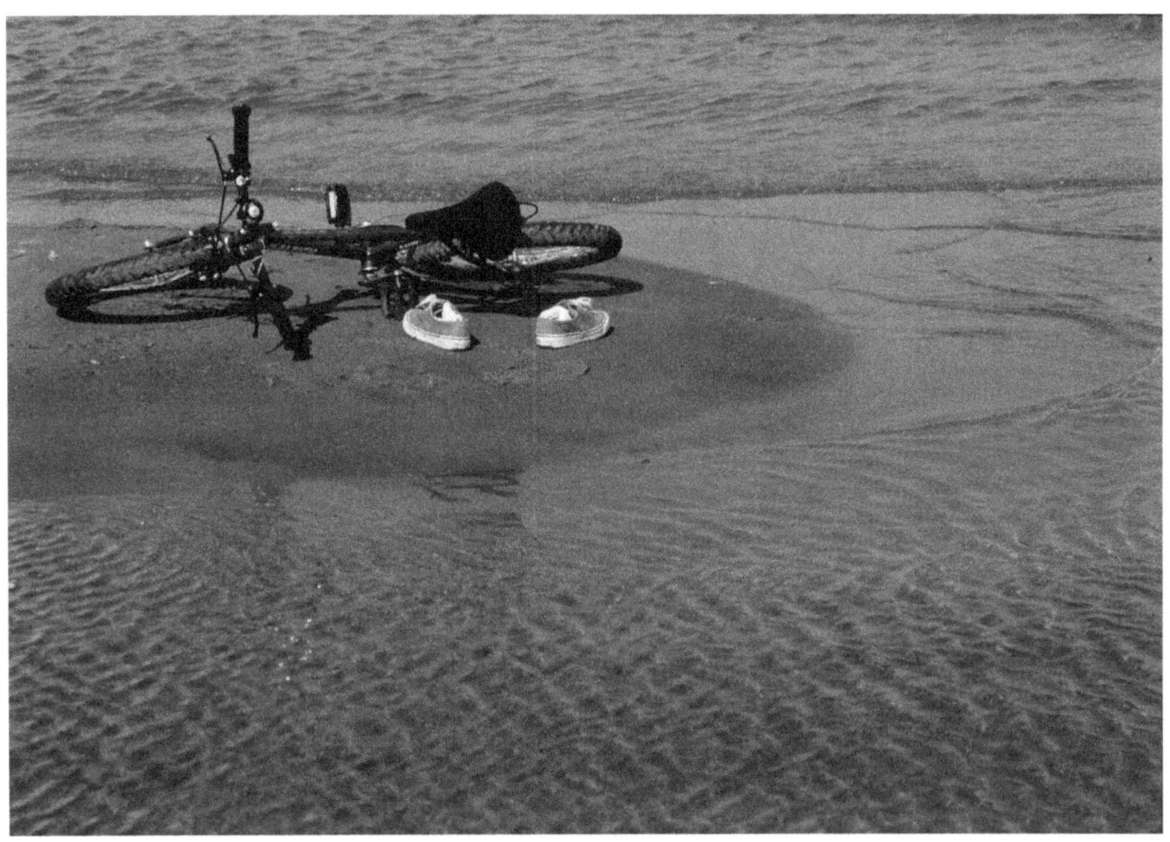

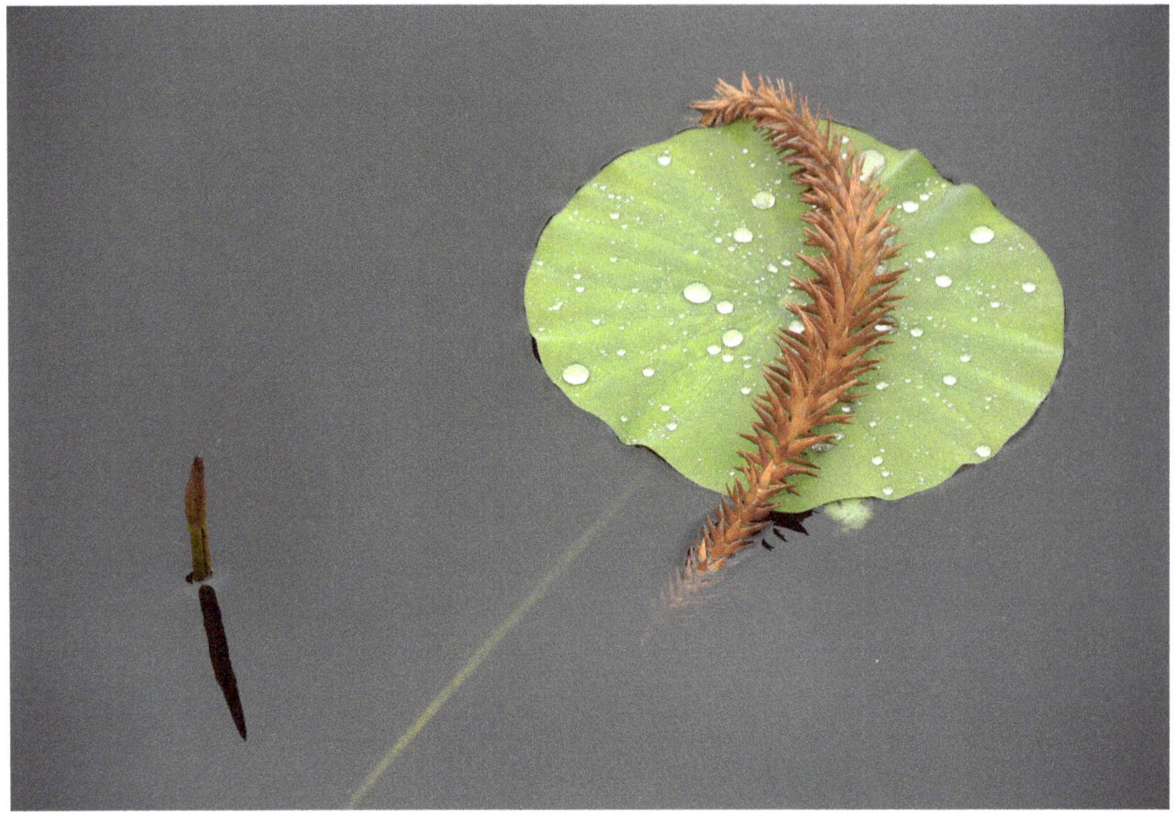

Assignment Seven: Drala

The only magic that exists is this life, this world, the particular phenomena we are all experiencing right this moment.

—Chögyam Trungpa, *True Perception*

Drala is a term and teaching from the Shambhala tradition, originally presented by Trungpa Rinpoche, and now manifested by Sakyong Mipham. There is more to be said about drala than what we present here; like other source teachings, we provide further resources in the bibliography.

Shambhala teachings present the human situation as based on sentient, heart connections. We are touched, and in touch. The experience of being human is felt through contact, communion, and communication. These three are the embodiment of our basic endowment: as birthright, all humans are fundamentally together and resourceful. In Shambhala, we call this *basic goodness*. Human society, which is also basically good, arises out of our individual basic goodness, and this combined goodness is the source of love, art, and more.

In Nalanda Miksang, we are focused on the ordinary art aspect of basic goodness; how ordinary everyday perception can be extraordinary, connecting to ordinary magic, and leading to vivid artistic expression. This transformation of the ordinary into the extraordinary is a kind of magic we call *drala*.

A literal translation of the Tibetan word *drala* is "above aggression." This translation is good to keep in mind when you are photographing, in case you slip into hunting or shooting mode. But the translation we will work with most in this assignment is a slightly less literal but equally accurate one: "ordinary magic." It is this understanding of drala which is the heart of Nalanda Miksang.

Ordinary magic is equivalent to, a facet of, basic goodness. Basic goodness is a human sensibility and capability to be awake, which is always already available. Drala is a subtle, deep resonance, a cosmic power teaching, which also works with what appears to be mundane. Drala reveals the ordinary as magic. The ripples of drala help us contact our basic goodness. Where basic goodness is the background, the experience of drala is the spark, the light, the heartbeat of the moment which helps us realize it.

How do we connect with, embody and manifest the intrinsic heart reality of drala?

In the drala teachings, we actually talk about inviting drala in. Why would we not invite it in regularly? Because we judge ourselves, believe our spaces or states of mind aren't good enough. It takes courage and warriorship to stand up to the inner bullies that believe in our inherent badness, judge our lives and spaces as not worthy, and make space for the already-existing magic to emerge. And when we can value ourselves, we can also contribute back to the world in ethical and powerful ways, whether that means making an inviting home or fighting against environmental injustices. When we are busy trying to ignore our personal homes, or the world at large, because we are overwhelmed or feel ashamed, we miss out on a lot of connection and power.

The same is true in meditation. One of our responses when we start to see the outer content of our mind is to say things like "Ah, yuck! It's nasty in there." But, with space and practice, we cultivate the curiosity to actually change our relationship with our mind, which also changes the mind. One of the words in Tibetan for meditation, in fact, is *gom*, which means, "to become familiar with." In this case, familiarity breeds contentment, not contempt. Nothing "out there" is static and nothing "in here" is static.

Chögyam Trungpa's *Shambhala: Sacred Path of the Warrior* is a wonderful source for exploring drala through contemplation and meditation. It is a root text for Nalanda Miksang. We explore the view of drala quite deeply in our first book, *Looking and Seeing*. For this assignment, however, we want to engage drala directly in our Nalanda Miksang practice. Using parts of *Shambhala: Sacred Path of the Warrior*, we present it as a two-step assignment: Perception as Drala, and Phenomenal World as Drala.

Perception As Drala

We contemplated the following Chögyam Trungpa quote in the Dot-in-Space teaching in our first book, *Looking and Seeing*: "When we draw down the power and depth of vastness into a single perception, then we are discovering and invoking magic." In terms of view, this describes the dynamic quality of on-the-spot Nalanda Miksang perceptual opening, practice, and presentation. Although these may seem like single, discrete moments—having a flash of perception, taking the equivalent, viewing it later—this process of our practice actually draws down something bigger than "just the object or subject" we are observing. A Flowers and Weeds photograph is more than a documentary shot of a flower or weed. There is something there, a felt sense which is larger than the sum of its parts. That's the vastness. That's the magic, drawn down into a single, simple perception and image.

What does it actually feel like to discover and invoke magic? It's good to remember what we mean by magic. Here, it is neither of the two conventional views. It is not the alchemy of turning one thing into something else, like lead into gold. Nor is it simply a magician's trick: presenting something as happening that actually does not happen, like pulling a rabbit out of a hat. Magic here points to depth: this image and experience opens your power and empowerment in resonance with the creative power of the universe.

We simply (but profoundly) mean seeing the ordinary as magical. This is such a subtle turn as to get overlooked—literally—when we take our lives or practice for granted. As the text says:

"By magic we do not we do not mean unnatural power over the phenomenal world, but rather the discovery of innate primordial wisdom in the world as it is." Contacting drala brings a union of depth and surface; we draw down the vast and profound to our phenomenal everyday lives. Our practice is to continually unify the primordial and phenomenal world. This is the magic we touch in Nalanda Miksang. It is both as simple as being present enough to experience a flash of perception, photograph it, and share it and as complex as unifying many layers of experience into the single, quilted, visual richness of an image.

Like the Zen Aesthetics assignment, the Drala assignment is more oriented to a view, a sensibility, and an approach. Rather than a specific subject matter, like Flowers and Weeds, Drala works with some of the natural inner energy of the phenomenal world. It is more of a pointing out instruction than a photographic exploration.

What do these images look like? The just-that of a set of salt and pepper shakers, with a sugar container and plastic cigarette ashtray on a café table, illuminated by the late afternoon sunlight. Expressed in an equivalent image, just-that delivers the just-now, the just—there, and the just-so. It is ordinary magic.

As Chögyam Trungpa says in *Shambhala, Sacred Path of the Warrior*:

One of the key points in discovering drala is rewalizing that your own wisdom as a human being is not separate from the power of things as they are . . . therefore there is no fundamental separation or duality between you and your world. When you can experience these two things together, as one, so to speak, then you have access to tremendous vision and power in the world—you find that they are inherently connected to your own vision, your own being. That is discovering magic.

Often we have been experiencing perception as drala already. We may not label a photograph as being mainly a "drala image," but once we start looking at especially the Level Two images through the lens of drala, we can see how, for instance, drala is brought forth by light, by color, by the resonant appearance of dot-in-space. In fact, in a sense, all of Level Two images have drala as perception as a part of the experience of perceiving, photographing, and viewing.

But how do we know for sure it is drala we are contacting?

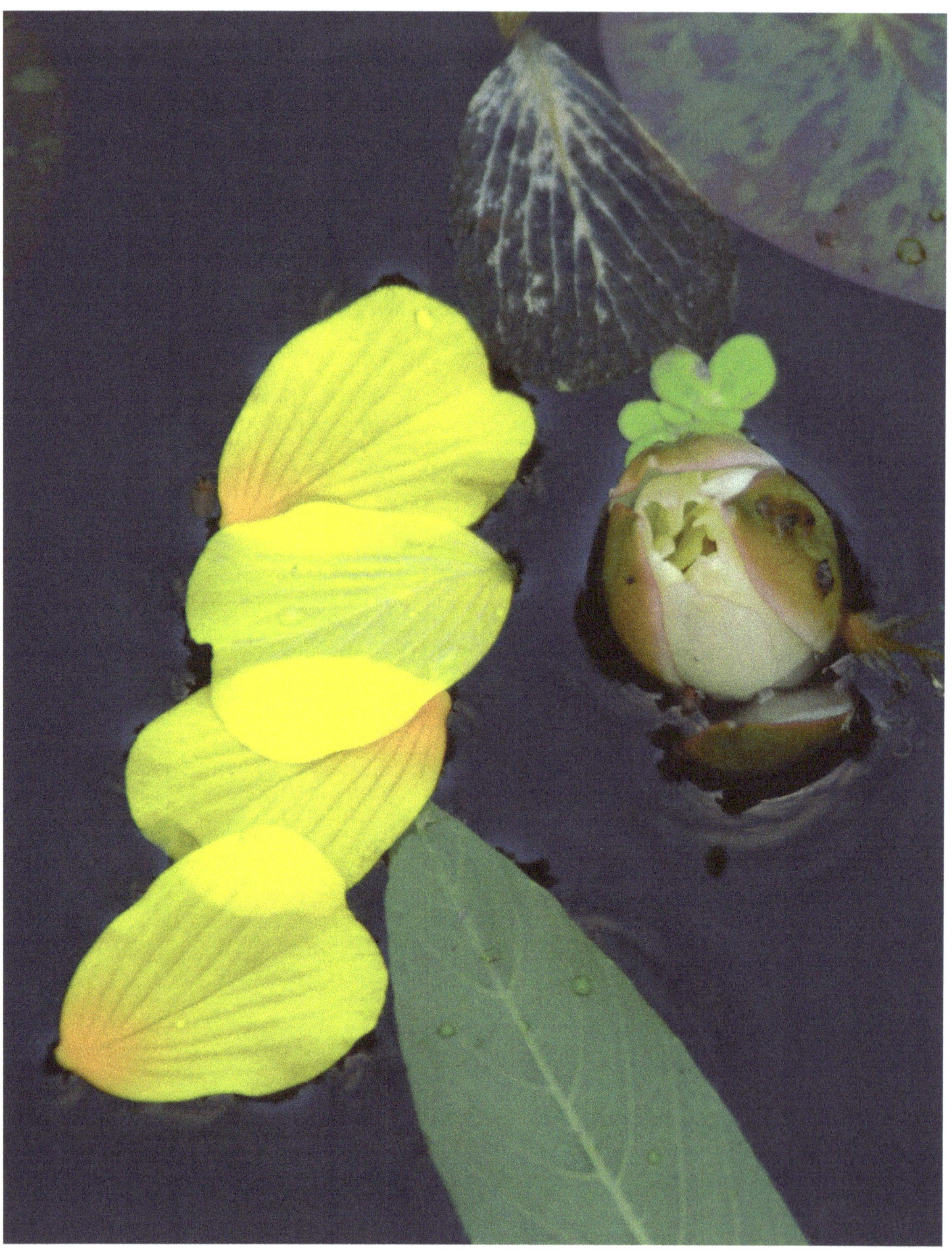

Phenomenal World As Drala

How does drala actually work in Nalanda Miksang practice? One formal way is through the flash of perception and dot-in-space expressions. In a more informal way, how does the magic work as a lived and experienced way?

The lived way to drala is not separate from flash of perception or dot-in-space, but it is more expressive. We are moving in to the way of the phenomenal world—the locus of the perceptual display, which is no different from what we actually experience. Again, Chögyam Trungpa, in *Shambhala, Sacred Path of the Warrior*:

The dralas are the elements of reality— water of water, fire of fire, earth of earth— anything that connects you with the elemental quality of reality, anything that reminds you of the depth of perception. There are dralas in the rocks or the trees or the mountains or the snowflakes or a clod of dirt. Whatever is there, whatever you come across in your life, those are the dralas of reality. When you make that connection with the elemental reality quality of the world, you are meeting the dralas on the spot: at that point you are meeting them. That is the basic existence of which all humans are capable. We always have possibilities of discovering magic.

In other words, our lives can be directly realized as basic goodness, often through direct perception. We can sense the connection to our basic goodness—and the basic goodness of everyone and thing—through drala when we feel the following: a synchronization of something simple or elemental with a felt sense of depth; direct contact with the phenomenal: rocks, mountains, snowflakes, clods of earth; elemental insights which arise from directly experiencing the water of water; a personal embodiment: "Whatever you come across," "When you make that connection, you are meeting the dralas."

If you go looking for drala, you won't find it. Instead, spend some time contemplating the power of the images you have taken so far in this practice, especially during your journey into the heart of photography. Lean into that with direct experience, felt sense, not trying to analyze or understand why. Take that deep heart connection to mystery and magic with you as you go out to practice. Then you will find drala, as you have been finding it already, and be able to recognize it as ordinary magic. Trust the magic. You are always already connected with drala, so just go with that.

"Anything that connects you with the elemental quality of reality . . ." Go with that.

"Anything that connects you with the depth of perception . . ." Go with that.

"When you meet the elemental quality of the world . . ." Go with that.

"Discovering magic . . ." Go with that.

Go with that. *That* will be drala.

PART SIX:
METROPOLITAN BEAUTY
AND FOUND CALLIGRAPHY

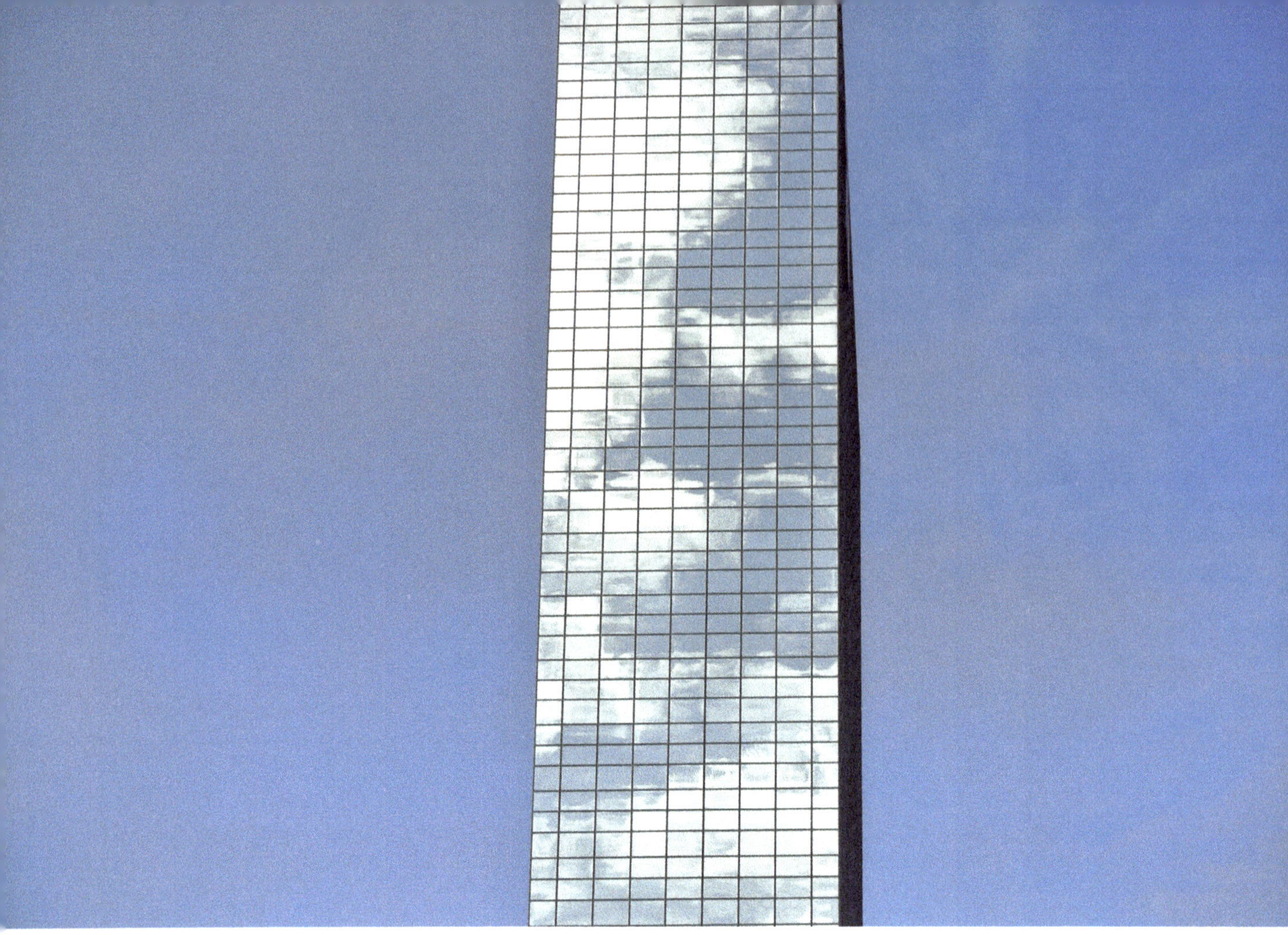

These last two assignments before our final assignment give a chance to explore some of the rest of the inter-related fields of perception.

Assignment Eight: Metropolitan Beauty

Some photographers locate the nature of beauty in the beauty of nature. In Chinese and Japanese contemplative traditions, nature is a prime source of inspiration, and this is the case in much of the Western art tradition. Impressionism is a strong example: it is primarily inspired by nature. However, most of us live in some kind of metropolis, or at least a village or town. Even if you live in a village, you live in an urban-driven media world. It is core to our view of contemplative photography that connecting with pure perception isn't as much about where you are (i.e., city versus country) as much as *how* you are with where you are. It is a matter of clear seeing and appreciation. So while much of Level Two focuses on nature, we would like to take some time to engage the city's beauty directly.

This assignment is very general, but the view is specific. You explore the urban environment, but in a contemplative photography way. Be open to manifestations of phenomenal expression, rather than seeking images in a world full of things. We have some experience with seeing objects through flashes of perception, but so far it's been mainly small scale. Here, open up to a larger scale—don't see a building, see the many ways it manifests visually.

That is the general approach. There are other more focused contemplative orientations to the urban setting. It is helpful to throw out the distinction between what is beautiful and what is ugly/raw/crude and, therefore, not normally considered beautiful. A back alley is no less beautiful than a high-fashion street. Don't look for a version of urban beauty or aesthetic. Just look through the urban as perceptual manifestation, and then you will discover perceptual urban beauty.

Commercial streets provide endless displays of vivid visual phenomena. Modern urban commerce centers with glass towers and urban geometry provide a formal aesthetic, and even impressionism. Stone and brick work bring out form and structure in a large-scale play of light.

Don't forget about back alleys and rugged industrial areas. These locales are a perceptual gold mine, because seeing real beauty depends on non-conceptual perception. In these kinds of situations, there is a more direct and deep lesson in contemplative urban beauty. These are our rejected areas—full of trash, set aside from what is considered façade-worthy. These areas are a great place to challenge your concepts about what is beautiful and what is ugly.

We live much of our life in these visually intense and dense urban settings. Sometimes this can seem overwhelming and oppressive. But your perception of these environments can be transformed into a constant source of perceptual adventure, contemplative enrichment, and aesthetic images through your practice.

Learning to relate with even a back alley—this is Nalanda Miksang magic and liberation. Rather than separating, taking a break from city life, instead you plunge right into it, even deeper, but with clarity. Clear perception itself is the tranquil oasis in the ongoing flux and intensity of the urban phenomenal matrix. The vacation you seek, the break you desire, is actually right in the middle of the fray and not separate from it. The intense urban world is transformed as a resource for your personal contemplative harmony and your artistic brilliant image manifestation.

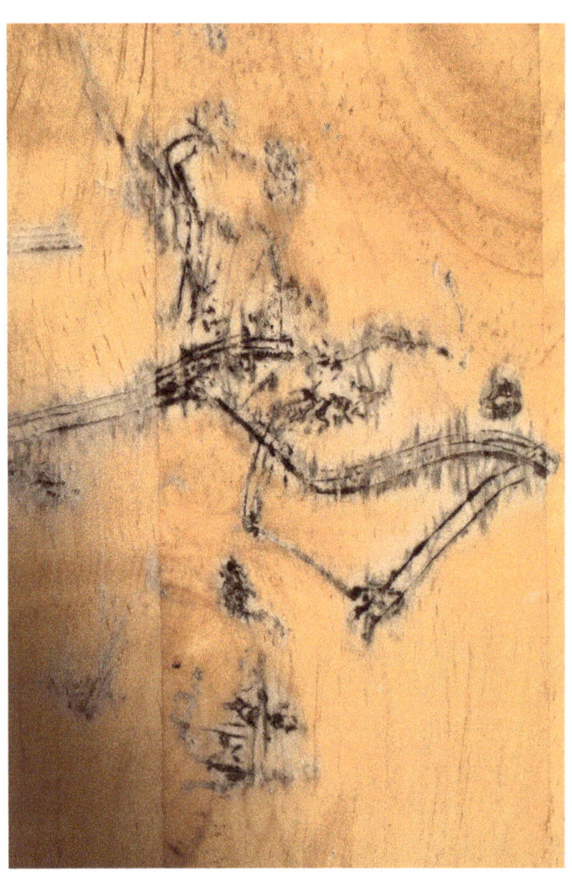

Assignment Nine: Found Calligraphy

The fields of perception of Level Two are very fluid, overlapping, and interpenetrating. For example, the salt and pepper shakers on a café table in Ordinary/Personal World can also appear as an urban artifact and a feature of the Metropolitan Beauty assignment. In addition, we find subfields within the larger fields of perception. We see this with the psychedelic ducks sub-assignment, which emerges from the Impressionism exploration. There are fields of perception within fields of perception.

Found Calligraphy is also one such sub-assignment, so to speak. It refers to the contemplative and artistic tradition of calligraphy. Calligraphy is one of the major traditional contemplative arts. It takes the ordinary activity of writing into the expressive realm of a contemplative sensibility. As with Impressionism, however, it is a found art—finding scratches and marks, reeds and clouds that appear as calligraphy-like within the urban and natural environment. It is a mash-up of the urban contemplative exploration and Zen aesthetics, and an assignment in its own right.

In this assignment we are not doing calligraphy, and we are not documenting traditional forms of contemplative calligraphy. We are looking to the secret manifest displays of such spontaneous calligraphy in the everyday world. For famous photographers who worked in a contemplative way we can look to abstract expressionist Aaron

Siskind, who often found expressive gestures in tar.

Our view is that the calligraphy manifests as the spontaneous embodiment of the spontaneous mind. It has a felt quality similar to the flash of perception in Nalanda Miksang. Chögyam Trungpa is famous for saying, "You could actually sum up the history of your life in one stroke," paralleling his teachings on perception drawing down the universe into a single instance.

There are endless sources of found calligraphy in the urban atmosphere, but two good starting points are these: graphic aspects of advertisement (noticing not the whole message but parts of expression through line and font), and urban graffiti, specifically, lines of gesture.

You have to be careful with graffiti. It is not as simple as documenting someone else's artistic work. You need to find your own fresh perception within that graffiti art expression. It must be perceived and delivered as calligraphy. While neither ads nor graffiti are intended as formal calligraphy, they can be seen as forms of an expressive dot-in-space gesture. A graphic gesture often expresses a fluid form of dot-in-space, with a certain point extended and modulated in a gestural way. It still has a foreground and background, but as a more dynamic expression than a regular dot-in-space.

Even just in the urban realm, this assignment is not limited to signs and graffiti. The adventure of the assignment is to find visual calligraphy that was not intended as calligraphy. Open to the possibilities: scratches on a car door, wires, vines; there are endless manifestations. It is an adventure assignment.

In terms of taking this assignment into nature, you will quickly find branches, waves in water, even fish making calligraphy right in front of you, once you tune into it. These expressions, paralleling our human communications, are always speaking to us, if we simply tune in to listen or, in this case, look.

As always, it is a perception assignment. The found calligraphy will only appear through your perception in that moment. It is a spontaneous collaboration between an expression only you are seeing at that moment and your flash of perception as an opening between expectations and judgments, finding a new communication—ephemeral, often quite beautiful, and full of resonant energy.

PEOPLE AND OTHER SENTIENT BEINGS

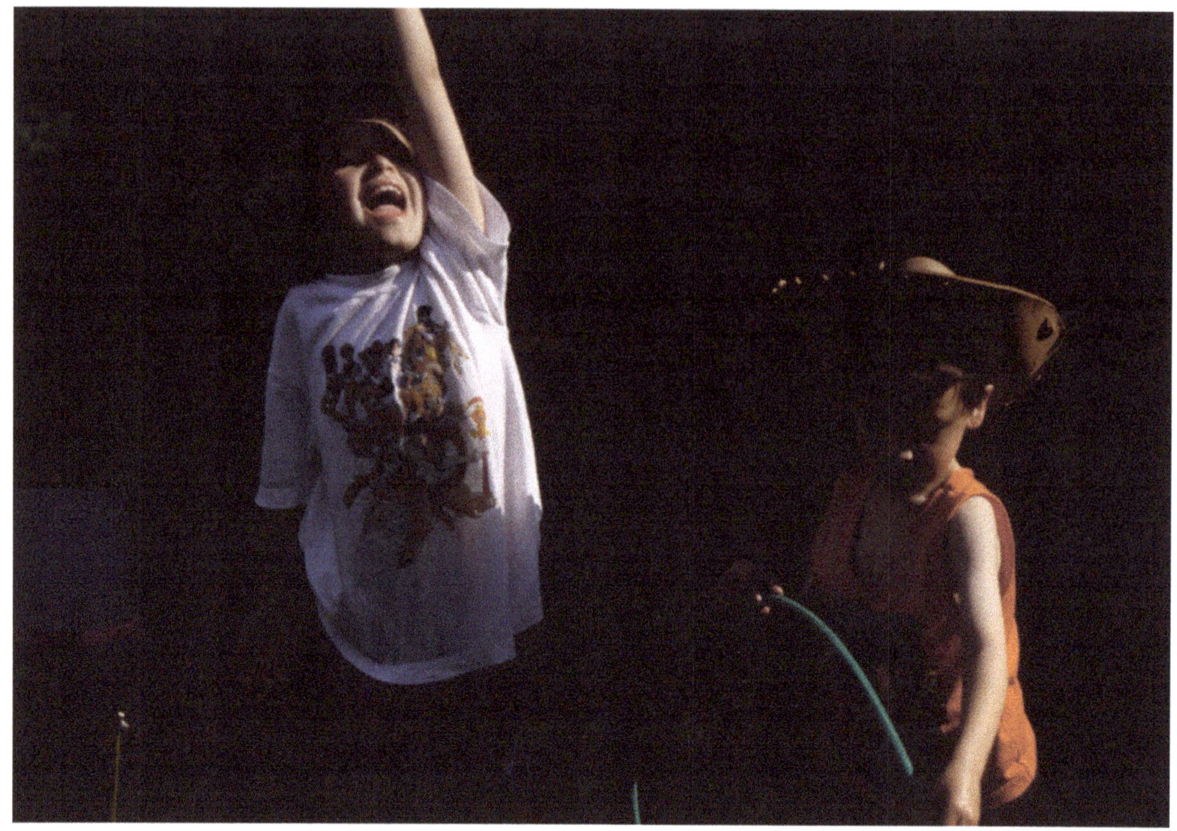

Assignment Ten: People And Other Sentient Beings

Welcome to the final assignment in this Heart of Photography exploration: People and Other Sentient Beings. Sentient beings are beings that perceive and feel, that have a sense of self and other, and the relationship between self and other. This assignment includes people, but it also includes other sentient beings, from elephants to ants.

Although, in principle, all sentient beings are included here, our focus is not as much on wild beings. That is a special topic for those who live among wild animals. Because most of us live alongside other people and domestic animals, we tend to focus on domestic friends—our pets, such as dogs and turtles; domestic companions, such as horses; or domestic animals, such as cows and sheep. No matter what the name is of the relationship, the point is the interrelationship between other sentient beings and ourselves.

Although we have explored some perceptions of living things—mainly plants—the most personal and pragmatically challenging aspects of our contemplative practice arise in this final assignment. There are many.

There is the question of what counts as

contemplative within this subject matter. There are also the many ways that the human subject has been treated over the lifetime of photography: portrait, artistic, photojournalism, recording of occasions such as weddings and graduations, snapshots, police mug shots, selfies, and so on. On just the sheer level of practicality, it is tricky to photograph people. For one thing, they move. They are active and expressive. For another, when confronted with a camera, they (and often you) become self-conscious rather than natural and expressive. The solutions of conventional photography include either posing sentient beings as subjects or capturing them in a candid way. Neither of these is really the contemplative way.

So what of the contemplative way? As always, it is based on direct and clear perception. When it comes to humans and other sentient beings as subject matter, the decisive point is that humans are not exactly an object, like a chair, or even another living thing, like a flower. In terms of Nalanda Miksang, the difference is that the human we are perceiving is also a perceiver, and self-conscious.

This reality generates many dynamics between the contemplative photographer and the photographic subject, including the way the subject reacts to being photographed, the ethical issues of making an image of someone, and the subjective issues of the photographer's intent. Specifically, it is important to look at the photographer's state of mind and emotions, especially gently noticing if aggression or self-consciousness arises in the contemplative photographer when making an image, as that changes the image and the situation dramatically.

Another main pragmatic difficulty of working with human subjects is that they react to the event of being photographed. When they react, the spontaneous perception evaporates. So we provide various skillful means for working with this situation.

We start simple and small, with curiosity and with the right view. The best place to start is actually with other sentient beings. This is because we tend to be less self-conscious when photographing them, and though they sense us, they tend to be less self-conscious about being photographed. The connection between humans and other sentient beings is powerful, and a joy to explore.

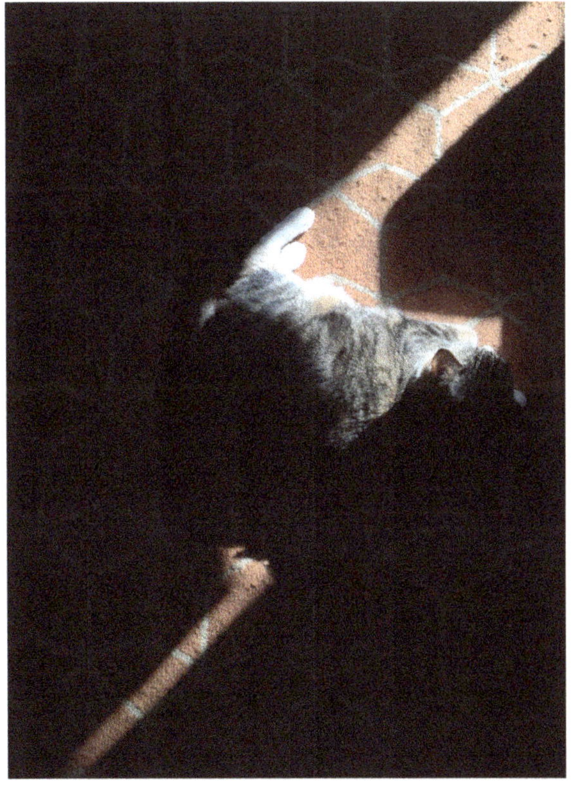

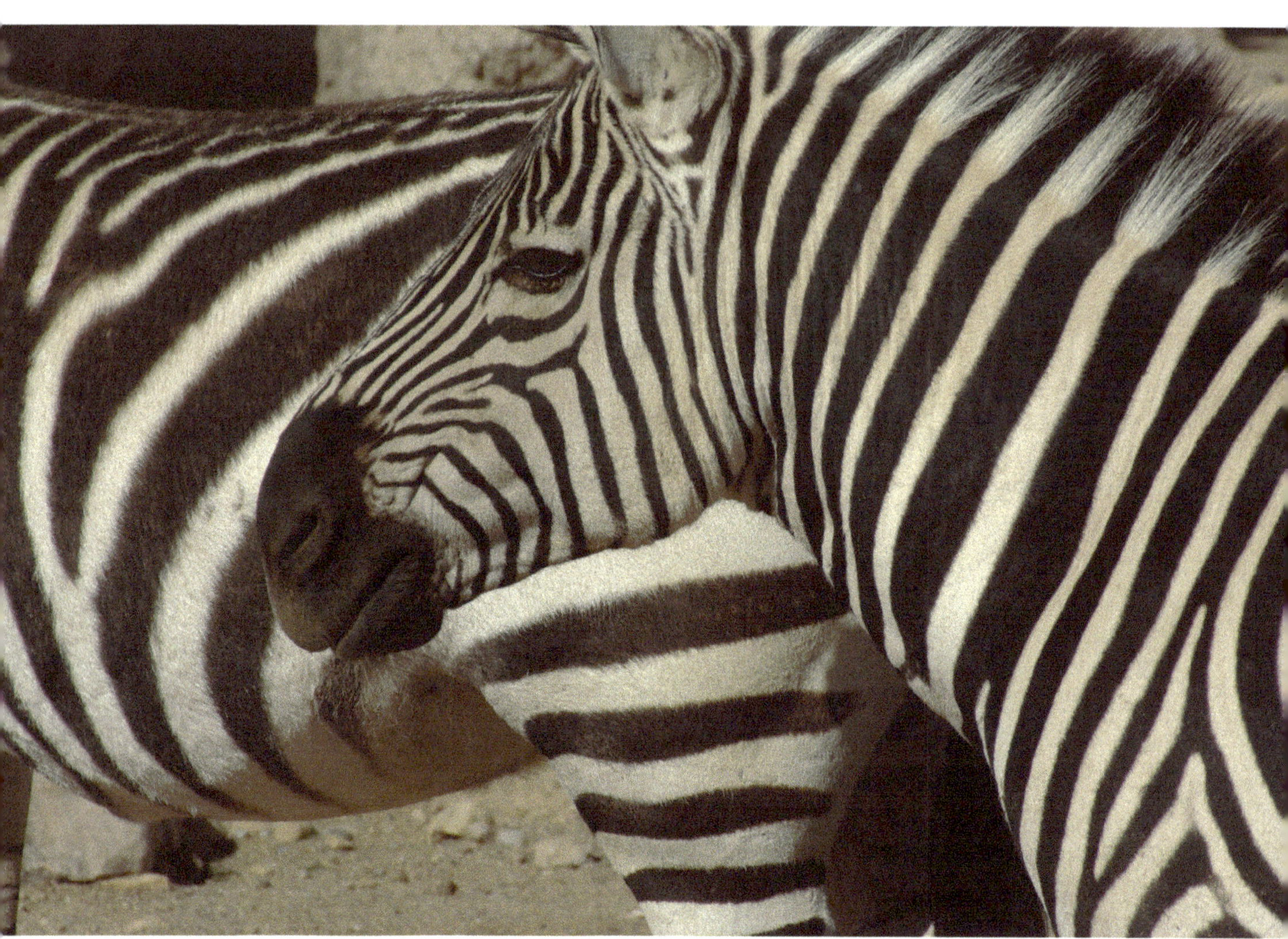

Starting Out: Other Sentient Beings

We strongly suggest that you start with nonhumans, otherwise known as "other sentient beings." Photographing our friends, like man's best friend, the dog, as well as cats and other household friends, such as hamsters, rabbits, and so forth, is especially powerful and intimate. We can also extend this assignment to domesticated animals such as horses and cows, to insects, to animals at the zoo—to any sentient being, including a vast array of living beings, from elephants to ants.

Logistically, many places are good for this assignment, even if you don't have sentient beings in your ordinary world (e.g., pets or backyard wildlife). Go to a dog park or a zoo. If you live in the country, explore your area for wildlife. Especially if the idea of photographing people feels nerve-wracking from moment one, start with other sentient beings.

What's important to keep in mind is that the approach remains contemplative. Usually, nature photography of animals is more documentary: "Look at the cute orangutan." The difficulty with a contemplative approach with our animal friends is the same obstacle we have with children: there's always the temptation to photograph something candid and cute, the kind of photos your mother wants of her grandchildren. Not that there is anything intrinsically wrong with candid and cute, it is just not contemplative.

As with children and flowers, the contemplative engagement with our animal friends is an opportunity to explore the fine lines between contemplative and conventional, between sensibility and sentimentality. Our animal friends are there with us: intimate, unique, and loveable. In the contemplative image, we need to meet them there in a perceptual way.

In doing this, you will notice right away how many technical obstacles arise with sentient beings, including the fact of their movement! We also notice the main psychological obstacle: we want them to keep a pose for us, hold a position, look a particular way. We might think, "It's going to be easier to photograph a squirrel than it is to photograph another human being," but when you interact with a squirrel, it becomes complex quickly.

We discover how often we want them to do it our way so that we can capture our flash of perception. We realize how quickly flashes of perception can seem to disappear. We have to let our relationship with flashes of perception evolve: they have to become looser and more flexible. Otherwise, when the moment passes, we get angry, feel regret, feel sad. We've completely left the flash of perception and entered into an agenda.

So now let's explore people as a specific topic.

Photographing People The Contemplative Perception Way

There are many photographic approaches to the human subject. The contemplative way, as always, is grounded in perception within the phenomenal world. We will articulate various possibilities of this way through perception master photographers like Edward Weston, Dorothea Lange, and Henri Cartier-Bresson, along with some tips from Nalanda Miksang.

Contemplative photography presents the human and sentient being as a perception and experienced event. The way of sentient beings is the way of looks, gestures, body forms, decisive moments and more, all found within the lived world of beings engaged with life and with the world. Above all, the topic may be people, but the subject, as always, is actually our momentary exchange or relationship with them—the subject is the flash of perception.

Aggression/Basic Goodness

I sat down to have dinner with my father. I asked, "Is there anyone else?" He replied, "It's just you and me." When my father said, "Just you and me," he was communicating the essence of society . . . When my father said, "Just you and me," somehow I knew that our ordinary exchange had implications for the world. He was trying to communicate that if we two could just be—be together, be relaxed, and be open—we would create enlightened society. The occurrence of this simple act would benefit everyone. Unlocking our own humanity would give humanity strength. Thus when I asked if anyone else was coming to dinner, and he answered, "Just you and me," he was really saying, "The whole world is coming to dinner."

—Sakyong Mipham, *The Shambhala Principle*

With this assignment we highlight aggression, because it is a decisive issue in how to be a contemplative photographer. Even as a contemplative photographer we are interested in making a great image, so there is a temptation to revert to the hunter mentality of getting the image. We see this aggression in the conventional world of paparazzi photographers invading people's privacy. Clearly we are in a quite different space in Nalanda Miksang, but still engaging similar issues. For the subject matter of people, we need to include respect and reserve. We need to account for their situation and perspective within our interest of phenomenal displays. We will address this in terms of being sensitive to the situation and the ethical issues in the next section. But fundamentally, we also need to consider the way we approach making an image.

Making an image is not the main point of Nalanda Miksang. Making a contemplative image is an equivalent of a clear, direct, and communion perception. That is the point. And to return us to the core reason for this practice, it is important for us to connect with our view, our intent, and our motivation. In photographing people, our intent is oriented toward basic goodness. We must begin to trust our photographing people as part of a practice of relating to others' basic goodness. Miriam's wife often feels uncomfortable when she photographs people in public because it draws attention to them. But Miriam's view is one of connecting with others, rather than distancing from them. While the person being photographed can't always feel this, our view that approaching other people through a desire to connect and see their basic goodness makes a fundamental difference in the tone of the interaction.

Secondly, our intent must express non-aggression—this includes not only toward the subject but also toward ourselves. If we feel nervous about photographing people, we need to recognize and respect that. We will give you ways to approach this assignment that are less intimidating than, say, strangers' faces. Noticing when you become nervous, anxious, or agitated, slowing down via the flash of perception exercise or synchronization exercise—this kind of gentle awareness goes a long way in helping you truly relate with other beings.

Finally, our motivation is connection. We do this practice to connect. If at any point you find yourself photographing people in order to accomplish anything other than connection or relationship—for example, you start pitying your subject, or wanting them to hold a pose—it's a good time to stop, remember the motivation to connect, and drop your agenda. When you drop your agenda you will find that you are just there with another person in an ordinary perception situation, and that feels good.

Permission And Ethics

There are some formal and informal ethical issues concerning photographing people, especially children. Here are some guidelines and suggestions.

If you do photograph strangers, the idea is to photograph without necessarily asking permission, because if you ask permission it changes the whole situation. If you ask, "Can I take your picture?" they sit there and smile for you—they think that's the kind of picture you want to take. However, the fact is, for most of us, asking permission is the only way we feel comfortable photographing strangers. So if it helps, ask. Just notice the difference between subtler ways of asking, such as holding up your camera at a distance from the person, then pointing to it, smiling, and nodding, instead of going up to someone and directly addressing them. Experiment with what level of permission feels important to you. And consider that you don't always have to photograph faces; see later assignments in the text that focus on non-recognizable parts, such as feet and hands.

All this points to laws and ethics regarding photography of people. Laws in most countries say that as long as someone is in public you can photograph them. You can also sell their likeness as art, but not to advertise a product. However, most of us, ethically, are more conservative than the laws; most of us would be unlikely to sell someone's likeness, even for art. Find your own ethical relationship and boundaries and use those. Also, make sure to respect local customs if you are traveling in another country. In some places it is considered a violation of someone's soul to take a photograph of them. In those cases, it is good to ask if the other person would feel what you are doing is connecting, or if it is better to leave your camera unused and relate with no barriers in between.

The Self-Conscious Photographer

With perception engagement and as a photographer, you may have personal reservations about making other people your subject matter. This is related to the ethics issue just addressed, but is more personal and on-the-spot.

Most of us have no emotional or ethical issues with photographing flowers in someone else's garden. But photographing another person, especially a stranger, can seem quite intimidating. Just note the language: as photographers, if we say we are "shooting flowers," that seems fine. But as soon as we say we are "shooting people," there's an uncomfortable resonance with deep aggression.

You may experience anxiety with this exercise. We all have anxiety, and we work with it regarding one topic or another, but it is exasperated in this particular context. We may feel uncomfortable when face to face with the subject matter, especially when they react. We might think the solution is technology: if we just had a telephoto lens we could be unobtrusive. But this misses both the main point and the main opportunity. Being contemplative is being engaged, not disengaged. This is your chance to be with the there through the there in a very direct and personal way. If it is still not working out, you can just say "thank you," or "sorry," and move on.

We need to just relax into the way of perception. Before our various takes or opinions on a situation—what we like or dislike, whether we are comfortable or uncomfortable, whether we should go this way or hold back—there's a direct experience happening. So relax and work with the way things go. Work with the way of perception and the phenomenal world.

As an example, a few years ago, Miriam was teaching in Seattle and went to a garden to photograph People and Other Sentient Beings with her students. She was agitated and couldn't settle. First, a few squirrels appeared, hoping for a snack. When she raised her camera, they squirmed away, hiding from her agenda. She got frustrated and ran off, trying to find a good position for photographing some playing children. The mothers caught sight of her and made faces, indicating they didn't want their kids photographed. This wasn't going to happen, and here she was, the teacher! Finally, she remembered from experience that running around only added to her anxiety and interfered with her connection.

She sat down on the steps of a historic building, sort of giving up. She put down her camera and pulled out a map of the huge park. Just then, she felt, more than saw, a movement out of the far corner of her right eye. She glanced down at her camera to check the settings, slowly lifted it to her eye, and slowly turned, not knowing what she would see.

A dog stood stock still at the end of a lead, sniffing the ground just a couple of feet from her. She smiled, and as she adjusted her focus on the dog, he looked up, his tongue popping out with curiosity. The shutter went and the image popped up on the screen. The person walking him, a tall woman on her cell phone, chatting away, missed the entire exchange. Miriam nodded to the dog, who lowered his head and lumbered back to his distracted owner. Honestly, the photo didn't turn out that great, but the moment was a precious break in the clouds of her confusion, and the rest of her day opened expansively thereafter.

Even if you feel pretty at ease with other sentient beings, if they are pretty straightforward for you, if you are already aware that when you go to photograph your cat or dog, they never do what you want them to do, we still suggest approaching this whole assignment through nonhuman sentient beings first. It can help you apply what you have learned so far in Miksang and in Level Two to living, breathing, moving beings. In the next sections we offer some suggestions for photographing people, which can also be applied to photographing other sentient beings in a contemplative way.

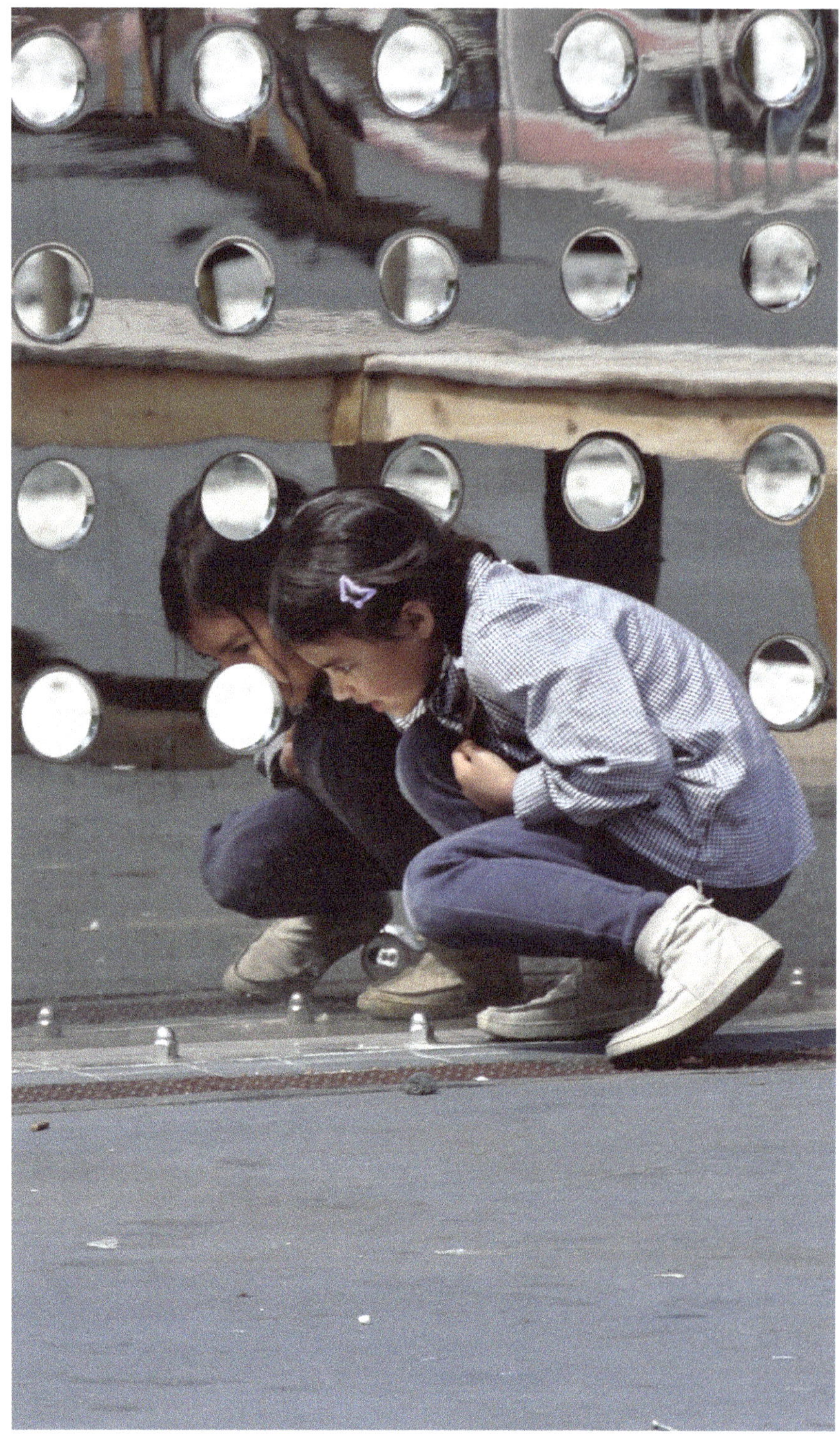

Photographing Children

This assignment is especially great with children. However, the ethical issues are even stronger with children, especially ones you don't know. If you do photograph children, it's better to ask permission from the guardians if they are nearby. Ethically, it is best to never put a picture of a child you don't know on the Internet without permission. You have absolutely no control over what happens with images on the Internet, even if you use watermarks and upload small file sizes, and children should be respected in this way.

All of that aside, photographing children can be lovely. For the most part, they don't pay attention to the camera, especially after a few minutes. First they may mug for the camera, but then they drop it. If you have time with a niece, a nephew, a friend's kid, or your own kid, after a while, they can really open up.

It's best to start with familiar children. John recounts that once he had two children, his mother started demanding "real" pictures of her grandkids. John's photos of his children were primarily Miksang—the light and shadow of blinds on his son's belly, the pink of his daughter's dress against the pink of plastic flamingos in the yard. Most parents really enjoy a "different take" on their kids, and photographing children you know can really bring out the playful aspect of perception and relationship.

Now, having said all of that, we can proceed to how to approach this assignment, with some inspiration from classic portrait artists, and go more deeply into the view.

Masters Of Contemplative Photography On The Human Form

Lange, Weston, And Cartier-Bresson As Inspiration

One thing that is lovely about people as a photographic subject is that while our approach varies quite a bit from traditional portraiture and candids, there have been other photographers who found ways to work through the perception of the human subject. Since Nalanda Miksang doesn't hold the franchise on clear seeing, we can take instruction from these perception masters. Nalanda Miksang can anchor itself in embodying these pure, expressive, and dynamic expressions of the human field of perception.

Three decisive photographers for Nalanda Miksang are the artistically pure Edward Weston (who worked with the body as incarnate tangible forms), the expressive documentarian Dorothea Lange (who explored the communicative body), and the dynamically active Cartier-Bresson (who opened up the occasioned expression).

These photographers were perception warriors. They entered the way of perception, found ways of seeing, and made decisive images. A good place to start with this assignment is to contemplate their images of people.

This section on People and Other Sentient Beings is not so much broken down into particular assignments as providing some approaches, or skillful means. After we explore the work of Weston, Lange, and Cartier-Bresson, we will offer a potpourri of perceptual ways with the human subject and other sentient beings, including some pointers and practical suggestions.

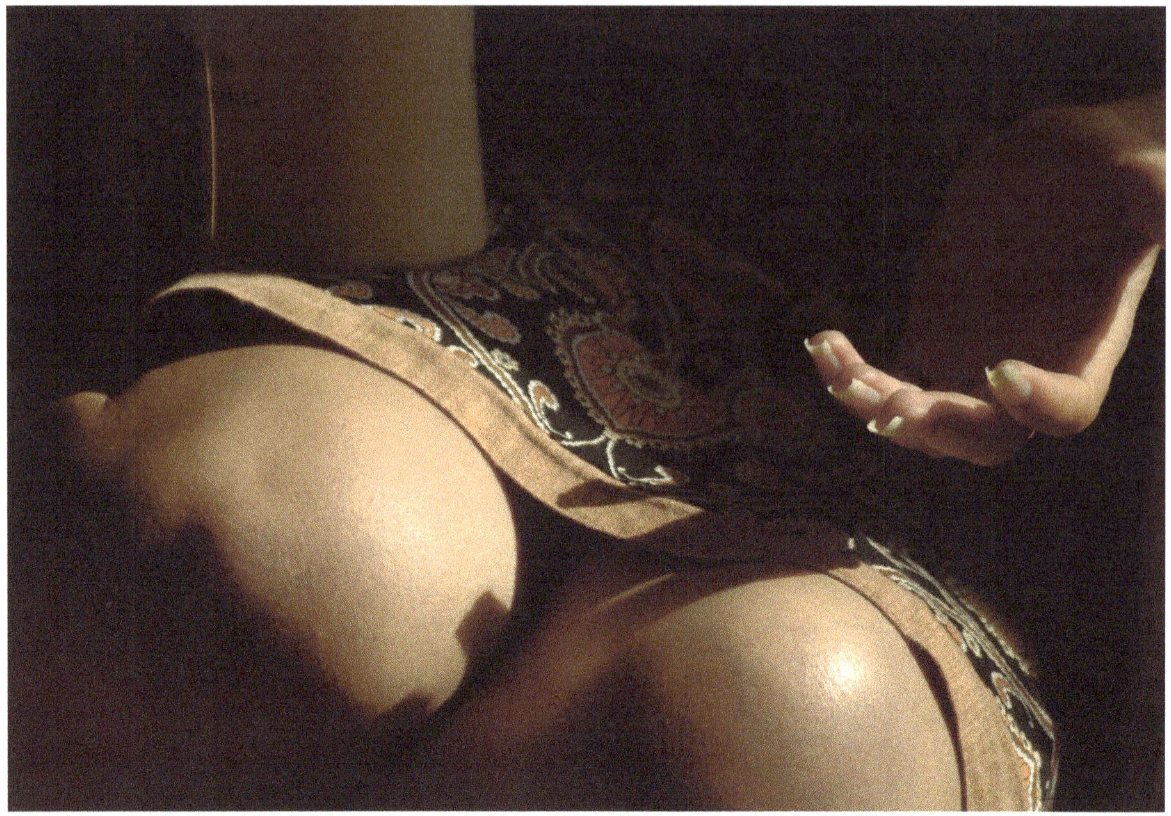

The Communicative Body—Dorothea Lange

Humans communicate. To a considerable degree, we express ourselves through bodily gestures: smiles, frowns, grimaces says more than what the mouth is speaking. Eyes are, as is said, the windows of the soul; their crinkles, winking, tension, or openness communicates volumes. Not to mention touch: we are sentient, which means both in touch and touched. The way we touch ourselves and each other says so much. These embodied expressions are the animation between the sentient and the sensible, subtle intimate communications. Gestures are minute expressions of embodied communication. The documentary photographer Dorothea Lange was a master of highlighting the evocative quality of a gesture.

Lange often made images of parts or features of the human body and human expression: just hands, the gesture of hands; just the eyes, the way of eyes. Just the mouth. Just the hair. Lange had a particular fascination with feet. Lange was more interested in the expressive sentiment than in deep formal carnality of embodiment.

When you look at her work, you find gestures as ways of seeing:

The way of hands: touching one's face or another's face, the way people hold hands or embrace each other.

The way of eyes: looks, stares, and glances.

The way of a mother's gestures with children, and the way of a family gathering together.

All the bodily postures and positions: gentle or aggressive, subservient or dominant, abject and celebratory, constrained or open.

In all these ways, gesture and posture display emotion through incarnate expression: joy, sadness, fear, despair, contentment.

In discussing Lange's work, we are not asking you to imitate her work. Rather, take an inspired perception approach. Each gesture can be expressive in its own way; the possibilities are endless. You can ask a friend to simply sit with you while you explore their gestures, having a casual conversation so they become less self-conscious. Don't pose; simply notice the gestures that bring forward their humanness. As you start to feel more comfortable, you can explore what we call "hand or foot conversations"—the simple and often humorous interactions that hands and feet have with each other. For instance, when out walking, Miriam loves to pull out her camera while waiting for a stop light. People have no idea she is photographing their feet and legs while they are in conversation. They think she is just checking her camera or phone. It can be a really simple, easy entry point.

There's a side benefit to photographing this way, especially if you are photographing strangers. Generally, across most cultures, so long as you don't photograph someone's face, it's acceptable to photograph them, even if you don't ask their permission—especially feet; feet are pretty fail-safe for photographing.

If some of the people you are close to don't mind having their picture taken, it's fun to photograph them. It may take them a bit to settle down and stop posing, but eventually they relax. Your fear around photographing strangers can go way down, although, of course, there can be some anxiety in photographing friends and loved ones because relationships are going to be mirrored back to you. A familiar relationship you already have with the person is mirrored back, for better or for worse, but that can be another way in.

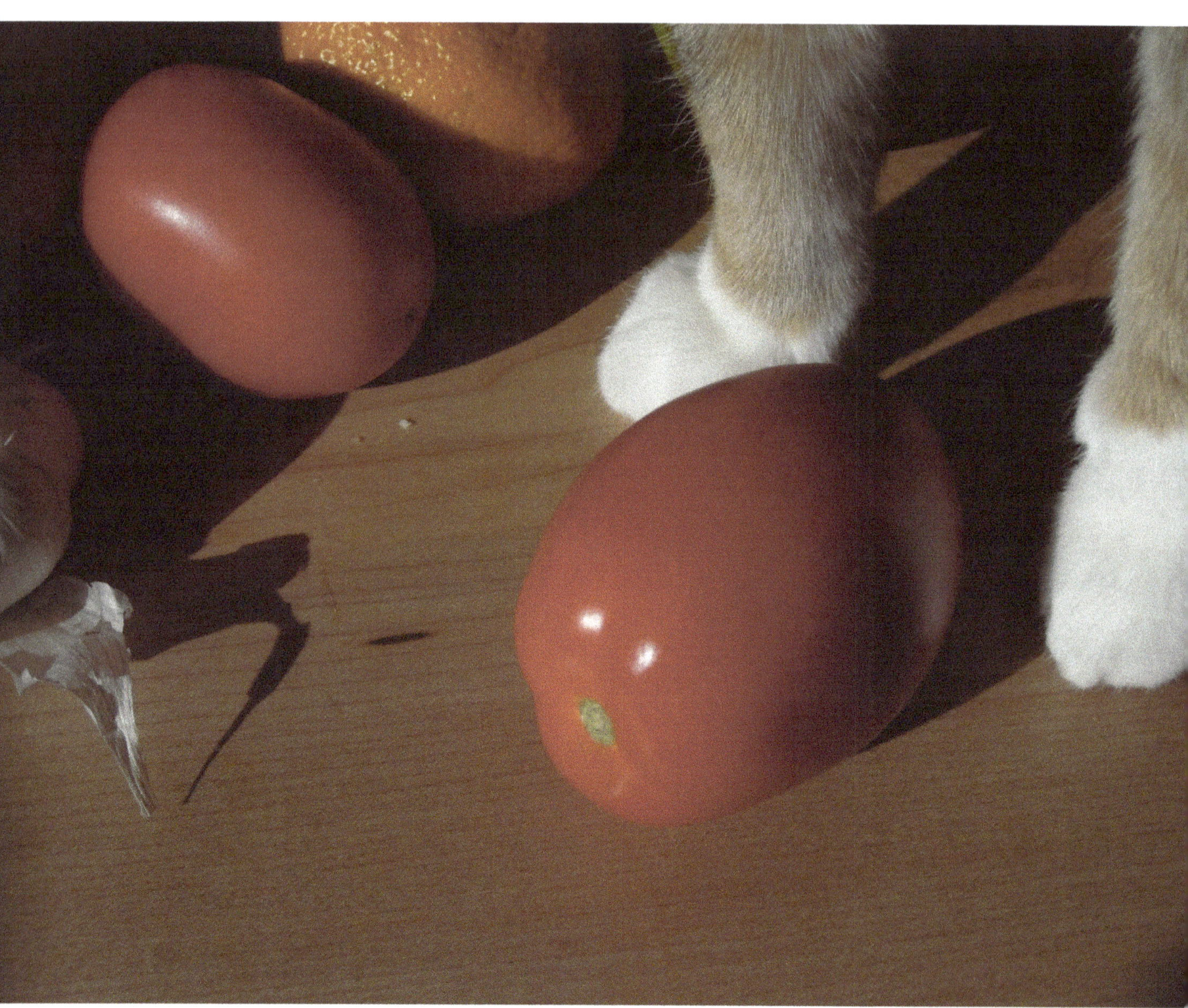

The Body As Tangible Forms—Edward Weston

Another photographer we can take inspiration from is Edward Weston. His is a somewhat Level One approach to the human body. Rather than trying to see the whole animate personality clearly, we can explore formal aesthetics of the human body, in a visual sculptural way. Edward Weston is one master of this approach. In his early explorations, he broke from conventional photography; he deconstructed the conceptual sense of the whole body into the partial values: shape, volume, texture, and tonal—the shape of a hip, the elegance of an arm, the force of a posture. He explored the tangibility of the human body in the same way he explored the tangibility of other forms, such as rocks and vegetables. In one famous statement describing his work, Weston said: "bark is rough, stone is hard, flesh is alive."

After exploring parts, Weston opened up to the whole body as a formal value—its overall shape, volume, and tonal degrees. He perceived the human body as living sculpture, as a living flesh form of the forms and elements of all phenomenal reality, like rocks, trees, plants, and vegetable forms.

In Weston's later explorations of a fuller human expression and personality, we can see his early formal approach. These images display a sensual, even sexual, presence, but they sustain a certain formality that is not artificial but rather attests to the tangibility and inner stillness of the human form. Here we see a deep contemplative structure and manifestation: the union of stillness and sensuality.

So, in practice, like Weston, we can work with a cooperative subject or just tune in with ongoing situations. The way Weston worked was to have a cooperative subject assume various forms. Then he would note aspects, whether formal or dynamic, of that human form. You can try this, but it is not our starting recommendation. Instead, you can simply have a sensibility for this way of seeing. Notice a gesture of an arm, the turning of a head, and so forth. Work with that, those detailed embodied expressions.

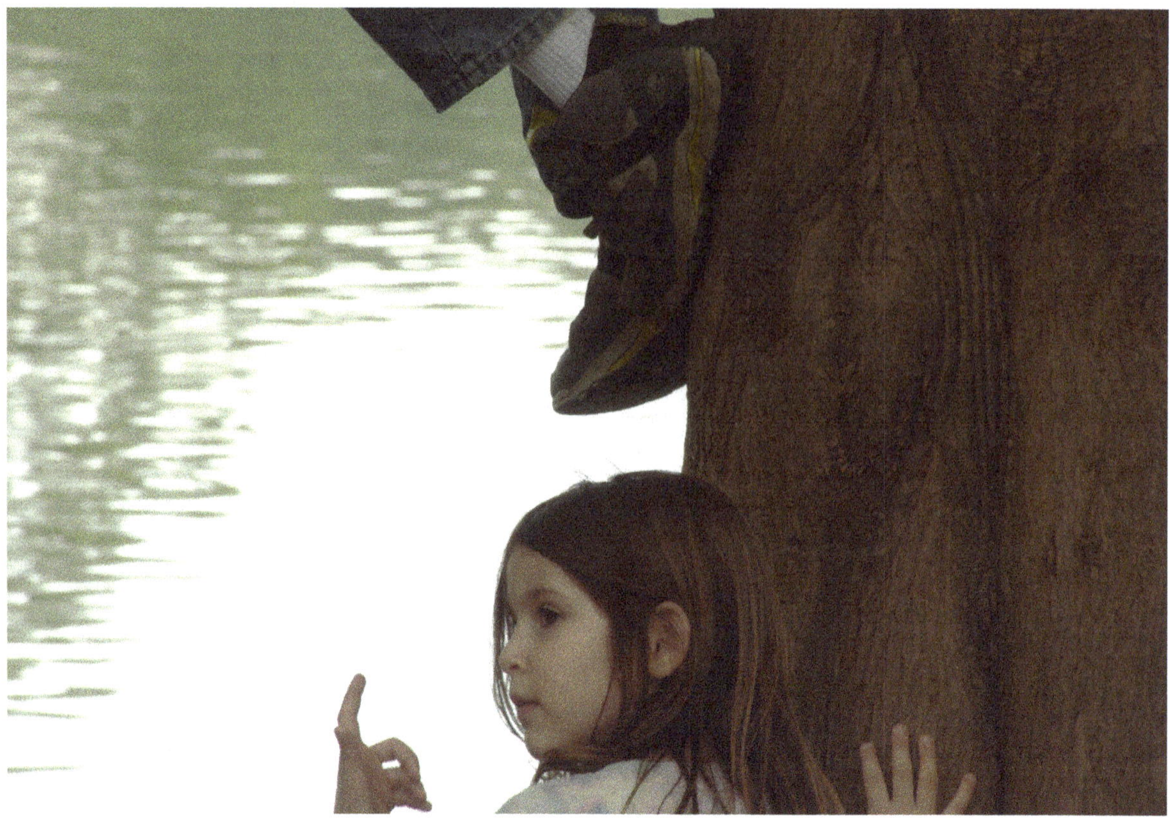

The Decisive Moment—
Cartier-Bresson

Expression is always an occasioned event. It is a happening, and there are two basic elements to this expressive happenings: the event, and the context of the event.

Much has been said and written about Henri Cartier-Bresson and his approach of the decisive moment. His view has a lot in alignment with Nalanda Miksang teachings. One quote of his that is particularly relevant here is this: "A photograph is neither taken or seized by force. It offers itself up. It is the photo that takes you. One must not take photos."

His approach has been compared to Zen arts, wherein spontaneity of engagement is highlighted. Indeed, this resonates with the contemplative teachings on "first thought best thought," or "flash of perception." However, in our view, many commentaries misrepresent decisive moment: they see it as a feature of the real, objective world—a particular event out there.

We suggest this instead: through the decisive moment, the perceiver responds directly to an auspicious moment of the phenomenal world. The decisive moment is isomorphic with the flash of perception. It is not a recorded event but an equivalent of the result of the perceiver and perceived being there together. As Cartier-Bresson said:

To take a photograph means to recognize—simultaneously and within a fraction of a second—both the fact itself and the rigorous organization of visually perceived forms that give it meaning. It is putting one's head, one's eye, and one's heart on the same axis.

Cartier-Bresson discerned situations that seemed to hold perceptual possibilities. When he established the place for the possible happening, he did much of the contemplative work. These discerned settings or circumstances of his decisive moment are often overlooked or underplayed. It was not simply a matter of being on the spot for a chance occurrence. Cartier-Bresson was not a photojournalist. He was a contemplative action photographer.

He then waited for something to happen in and through these visual environments. What is crucial in Cartier-Bresson's contemplative practice is not only the decisive moment but also the decisive context, and the contemplative discernment of a situation as the decisive moment.

There is a subtle contemplative practice in recognizing when something happens, especially when it involves people who are on the move. You can learn many tactics to be prepared, and we will offer some in a bit, but at the perceptual level, this can only happen how it happens. It is somewhat unconditional, and has the quality of a flash of perception. You then make your equivalent image of the moment.

When Cartier-Bresson recognized something had happened, he was there with the way it was. Being in the context of that moment is the only way. That is the decisive moment. This is the deep contemplative decisive moment. The happening is not the decisive moment; the decisive moment gathers the whole situation, including the viewer, who is not really separate.

There is an interplay between the contemplative intention, the contemplative situation, and the contemplative event. For example, in Cartier-Bresson's work, there is the famous image of a man jumping over a large puddle of water on a city street. Most people focus on the man jumping as the decisive moment and forget the setting of the water, street, and city. They forget the most decisive feature of the decisive moment: Cartier-Bresson himself. His contemplative mind and complete contemplative practice as a contemplative action perception photographer. He was there with the there both before it was a there and as it was a there.

In Nalanda Miksang terms, Cartier-Bresson found and established a visual space for the occurrence of the flash of perception as a dot-in-space. The decisive moment is not just the moment when something happens. It is the whole orientation and engagement with the contemplative process: contemplative mind and intent, discerning the visual situation, contemplative waiting, the occasion and simultaneously recognizing the occasion, the equivalent image.

Often when we are out photographing moving beings, we are doing a kind of catch-and-release fishing. We even speak of "good fishing ponds"—finding places where people can easily try out whatever our current assignment is. Cartier was a visual fisherman who knew how to find the good fishing holes and how to catch the best fish. He knew catching was not simply bringing bait and a pole, but knowing where to go, the state of mind to use, and how to be patient for the whole process to come to fruition.

The Environmental Portrait—Cartier-Bresson

You can take Cartier-Bresson's approach as a formal assignment. Find an area, a situation, or a circumstance that has visual ambiance and holds the possibilities of visual action.

Part of this contemplative exercise is discerning the visual circumstance. In general, anything can happen anywhere, and that is a good contemplative attitude. In this case, however, you need to attend to the specific assignment of an environmental portrait, where the visual environment is part of the visual image. Some environments favor human actions. For instance, you are more likely to witness human action and decisive moments around a bus or streetcar stop than in a deserted after-hours parking lot. You should also consider the contemplative aesthetics of the situation: the environment should already be contemplative, containing simplicity, purity, and space. If you choose an outdoors rock festival, you will find plenty of incredible gestures, but not many situations where you can actually photograph the whole environment in a clear way.

For example, John once did this assignment by setting up at a beach boardwalk. The forms were there: the visual strata of the boardwalk, the sand beach, the water, and the sky. It was it was already a pure formal contemplative visual situation. Against this backdrop, there was the activity of people on the boardwalk, on the beach, and in the boats on the water. It was a good fishing hole. However, he didn't have an idea of what in particular he was going to shoot. He simply swam in the unknown potency and waited until

something occurred. If he had expected a specific something, holding out for that, it likely wouldn't have occurred, and he would have missed out on many other possibilities.

It is difficult to give instruction for this aspect. You are not merely taking snapshots or photojournalist documentary shots. That is not contemplative. The contemplative is not only the decisive moment but the auspicious moment, the moment of harmony and synchronization. It is a double synchronization: you are there with what is there. More often than not, you are not looking at it; you simply see it, and the whole perception hangs together. You are there together.

In this example, John noticed a young Asian woman in a white dress walking down the beach. In her hand was a red cap, moving back and forth with the rhythm of her arm, which was in tune with the rhythm of her walking pace. She really caught his attention, but he waited to take a photograph, not just immediately press the shutter. Simultaneously, he noticed, on the water, in the distance, a sailboat moving in the opposite direction.

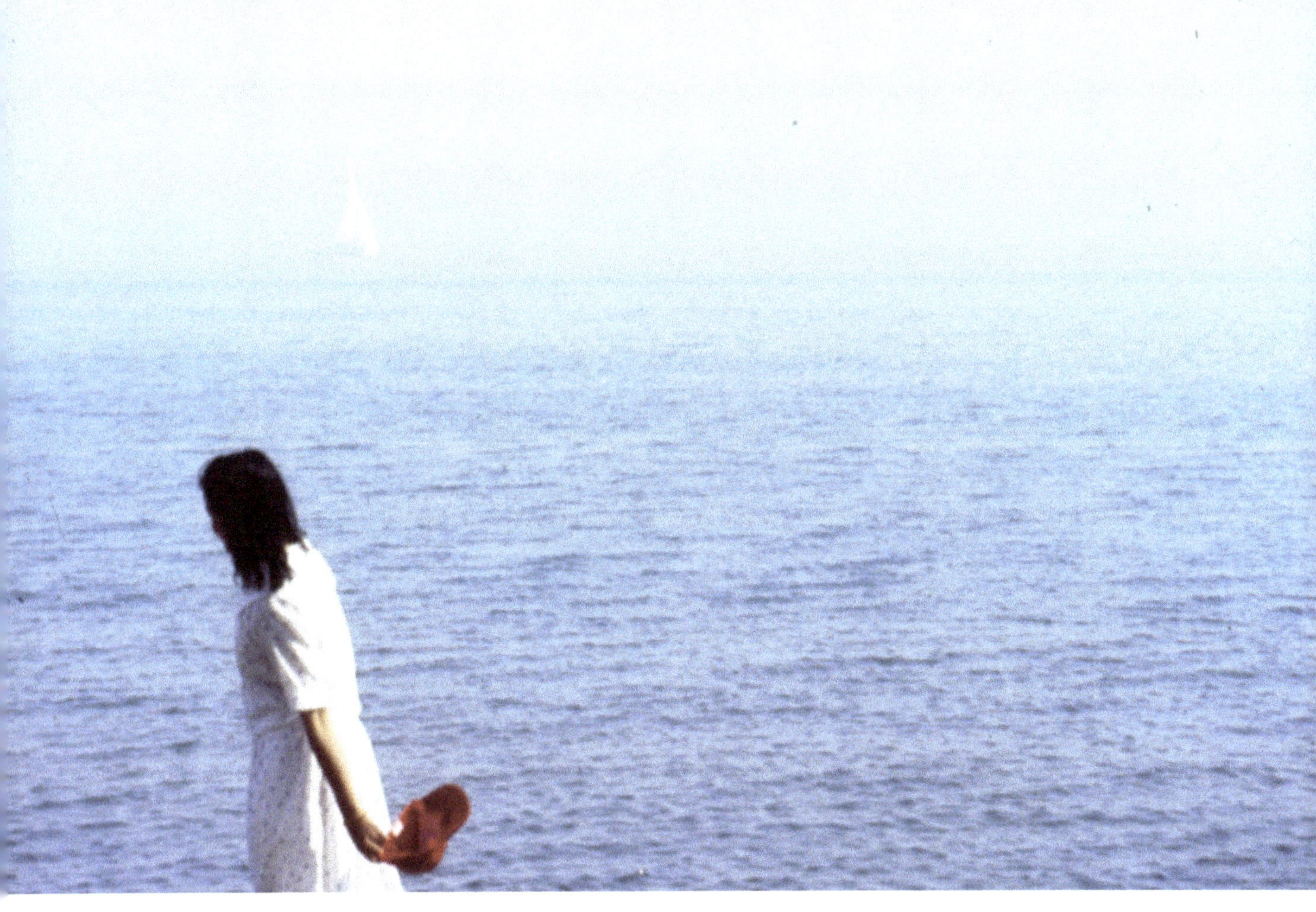

Without planning, at some point—a decisive auspicious point—the whole perception synchronized: the visual strata, the Asian girl with the white dress, the arm with the red cap swung behind, and, in the misty distance, the sailboat entering the whole visual scene. It became clear: now. And that is when he pressed the shutter. There is no way to know when now will happen before now is now. This is what makes it contemplative. This is what makes it a fun adventure, and part of what imparts ordinary magic into your life and images.

So this is the assignment: put yourself in a visual environmental situation with people, then relax and open to the auspicious decisive moment. As it happens of itself, try and just be there and make an image. Enjoy that special moment—it is ok to enjoy that special image. Every time John sees that Asian girl/red cap/sailboat image, he experiences an inside/out smile. That inside/out smile is the inner contemplative of contemplative photography.

That's the end of our presentation of photographing humans from some of the masters of this subject: Lange, Weston, Cartier-Bresson. Now we present more of a mix of recommendations and instructions gathered from our contemplative engagement with photographing the human phenomenal world.

CONTEMPLATIVE PEOPLE PHOTOGRAPHY: OTHER WAYS IN

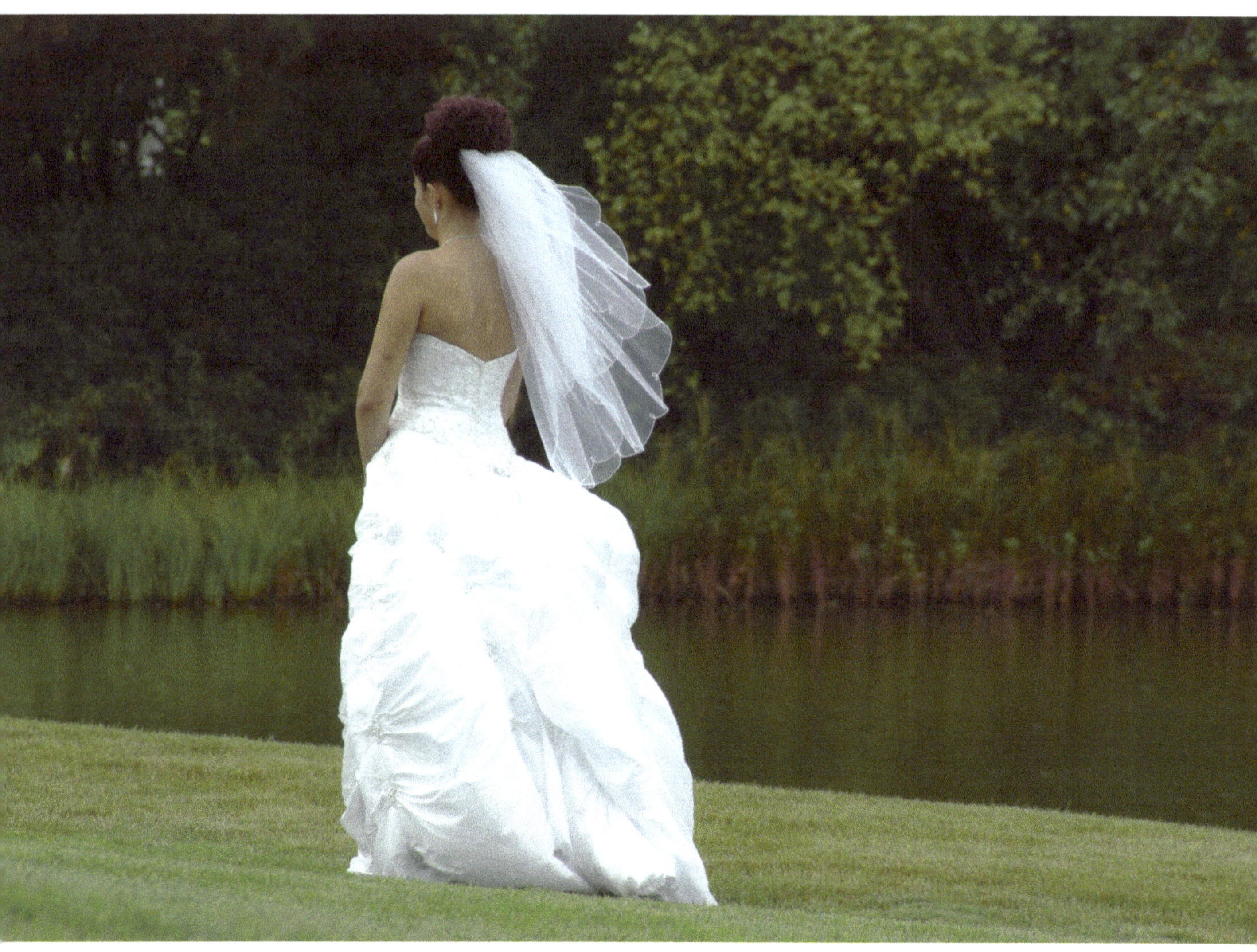

While Lange, Weston, and Cartier-Bresson inspired some forms to work with, there are also more contemporary situations and approaches to consider. As we have been doing so far, we present these from simplest to most complex, ending at the far edge of Nalanda Miksang for this assignment: Street Photography.

People Situations

This recommendation is a no-brainer. It is just common sense, but sometimes we miss the obvious. Here it is: if you want to work with people as a subject matter, you have to go to situations where there are people.

The key word here is *situations*. This is not quite as formal as the Environmental Portrait approach. Here we have in mind places and situations where people are gathered with a certain intent, not just in the general, to-and-fro flux of urban situations, like walking on the street, Rather, go where people are gathered for a specific practical engagement: a fair, a farmer's market, a parade, a demonstration.

These people are preoccupied, and there are many other cameras of camera folk around. So this can help with feeling self-conscious, for both you and your subject, as they are preoccupied and have a tolerance for cameras. You can just hang out as part of the whole situation and scene and wait for something to arise. As we mentioned earlier, this carries with it the trickiness of a busy scene; often there's quite a bit more going on in these photos than in Environmental Portraits. That's ok, it's a different kind of shoot, but one you might want to work up to.

Michael Wood, John's early Miksang colleague, was a professional photographer. Part of his practice was wedding photography. Like many photographers in Toronto, he would stage his shoots in a park called Edward Gardens. After he was done with the professional session, he could engage a more Miksang approach to photographing people than for the other wedding events. It was a perfect situation: many people were very involved with their wedding and expected photographers to be there, both professional and non-professional.

Miriam found the same when she photographed the previous image of the bride turned away from the rest of the party for a moment's pause. When people let down their guard in a public place, if we also let down our guard, we can connect—even if not face-to-face—in a profound perceptual interplay in space.

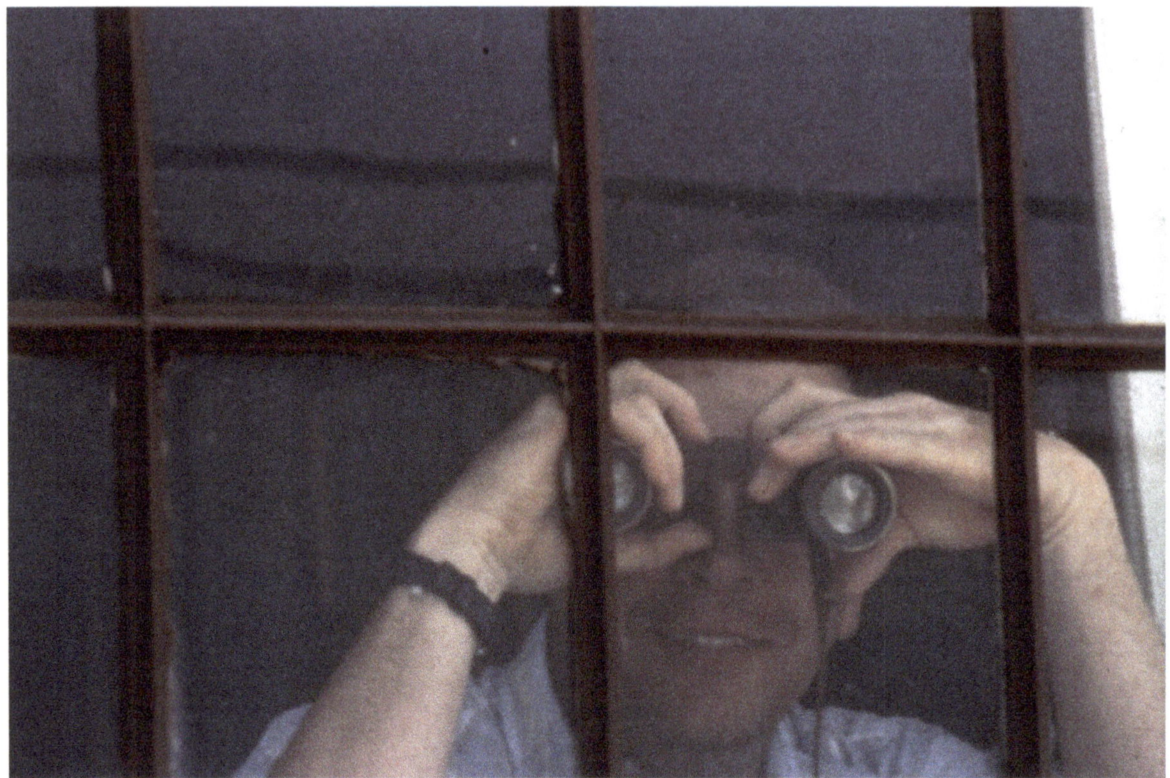

The Photojournalistic Take On A Decisive Moment

Although photojournalists generally have a different intention than contemplative photographers, they have their own version of a decisive moment. Because they are out looking for news, photojournalists are on the spot for a visual happening. For contemplative photography it is important that we do this in an unobtrusive way. There can be no aggression of getting the shot; we are not the paparazzi. What we can learn from photojournalists is how to be on the spot, how to be quick and yet synchronized.

These skills are helpful in crowded, unstructured settings, like street photography, an ever-growing popular form. In wide open circumstances like this, without a specific assignment, you must combine intent and camera craft. Your intention is to engage in a more spontaneous, candid exploration of the human subject and situation while staying ready and invisible. You want to get in and out of a situation unobtrusively. This involves a fair amount of working with your own desires, self-aggression or doubt, and self-consciousness, which manifests as a form of aggression. If you are anxious about wanting a shot to work, the subject will feel it; having a longer lens does not help, it simply amplifies the energy of your struggle.

It's also good to preset your camera to some programmed settings. There is often no time for deliberation, so the best approach is to set the camera at one focal length, say, the portrait favorite of $f/5.6$, and the corresponding shutter speed for the light of the day. Then you can spontaneously follow the spontaneous visual moment. You move in, you move out; you are almost not really there, but the there is there. This is the contemplative thrill of this kind of photography. It takes quite a bit of practice to ease into this kind of action, both visual and mental/emotional. It is not for everyone. But it is magical.

For example, one day, John was doing some beach shooting. He set his camera to $f/5.6$ and adjusted the appropriate shutter setting for the time of day. At one moment, he sensed someone watching him. He turned to see a man looking through a window with binoculars. That moment had huge resonance beyond the moment, as it paralleled the paintings of Alex Colville. There was a lot of depth happening in that spot, the depth of the now moment. John framed, focused, and clicked, and at the very moment John took the picture, the man with the binoculars picked up on John looking back at him and smiled. That made for a better image, even more spontaneous and connected than the initial flash.

For this kind of contemplative photography, you need to straddle the fence between photojournalism and contemplative photography. You are not trying to capture the moment; you are opening to being in the moment with that moment.

This is even deeper than the contemplative timeless moment. It is the timeless moment, but there is no sense of dwelling in it or on it. There is no time for dwelling. You are on the spot with this on-the-spot. Because you cannot plan for it or predict it, because you must let go and move on afterward, it is not so easy. But when it happens, it cuts through mental chaos and preconceptions about photographing. When it cuts through, then it is direct, vivid, personal, and resonant.

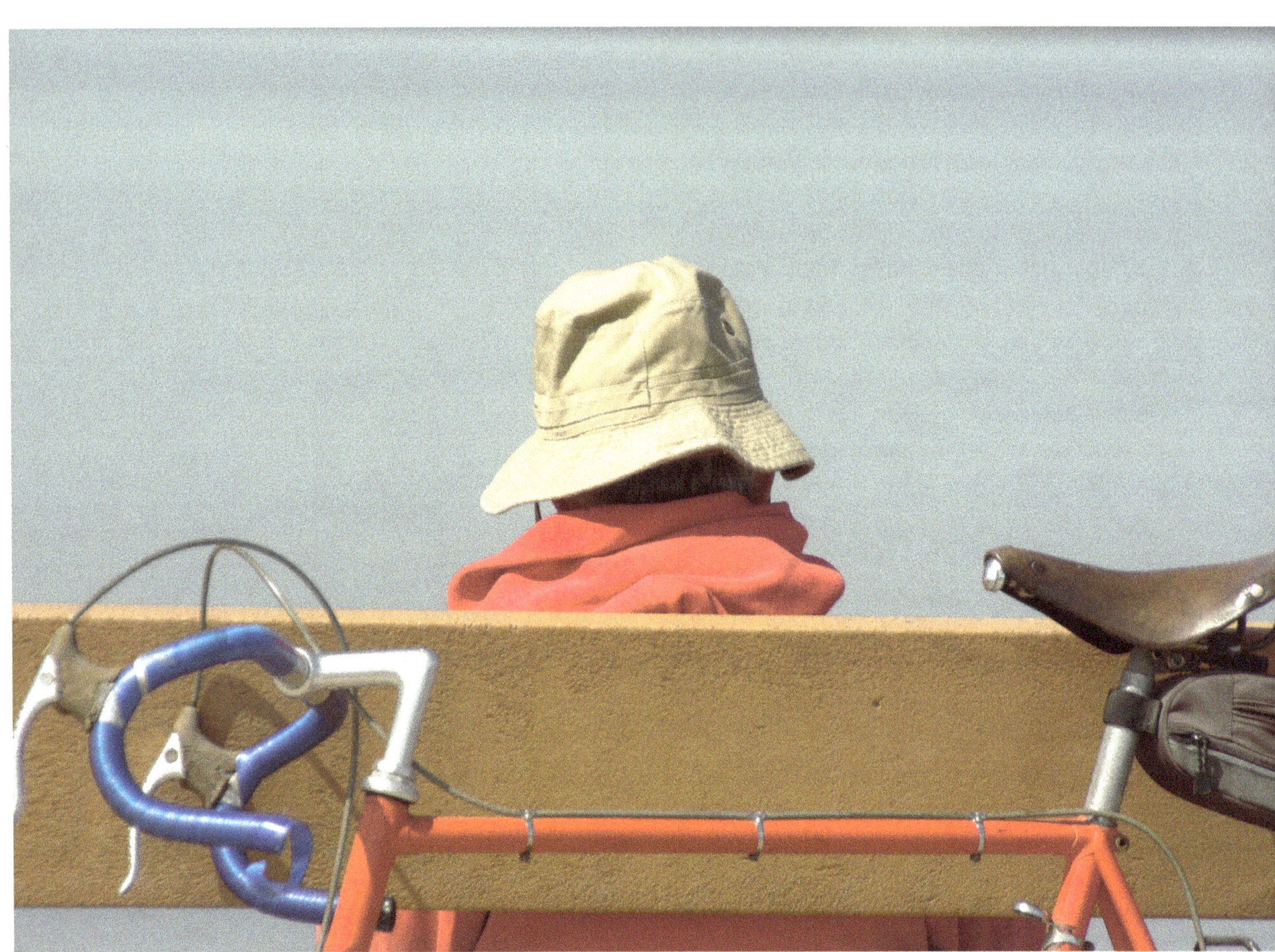

Photographing From Behind

Again, this can be somewhat obvious, and again, we often miss the obvious. One direct way to solve both your feeling self-conscious and your subject becoming self-conscious when they see your camera is to make the image from behind them; the person seen does not see you. You are just seeing what you see. This also helps eliminate the ethical issues some people have with photographing strangers: usually photographs from behind do not render the person recognizable.

This approach has a contemplative mind element as well: it breaks with the convention that we should always make images of people from the front. It also treats the human form more as a form, rather than as a person or personality. As we have noted with Weston and Lange, the human figure perception is a multidimensional manifestation.

This shooting from behind has become one of John's ways in with human subjects. He appreciates the relaxation factor—the lack of stress and reaction issues—and the different perceptual vector.

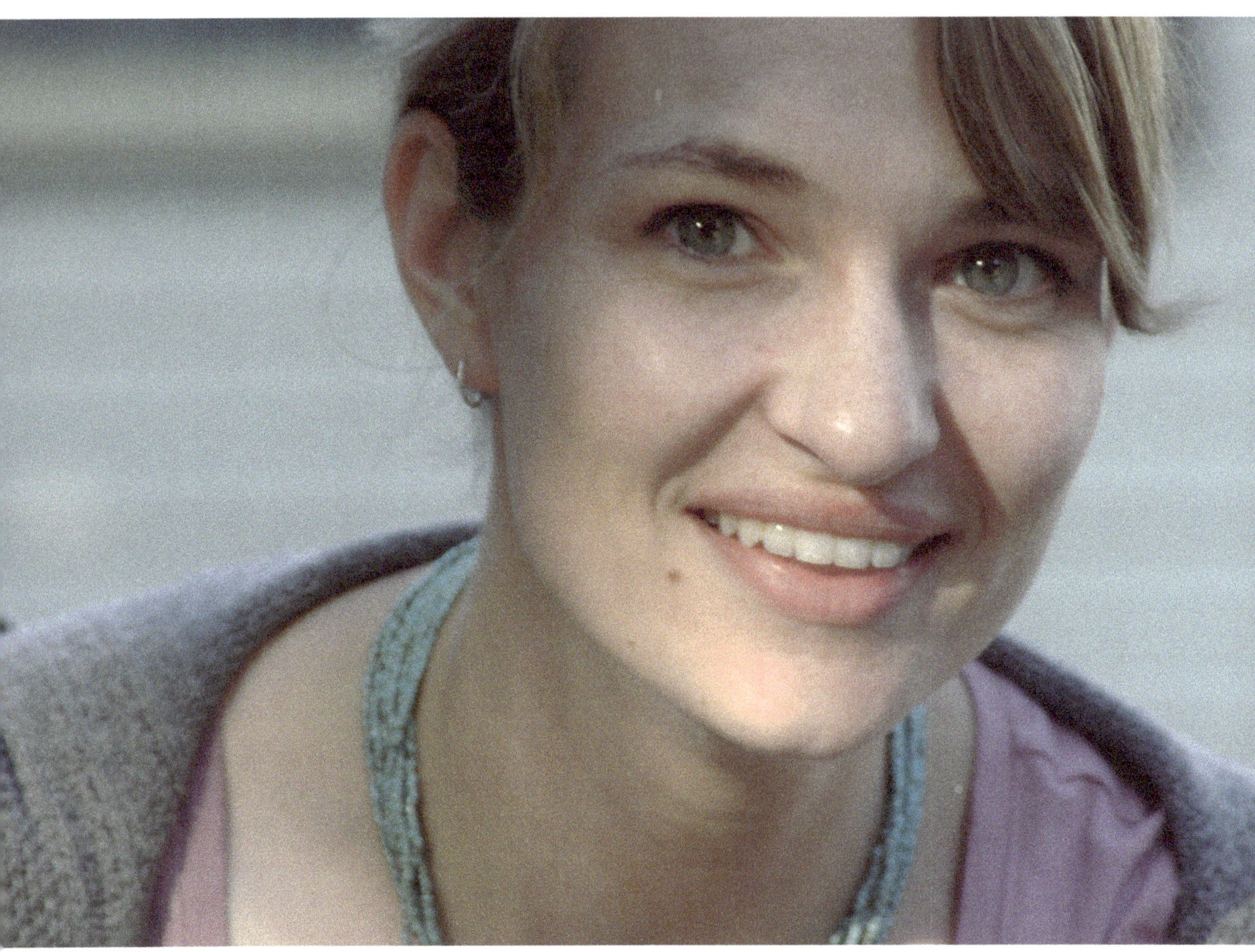

The Contemplative Collaboration

The most direct way to photograph humans in a contemplative way is to collaborate with them in a contemplative way. This is the contemplative version of portraiture. In conventional portraiture, one person poses and the other photographs. But our way is not a photo shoot. Instead, you enter the process together. There are different approaches to this way: Miksang community, partner collaborations, and face-to-face portraits.

In Nalanda Miksang communities of contemplative photography practitioners and friends, when we are gathered, say, on a field trip, we can photograph each other. We trust each other and understand the way of Nalanda Miksang, so we can relax and let the process happen. This is one way we start out before going out to photograph strangers. It helps us to understand just how powerful the energy exchange and relationship between the photographer and the person photographed is, and we also learn to relax and let go.

Another way is again inspired by Weston. He would have a willing subject go with the flow—move around, enter postures, and so forth, and at some point he would tell them to hold. He was asking them to pause at his decisive moment. This is not strictly Miksang, but it combines structure and flash of perception/decisive moment.

Finally, there is an even more deliberate approach, grounded in some approaches of formal portraiture photography: you set up a formal situation and wait for, or even solicit, the decisive moment. We have adapted this in a more relaxed contemplative way. It is similarly formal, where a portrait situation is set up. The difference is an understanding that this is a contemplative engagement. Subject and photographer both wait for the release and relax into the now moment when we are both there together.

This is as much an exercise of mind as it is of vision. As participating photographer and subject, we are partners to this process of relaxation, opening, and trust. Then we switch positions so that we each have the experience of both orientations. In this way we mix our contemplative minds and hearts.

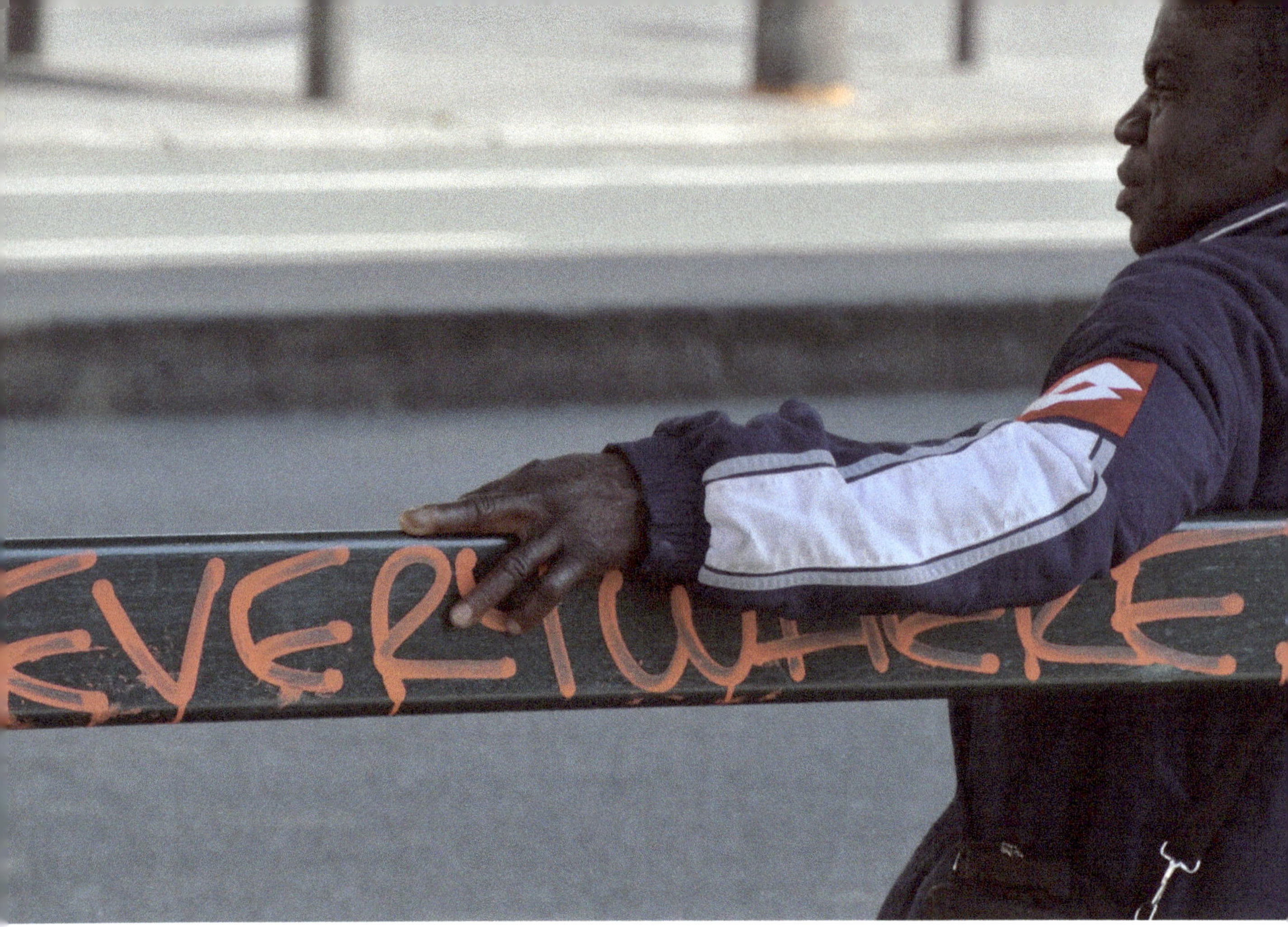

Miksang And Street Photography

In recent years, what is referred to as "street photography" has become increasingly popular. There are many videos and classes, books, and offerings out there giving instruction on how to approach photographing people candidly on the street, in public. The focus of a lot of street photography is on "how" to do it; much of that strategizing has a different view than Nalanda Miksang. This is a growing edge, both in terms of working with our minds as practitioners and as a community for Nalanda Miksang International. We invite you to explore it with us, if you feel ready, and to not touch it with a ten-foot pole if it feels ethically or otherwise restrictive to you. In other words, this far edge is not for everyone.

A bit like environmental portraits or people situations, the main preparation for street photography is going to a good place, somewhere with potential, and waiting for something to happen and photograph it.

The thing is, you don't know what's going to happen. It is far more spontaneous and far more edgy than photographing your cat. The gap between photographing your dog and photographing strangers in public is huge. At the same time, the same issues come up. With your dog, you know the situation, and you are familiar with the being. Out on the street, you have no idea, no ground for what is happening, so anxiety and aggression can arise very quickly. One of the ways people sometimes compensate for this is by using the camera as a shield, to block themselves from the situation, to make who they are seeing—a homeless man, someone in an unusual outfit—into the other. It is crucial when photographing in any situation, and especially with other beings, to find the union and the connection, rather than increasing the distance with the camera.

When we engage with this assignment we're exploring the phenomenal world, which includes our own mind and the energy that our mind is expressing, the way that our thoughts are working. Work with those things so that there is less intimidation, because for most people, even professional street photographers, this activity is pretty intimidating. It's easy to blame this feeling on our contemporary urban world. While it is true that most of us are intimidated by relationships, any time we encounter another sentient being we simply have reflected back to us what is happening externally as well as inside of us. In street situations, in urban complexity, what is often reflected back is less a sense of harmony and more an orderly chaos, in a visual and also physiological way. The busier, the louder, the more complex the situation, the harder it can be to trust pure perception. However, it is always there—your connection, your interdependence, and the basic goodness of all beings. Practicing this far out, at this edge, if you can do it, can be some of the most rewarding practice for Nalanda Miksang.

However, some of the people drawn to doing contemplative street photography are also what Miriam's shastri calls "discomfort junkies." If you find yourself wanting more complexity, more challenge, looking for harder assignments, it's a good time to ask yourself if perhaps what is challenging for you is, in fact, harmony. Some of us are more naturally drawn to urban, complex situations and contemplative street photography; some of us feel more at ease in the country, with flowers and weeds. Finding where your edge is, which might be what others wouldn't consider "edgy," is crucial. Keep growing in your practice, checking in to see what topics you have rejected as being "too boring" or "too hard," gently expanding your edges in these never-ending fields of perception.

Contemplative Photography And Human Relations

One of the most basic aspects of being human is relating to other human beings. Even now, with the Internet, smartphones, and other technologies that let us communicate less directly, communication is still human to human, which is a heart connection. In *The Shambhala Principle*, Sakyong Mipham Rinpoche says a good society starts with personal connection between two people: heart to heart.

Relating with others is both wonderful and challenging. Sometimes it's even challenging when it is wonderful, like when falling in love. Human relationships can be difficult because they are basically true. Others mirror back to us our own perspective and energy, just as we mirror back their perspectives and energy. Sometime we can get lost and confused in this hall of mirrors.

But Nalanda Miksang as a practice can directly impact your capacity for compassion in these relationships. The contemplative photography relationship is different from many conventional human relationships of direct reciprocity, like between marriage partners, parents and children, teacher and students, and so forth. Contemplative photography is grounded in the relationship between the perceiver and the perceived. It is not a personal relationship; it is a perception relationship. That does not mean it is not intimate—quite the contrary. The practice of this assignment is how to discern and express the intimate and personal *within* the relationship of the perceiver and perceived, via an image.

What we often fail to understand as photographers is that taking a photograph of another sentient being is a conversation. Even if the other person does not know we are speaking to them, they are communicating something and we are attempting to accept and convey that communication.

Shambhala teachings speak of our personal soft spots. Basic goodness may seem like an abstract or philosophical notion, but because of our soft spots, we know what it is like to feel. When we touch and are in touch, the *touch* is the connection via our soft spot with sentience, which is feeling. That is our direct connection with basic goodness. Even though it does not always feel good to feel, it is how we know we are alive. We know what it feels like to be hurt or have wonder, to feel betrayal and unexpected kindness, to get wrapped in jealously or envy, to free-fall into romantic love, to dive into the warm embrace of family, to have pride in accomplishment, to twinge with the agonies of defeat; the possibilities of our feelings go on and on. All of this is very direct and vivid and is very real to our experience. How to be gentle with our own humanity, and with other humans, is key to discovering our mutual basic goodness. This is the deep practice and insight of this assignment.

In Nalanda Miksang, our relationship to our soft spot connects us to a direct perceptual event. We connect through the soft spot to occasioned details of perceptual manifestation: a gesture, a look, the decisive moment, and so forth. Because of relationship, Miriam finds this assignment the most rewarding of all the assignments in Nalanda Miksang. She likes to think of the flash of perception becoming a "flash of connection" in this assignment—an opening between the soft spots of two beings, a deeply interdependent contact. The possibilities for insights and transformation of perceptions are most available here. In order to let this assignment transform us, however, we must open to it—at whatever level we can begin.

It might help to understand that, in our openness, through making and sharing our images, we offer something back. It is a heart-to-heart exchange. Nalanda Miksang is a perception way with this heart-to-heart exchange. It is different from, but resonates with, meditation. The ways of meditation provide a practices of Tonglen and loving kindness that also work directly with this kind of exchange. If this is of interest to you, please see a presentation of Tonglen in the appendix.

Something about a gesture is poignant and resonant. Something about a shy, self-conscious smile is poignant and resonant. Something about the way the light plays in a person's hair is poignant and resonant. Phenomenal poignancy and resonance are endless because something about the detailed perception of heart moment–to–heart moments in human relationships is poignant and resonant.

This endlessness is the stream from which we draw an equivalent image. This image expresses this heart perception to share with and enrich others. It is both an image of a single moment and an image that resonates with our connection to all moments. This is the heart of photography as the heart manifestation of sentient beings.

CONCLUSION

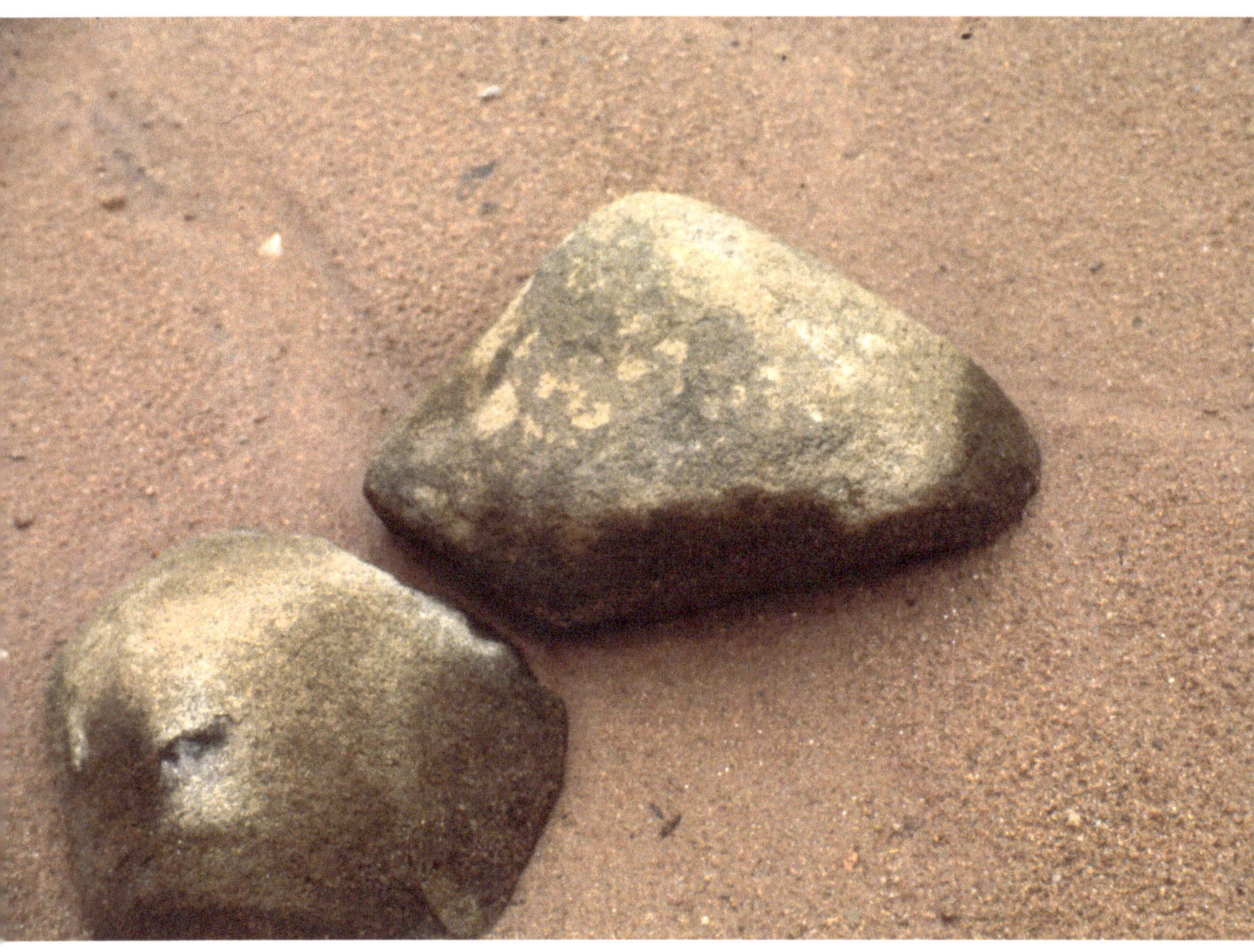

In daily life we don't have to create the concept of letting go, of being free . . . we can just acknowledge the freedom that was already there . . . there is a quick glimpse. A sudden glimpse. The sudden glimpse of awareness that occurs in everyday life becomes the act of compassion . . . The practice is the recognition of the glimpse and its qualities. . . that glimpse, if you analyze it, takes one-sixtieth of a second. It is so fast and sharp. The sharpness is the intelligence of compassion. Compassion also means being open and communicable. It contains warmth, because you have the desire to do such a thing.

—**Chögyam Trungpa, *Glimpses of the Profound***

Enriching

The teachings in this book point to the heart of Nalanda Miksang, which includes the way we are in touch and the way we are touched, and the sense and sensibility of true perception.

The images are important. After all, we are practicing contemplative photography. These images don't just show what we see, they express our vision. Vision joins eye and inspiration. Inspiration joins heart and creativity. Our images show this heart vision and creativity.

In practicing Nalanda Miksang, we gather appreciation, insight, and wisdom. Each field of perception gathers its own unique experience, insight, and brilliant images. Through the practice, we appreciate and enrich our lives, and through the images, we enrich the life of others and the larger culture. It is that simple, and that profound.

Nalanda Miksang Level Two is what Shambhala calls an enriching presence practice. Enriching presence practices help us connect deeply with the natural richness of our world. They don't enrich through projection; they help us appreciate all that is already there. Another way of defining the word *appreciate* is "to give something value." For example, when you invest a sum of money, its value increases; it appreciates.

Here we give value to our ordinary experience, perception, insight, and images. Unlike monetary value, appreciation gives true value, showing that our personal lives, flowers and weeds, people and other sentient beings are all worthwhile. By being truly present in our lives, we practice enriching presence—mixing with the richness that always exists. Amazingly enough, it is just what is happening, but that it is happening is extraordinary. It is just a matter or tuning in and appreciating. Appreciation is enriching. Through your images, your life and the life of others is enriched. This is what you are doing when you engage true perception and make resonant images.

Nalanda Miksang begins with the phenomenal world and is oriented through the phenomenal world. We let the phenomenal world make the first move, and our practice is a response. Our practice is a thanks for the gift of the phenomenal display. Our practice is a thanksgiving.

This is why you not only feel good; you also feel fulfilled. Enrichment is a sense of well-being, completion, and enhancement. This is an integral aspect of contemplative practice and of contemplative photography. In formal terms, it is synchronization which erases the dualism between the perceiver and the perceived.

In experiential terms, this enrichment appears in a very ordinary and available way. Usually you simultaneously realize two aspects. One is that you are not bogged down with your stuff—stuff is on hold and out of play, and that feels light and spacious. You are no longer carrying that load. You feel released. What is released is not just the load of discursive mind and self-preoccupation but also the habitual filters of interpretation and preference. The second aspect is that you feel open, bright, on edge, and inquisitive. Your deepening of appreciation resonates and radiates out into the world.

Resonance And Radiance

Level Two images set up an awake contemplative resonance, like a tuning fork vibrating with wine glasses. They also have an intrinsic aesthetic, a pre-existing, natural aesthetic that expresses the experience of space and the phenomenal world. Each perception is an opening infused with a visual manifestation. What you see is this visual manifestation: a field of tulips as a field of red dot forms, impressionistic colors in the reflection of water, and so on. These are all specific and unique happenings that help you experience endless phenomenal manifestations.

The heart of photography is an infusion of perception and aesthetic. It is like a rainbow: the colors and the transparency of the rainbow space are self-same. This is actually how experience manifests. Experienced perception and is full of the elements of the phenomenal world (what we work with in Level One, or *Looking and Seeing*): light, color, and other forms. *Heart of Photography, Level Two*, explores the way these forms become

the light, color, things of the world: fire engine red and a red fire engine, tuning into this inherent aesthetic expression that is not different than the experience itself. Direct experience is detailed and inexhaustibly rich. It is just a matter of tuning in rather than tuning out.

As photography and photographic image this is what you express. Your images don't just record something you see, they express your seeing itself and embody the sense and sensibility at the heart connection of your vision. This is a resonance that happens both "out there" in the world and also in you, vibrating the strings of your heart through direct sense perception.

As we have explored, there are the contemplative aesthetics of resonance: sabi (poignancy, subtlety, subdued, delicate), wabi (simplicity and time-seasoned character), and yugen (quiet mystery of an image that holds the mind as it releases the mind). These manifest in endless ways: the dewdrop mind, the bird-on-a-wire mind, the rainbow mind, the ebb-and-tide-flow mind, the cat whiskers mind, the impressionistic fleeting-and-floating mind, the open-window and open-field minds, the childlike-wonder mind and the wise-beyond-years mind, the flower and the bee minds, the sun and the moon minds.

This infusion and radiance are what is heartfelt in your images, the heartbeat of your images: contemplative, heartbeat beauty. This is what moves others' hearts. It shows the heart of the world because it is the heart of the world.

The Shift

Beyond the images, and through the images, we see that the expression of the phenomenal world is worthwhile. That includes us. For the contemplative, we make a decisive shift. We leave behind the concept of a static "thing world," which is understood to be there in the way we need it to be, as a functional situation. We journey into the experienced phenomenal world, which is always there in the way it is there, manifesting in its rainbow, ever-shifting ways.

This shift is the shift to living in the lived world. It is the shift to the experienced world as the phenomenal world and the phenomenal world as the experienced world. It is the shift to seeing that the experienced world and the phenomenal world arise together. They are both fresh and free. It is not abstract or conceptual; it is simply the way it is with the experienced phenomenal world.

A haystack is never just a haystack. It is the haystack with the way of the seasons, the daily cycle of sun and shadow, the way of the weather, the way of the light, and so forth. Never forget, it is also the haystack with the way of your mind, whether you are actually there with the there or lost in the drift and obscuration of various discursive distractions and conceptual filters.

We always still have an ongoing pragmatic way with the thing world, which is a feature of how we are, and how we work, within this world—how we operate as humans in this human world. We sit on chairs, and so forth. But this is not the whole range of our experience. Indeed, in terms of experience, it is a highly limited range.

Our contemplative practice is not in any way against the pragmatics of living. Rather, it offers the idea that we can relax about pragmatics and open more to the open experience of living. Then your experience is not so much the same old, same old—the same old thing world and the same old routines. Instead of the static thing world and the drag of the habitual life, more and more, you orient toward the ordinary, everyday adventure of the experience world, a live-wire world.

Even without formal practice, we can notice ongoing moments that break the momentum of routine. We pause and find ourselves relaxed, settled, and open. No big deal. Quite ordinary. Simply noticing how hot it is, hearing that bird chirp. As we pause for no particular reason, we can tune into the personal details of our experience. Those pauses become gaps in the daily program. You can find yourself in that gap. In that gap, you find you are with yourself and with the world and realize this is always, already the reality. Nalanda Miksang practice just focuses and intensifies natural everyday openings and ordinary appreciations of being there and being alive. As a bonus, it produces photographic art to share this connection with others.

In Level Two, we deepen this shift to the phenomenal world. We explore, appreciate, and express this experiences. In fact, we let the phenomenal world make the first move. It comes to us in its own way. We are not trying to capture or create a great flower image; we can let the phenomenal flower display itself in its own way—just those flame yellow petals in space, spontaneous and unique. From that, you make an equivalent of a completely free and unique perception, expressed in a completely creative and unique photo. This is Nalanda Miksang.

Through our images, we appreciate this every day, ordinary miracle and radiant beauty. It is not just seeing clearly, and it is not just seeing the beautiful; it is seeing that seeing itself is beautiful. This is the deep contemplative way: the way of seeing is always already radiant and beautiful if you can see it that way.

The more you engage, embody, and manifest the way, the more it enriches. The more you engage, the more you are engaged. There is a shift and a momentum. You enter the path as the path. Your habitual patterns shift out of ho-hum and into appreciation. This appreciation increases as it increases, and your orientation gradually changes, more and more toward the fresh and free. Like a ship turning just a few degrees in the sea, our course changes dramatically over time through subtle but ongoing practice. Eventually, we arrive at the continent of the fresh and the free.

Being, Feeling, Expressing

This freedom leads to a surprise free fall through the visual phenomenal world. It is an adventure of buoyancy, deep electric stillness, lively, inquisitive joy. That is the experience, and what we really want to understand is that this experience is our birthright, ordinary, natural mind. This is the way it really is.

In formal terms, it is a threefold process: being, feeling, and expression.

First, you are just being there with the there through the there. Just that color, just that dewdrop on a leaf; as we have explored, there are various terms for this, like *suchness, being present,* and so forth. But it is best to stay loose and simple—accept it as it comes in an ordinary magic way. Being there is not abstract; it could not be more intimate and sensuous. It is the feeling and realization of engaging something worthwhile. This has at least two ways of manifesting.

It can come through your life experience— nothing added, nothing taken away, totally complete. You feel like you. You feel alive, at least for now. It can be on the spot, momentary: just that perception, experience, and image. If Nalanda Miksang resonates with your previous life experiences, then you know how this happens without practice.

But practice can help solicit this experience, invite it. A sense of really *being* can arrive in a more reflective way, in the case of Nalanda Miksang, through photographing or sharing images. Sharing this experience of goodness is sharing basic goodness, which is at the heart of being a Shambhala contemplative. This is the vision of enlightened society: an awake culture in which each enriches each.

Second, there is the feeling aspect. When we are there with the there, there is sense and sensibility; this is the heart of Level Two. Our senses deliver the way things are, the feeling of the phenomenal world: that red is hot or flat; a stop sign red; an electric, seductive, flash red; a subtle, blood red; rose red.

Level Two images are suffused with feeling tones. Light creates a mood, simplicity and space play together, phenomenal focus draws us into details: a hand touching a face, the look of eyes, rain drops making circles on the surface of a pool— it goes on and on in this way, it goes on and on. This is how we are moved, touched, and changed— through appreciation, delight, surprise, relaxation, discrimination, smile, pause, stillness.

There is a deep stillness underneath all of this. You begin to sense that our life experience is a surface of a depth. There is more going on than meets the eye, but it can only be met through the eye. You sense the paradoxical resonance. There is more meaning than can be grasped or said in so many words or expressed in any image, and yet, the image communicates an echo of it.

In contemplative traditions, this is called the heartbreak of trying to express what can never be fully expressed; something Chögyam Trungpa calls the "heartbreak of unrequited love." Our practice is precisely this: each pure, beautiful image will never be beautiful enough, and that is its resonant beauty.

Out of that depth of sensibility comes appreciation and enrichment. This is the deep enrichment, the insight that the phenomenal world is an ongoing gift. The experienced visual world never stops, and it is always varied, it is always full. It is fresh and free and a kaleidoscope. It is never the same old, same old. That is our real everyday experience. We live in a rich world. We all have won the lottery. We have the gift of life and. in this case, the gift of visual manifestation. It is a gift that keeps on giving whether we realize it or not.

Nalanda Miksang practice is to realize this. First you tune in, then you appreciate, and then you realize. Sometimes it is the other way around: you realize, are tuned in, and appreciate. That is being and feeling. Then the third phase is to express it. We express it through our personal connection and through the images.

In our personal life, we integrate this practice, experience and insight. We start to slightly shift our orientation and the momentum of our life. More and more, the everyday magic becomes our everyday path experience and the way of our being there. It is always there, but now we acknowledge and appreciate that it is always there, and we are there with and through that being there. That simple shift starts to change the direction of our

experience to perception and being out there with the way it manifests.

It is the difference that makes a difference. Just by shifting a tiny bit, we are turned in the right direction. We are less and less self-preoccupied and enclosed. Now we are out there. The direct perception of phenomenal world: red is red; red as feeling resonance; a bird on a wire. This is release and free floating. But more than this, there is the insight that this phenomenal world comes to you. It is a feature of the gift of life, your life.

Your simple contemplative image can express this profound universe situation. As Chögyam Trungpa put it, a dewdrop shows the whole essence of water. A dewdrop is a drop in the ocean from the ocean.

Going Deeper

If you wish to go deeper through study, you can. The mediation masters, the contemplative masters, and contemplative photography masters embody the way. Some study sources are in the bibliography.

If you don't wish to study, that is good enough, more than good enough; it is rich. You can engage clear perception, experience the free-fall joy of perception, and make radiant perception images. That is the contemplative photography experience. That is enough, more than enough. You are engaging the enriching presence practice, and that is good. That is Miksang, or "good eye."

Through practice and study, however, there is a deep contemplative shift toward seeing that the phenomenal world is the way in which the world manifests. Eventually, this shift is to live with that view and insight, with your allegiance and habitual response, staying with the ongoing, outgoing experience of the phenomenal world rather than with the gravity and absorption of the thing world and self-preoccupation. The shift is to orient outward, to free-fall float with the phenomenal world.

From the affirmative perspective, you experience a free fall through the experience world that opens in its own ways. Becoming a contemplative is precisely this shift: you shift your life orientation and connection more and more from the static-stress thing world and self-preoccupation to the open lived world. Now, more and more, you live in the actual lived world. This is being a contemplative, and this is being an artist. You become an artist in your life as your life. Your life is always an ongoing creation and adventure. Your life experience is creative, and you make creative works through your images.

To be contemplative is to orient toward the manifest priority and enriching presence of the phenomenal world. It is everywhere and every day. It is just a matter of tuning in and accepting and engaging its true value. There are many ways to the contemplative. Nalanda Miksang is one way that points the way.

If your intention is enlightenment, Nalanda Miksang will take you in the right direction, but we cannot deliver this. It can facilitate and express this, but it cannot deliver this. You will need to also engage one of the enlightenment dharma traditions, with their transmissions and practices. Nalanda Miksang is associated with Shambhala, but there are many other genuine dharma transmissions and schools.

Contemplative and meditation traditions work well together. The contemplative traditions can express modality meditation experiences and realizations. Contemplative practices can also catalyze meditation practices. They can spark to ignite the flame of insight from meditation practices. In turn, meditation traditions provide a vast and profound view for contemplative traditions. They help connect the contemplative dewdrop with the ocean of dharma.

Post-Practice

Especially in Level Two, we want to look at how we are after we practice. Our real engagement is in everyday, day-in-and-day-out, every-season life situations. The more we shift from living in the thing world, toward living in the phenomenal world, the richer our everyday life reveals itself to be. Every encounter every day is an occasion for being there, feeling there, expressing there, or just being cheerful on the spot.

This isn't even an intentional practice; it just happens on its own. The phenomenal world makes the first move. It wakes you up. As you commit more and more to a life of direct experience, your path becomes quicker, easier, and more powerful. The universe is working for you, with you, and through you. The more you open to it, the more the phenomenal world comes to you. This is the deep and effortless contemplative practice. Your images embody and express this ordinary magic.

So take your practices out of the camera, off the cushion or mat. Whether you engage in social media, work situations, family situations, or walking in nature, you can be practicing this non-practice of direct perception. On the one hand, we are always practicing—never perfect, never completely realized. On the other hand, there is no practice. You are in every moment, whether you are aware of it or not, and every moment is exactly as it is, completely perfect, without fault.

You experience a vast realm of perceptions unfolding. There is unlimited sound, unlimited sight, unlimited taste, feeling and so on. The realm of perception is limitless, so limitless that perception itself is primordial, unthinkable, beyond thought. There are so many perceptions that they are beyond imagination . . . there are endless fields of perception.

—Chögyam Trungpa, *Shambhala, Sacred Path of the Warrior*

LEVEL III AND BEYOND

Heart of Photography covers the majority of what we call the Level Two teachings in Nalanda Miksang, but there are more teachings where these come from. Still in Level Two, these include the huge world of contemplative landscape, going deeper into haiku, and more. Over time, Nalanda Miksang areas of study have proven to be as endless as the fields Trungpa Rinpoche speaks of. The further we go, the more mysterious these explorations are, but the more they open for practitioners in a real way.

Further volumes will capture the teachings of what we currently call Orderly Chaos, or Nalanda Miksang Level Three. These teachings turn what we have come to think of as contemplative

photography, and Nalanda Miksang, on its head. Exploring chaos, as Sakyong Mipham says in the following quote from the *Shambhala Principle*, is both tricky and simple. Regardless, it is key:

Modern chaos theory posits that even a small change can dramatically shift the long-term behavior of a system . . . with mindfulness . . . we can see the connection between humans and the environment, and therefore nature itself . . . Can we feel comfortable in our own minds and hearts? Compassion is not simply a feeble response to hard times. It is choosing not to pollute our own thoughts and our planet with the energy of aggression . . . What are the signs of progress? Our body, speech, and mind become more gentle. At times we are able to bear difficulty without complaint. We might even begin to welcome chaos as an opportunity to engage . . . When we consider chaos good news, whatever comes our way—good or bad—has less power to obstruct our journey.

If you have hung around Nalanda Miksang on social media enough, you have noticed mention of something mysterious, our sister school, Absolute Eye. Little can be said about Absolute Eye for now, but the basic explanation is that it is an investigation of what the modern art schools were exploring in the 1950s–70s, including abstract expressionism, pop, color field, and more. As we study these artists, we discover naturally occurring instances of art with similar feeling in the primarily urban environments most of us live in. Studying these artists and their works is another way to explore the edge of chaos and harmony, all focused on direct perceptual engagement.

The future of Nalanda Miksang is constantly unfolding. We are expanding our social media presence, with groups on Facebook and Flickr, hash tags and all the markers of this new generation of connection. Like our shift first from film to digital cameras, and now into phone cameras, the risks inherent with a sped-up life are prevalent. When we post our images quickly, we can forget our original intention to connect. Connection online, just as in person, can be addicting, refreshing our browser constantly to see if someone "likes" our images or reflections. Keeping a contemplative mind in this chaos, too, is an essential and natural extension of all we cultivate in practicing Nalanda Miksang.

Thank you for joining us on this journey into the Heart of Photography. We would like to close with a dedication of merit, a traditional closing at the end of a practice session to mark our desire that our practice be of benefit to all beings. This aspiration, to dedicate the benefit of our practice to all beings (ourselves included), lets us acknowledge how powerful even simple practices can be, how much of a change in direction small shifts can begin. This version comes from the Shambhala tradition, our tradition; if you feel connection to it, please consider closing your practice sessions with it. If not, explore other versions, or find your way to your own way to close, appreciating the richness, including the richness inside you, and dedicating its benefit to all this practice connects you to.

By the confidence of the golden sun of the great east

May the lotus garden of the Ridgen's wisdom bloom.

May the dark ignorance of sentient beings be dispelled.

May all beings enjoy profound, brilliant glory.

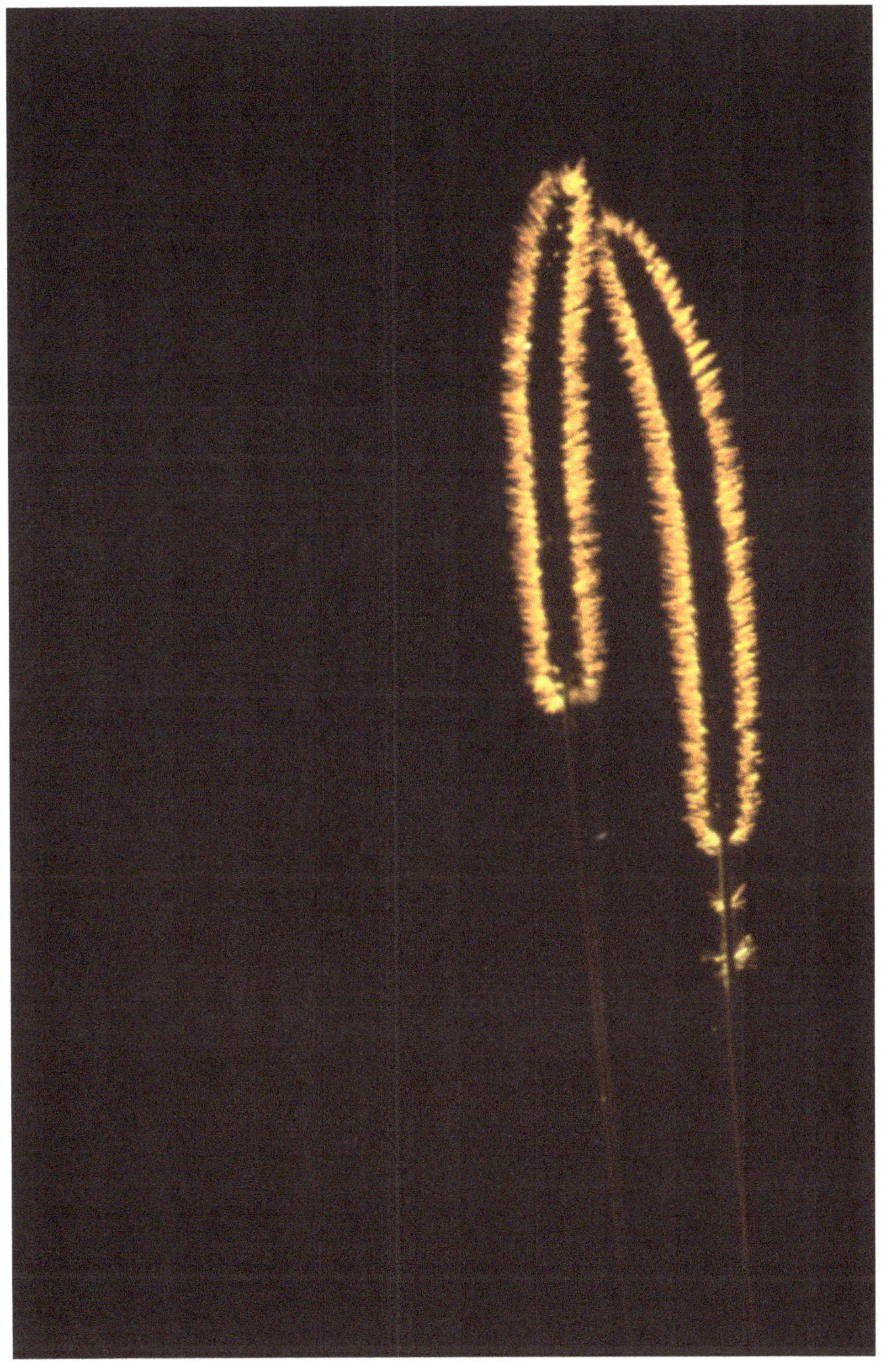

APPENDIX

The Basics Of Looking And Seeing

I.

We realize you may have picked up this volume having not read our introductory book, *Looking and Seeing*. While we recommend you give it a look, we want this volume to also be a doorway through which you can enter into the way of seeing. So we offer here a review of Level One principles, covered in depth in our first volume, *Looking and Seeing.*

Miksang is a Tibetan word that translates as "good eye." Nalanda Miksang is one of two founding schools of the practice of Miksang. Our school focuses on a way which combines perception and photography to connect with and express basic goodness. *Basic goodness* is the Shambhala tradition's term for our fundamental, unconditional state of being awake.

Nalanda Miksang embodies Chögyam Trungpa Rinpoche's presentation of the three levels of perception. These three levels offer a progressive purification of the false sense of separation of the perceiver and the perceived—in other words, the false sense that we are separate and isolated, rather than connected and in communion. This practice and teaching presents a photography way for realizing this connection and, from this communion, making brilliant resonant images.

In fact, the photography aspect of Nalanda Miksang is those brilliant images. Yet it is also much deeper than that. These vivid images embody and express the brilliance and enrichment of our human experience, which is basic goodness. This is what makes it a contemplative practice. Like many contemplative practices, it has an orientation which enriches and transforms one's life in very ordinary and available ways. At the same time as being ordinary, these ways are also magical.

Another key source of Nalanda Miksang teachings is the perception teachings of Chögyam Trungpa Rinpoche. These are, in large measure, presented in his texts *True Perception* and *Shambhala: Sacred Path of the Warrior*. There is much to be contemplated and said concerning these teachings. Here, our point is simple: these perception teachings of Chögyam Trungpa are not something he made up. These are deep, ancient teachings he presented in an available way.

These perception teachings open to much vaster and deeper principles than basic Miksang pedagogy, but all of them come from the same principle: what constitutes contemplative art is true perception revealing itself. If you are interested in exploring these deeper teachings, you can find sources in the bibliography.

Although true perception is a human birthright, it is not necessarily realized, expressed, or enjoyed in our daily human circumstances. More often than not, even if we are aware of it, we take it for granted. It is taken as a given—a power and resource we can use through our daily tasks.

There is a paradox here. It is true that this grant of life is a grant, and we can use this resource however we want. But a grant is a grant. It does not come from us. It *is* us. Here we do not necessarily need to default to a religious view that there must be someone or something who grants us this gift. Contemplatives just affirm and work with the reality of the grant.

Now we are getting to the point behind the point, the point this contemplative photography practice embodies: your creativity is most creative when it runs with the way it is. You become more creative when you let go and become you as you within creativity. Your images sustain and embody this creativity: stunning but absolutely simple beauty images.

This is very practical. Even in the ongoing demands of daily living there are enormous possibilities of ordinary joy available. At a minimum, it can give you some relief from stress. At a maximum, it can open to the meaning of life.

It is possible to cheer up on the spot.

II.

Good eye means clear eye, unconditionally seeing eye. In order to aid in understanding what seeing clearly feels like, Nalanda Miksang is structured into levels: Level One, Level Two, and Level Three, along with a few side programs, including Way of Nature, Contemplative Landscape, and Absolute Eye. Level One, the primary content of *Looking and Seeing*, covers the basics of how to practice Nalanda Miksang as well as the assignments of Level One, which naturally lead into Level Two. As the primary content of this volume is Level Two, we will review the basic lessons of Level One and its assignments here.

Level One is an exploration of pure perception. The most basic components include the practices of Flash of Perception and Synchronization (see sidebars for instructions). As far as assignments go, we work with the primary forms of perception:

Color as Color; Surface (Texture and Pattern); Light as Light (Patch of Light/ Patch of Shadow, plus Light on Form); Space; and Dot-in-Space.

Level One can feel quite formal at first, focusing on these forms. Rather than composition, the emphasis in Level One is on filling the frame with your flash of perception of these forms. Once we recognize we are having a flash of perception, we adjust our position and camera to best reproduce that flash. The most important part of this process is to understand that the flash of perception leads the way; it composes itself, rather than you thinking of a way to compose it.

Level One images are often abstract, not recognizable, separated from their "thingness," or "not of this world." While Level One images can be quite compelling and have deep merit in their own, this training in form is only one level of Nalanda Miksang training. These forms of perception—color, light, texture, pattern, space, and dot-in-space—are the notes that make up the chord of how we usually do what we think of as seeing. When we perceive, these elements appear somewhat isolated from one another, before concept glues them back together. While we may appear to see all of these things at once—the lit-up computer screen, the blue background—and also use our other senses—hearing, smelling and tasting—in fact, we receive each tiny iota of data bit by bit and string them together. These little pieces of information, called *phenomena* in phenomenology, the philosophy of perception, are themselves unbiased (not likeable or dislikeable), without identity (not a leaf or a tree or even "green") and, therefore, pure, simple, and spacious.

We stop the mind by stopping the eye; in Level One pictures, the eye should stay in the picture, not move a lot, be stable and open. There should be only one perception, though sometimes overlapping with a second, as in a textured red surface. It is helpful—and joyful—to practice this basic training, which is very simple but often hard for folks to "dumb" themselves down to, before moving forward into the other levels of Nalanda Miksang.

Synchronization Exercise

The Synchronization Exercise is a simple way to start your Nalanda Miksang shoot. Once you are ready to photograph, find a safe space where you can close or lower your eyes, taking your visual experience out of play for a few minutes. Focus first on sound—the obvious sounds usually appear first, not grasping for them, just receiving, noticing how the ears more easily accept sound, versus how the eyes search out things to see. Notice how, over time, subtler, previously unheard sounds appear, and let yourself connect and synchronize with this pure sound experience, without labels or preference.

Then let yourself sink into your external felt bodily sensations—the temperature of your skin, fabric of your clothes against skin, the wind or air around you; then the internal bodily felt sensations—your heartbeat, your breath, your digestive system. Once you have made clear contact with all of these, and rested there for a bit, open your eyes gently and slowly, with curiosity, wondering what you might see now that you have relaxed your vision, and now that your vision includes more than just your eyes.

Flash of Perception Exercise

What most people notice after doing the Synchronization Exercise is a sense of seeing the world fresh again once they open their eyes after synchronizing. The Flash of Perception is an abbreviated version of the Synchronization Exercise, and like Synchronization, rather than being an affect or way of making you see differently, it should be understood as a way of connecting with what you are already experiencing and often overlooking.

Again, in the beginning of a Nalanda Miksang session, find yourself a safe place to stand or sit and close your eyes. Turning or simply adjusting your position so that when you open your eyes you don't know what you will see, open your eyes and notice the first thing you see. That first glimpse, often something which catches our eye, has strength, simplicity, and nonconceptual clarity to it. This is the kind of sensation we want to contact in order to recognize when we have had a flash of perception or not. When in doubt, use this exercise again and again, although if you find you are flashing without it (secret: you always already are), you don't have to use it.

III.

In Buddhist terms, Level One Nalanda Miksang is the *shamatha* of contemplative photography, meaning, a very basic connecting form of contemplation, like shamatha is for meditation. It is not to be seen as something one does and then is finished with. Level I images have, on their own, a deep and important abiding energy, as well as a feeling tone or sense. The total clarity, simplicity, spaciousness, and purity of these images, while not entirely of the thing world, are deeply perceptual, deeply phenomenal, and deeply true. They can be very beautiful, aesthetically. Or they can be boring. Both are ok. Miksang practitioners who have done further levels are always encouraged to come back to the Level One forms and see how they change their relationship with the forms over time. The forms, as abstract and formal as they may seem at first when doing Level One, are far from unchanging, as our relationship with them, and the world itself, is always changing.

What is unchanging in Nalanda Miksang—infallible, without doubt, and made of total confidence—is the flash of perception, which is one of the first teachings in Nalanda Miksang. Though we teach it as an actual exercise, it is being used here in the sense of sparking awareness of our natural interaction with the phenomenal world, in other words, our direct perceptions. Nalanda Miksang focuses on direct perception. Each experience, coming into our minds through our senses, passes through these gateways of perception: the five "normal senses," as well as, in Tibetan phenomenology, the mind, a sixth sense organ. Data—smells, sights, thoughts, feelings, sounds—are all unbiased, not good or bad, not this or that, but pre-existing, before you sense them and long after you are gone. The moment of recognition of pure perception, a flash of perception, is also without judgment, and points out to us the joy of our everything being enough as it already is, including ourselves. Every second, every millisecond, according to ancient texts and modern cognitive psychologists, we are perceiving anew, constructing our world, and therefore we have a chance every millisecond to connect with our basic goodness, with the goodness of the world, through our senses.

This is truly a gift; one we often deny. We bypass our senses often and go straight to concept. What usually catches our attention first is like or dislike, desire or repulsion, happy or unhappy. In other words, our reactions are what we usually define as reality. One definition of the word *karma* is action. In the way we use karma in dharma teachings, these reactions are karmic action. If we interact with the world in the new, fresh mind of direct perception all the time, karma has nothing to feed on. It is only through practice and awareness that we can become confident that other possibilities, other states, or reactions or interactions, are possible and already present. There are choices all the time, every millisecond, and we are making them already at the perceptual level: red versus green, cold versus hot. Before we have even made conscious thoughts about these things, we begin to identify them, label them, and act accordingly. The Abhidharma, traditional Tibetan teachings on phenomenology, says this is when our egos begin to develop, occurring milliseconds after the myriad perceptions we are constantly experiencing. If we rely on our habitual tendencies toward bias and concept, they become our view, not only of how the world is but also of our solid sense of self. We believe in our biases and judgments instead of in basic goodness.

The good news is, because of understanding these troubling patterns, we have a choice, every moment, to pick something else, something other than habit, through bringing careful attention to what is always happening. When we begin to choose things as they are, and us as we are, in every new moment, the cornucopia of the phenomenal world begins to display its riches to us. They are always available, but we are not always willing to receive these gifts. This is one of the core messages of Nalanda Miksang: that there is an overwhelming generosity of the phenomenal world, and a way to overcome our blinders of habit so that we can partake in and then turn around and share these riches. The form of the practice of Nalanda Miksang gives us leverage to access the phenomenal world, which, without the form, remains distant from us because of our habits.

After experiencing the flash of perception, we need to actually frame a flash in order to make what we call an *equivalent*, which photographers will recognize as a classic term from Alfred Stieglitz, pointing to the fact that a photograph is never exactly the same as what we see. This equivalent is not the same as the flash, but it's as close as we can get. Holding the perception gently with the eye, we often (but not always) need to move in a bit in order to actually capture what we perceived, not what we saw.

We are interested in perception without direction, without concept, without label. Flashes of perception are small focuses, doubtless and stable. In any given moment we are actually seeing a lot (try taking a picture right now from where you are sitting or standing) but perceiving tiny bits and pieces. We actually are not able to perceive absolutely everything that is happening at once, so we fill in the gaps. In this practice, we notice those gaps and take advantage of that space to really be with the flash.

The slogan we use for forming an equivalent is "Fill your frame (viewfinder or LCD screen) with the flash of perception." Fill it with "fire engine red, not a red fire engine. If the red is what brought you to the engine, then photograph that." Stick to one thing at first: one form; simplicity.

Another basic guideline from Level One is to put our focus and practice into taking a clear photographic equivalent up front. Whether or not you use Photoshop or another post-processing program later, John likes to say Nalanda Miksang will make less work for later. We are always staying as close to the direct moment of flash of perception as possible. Reworking it later, especially if we photograph with the intent to change it later, even if it is to "make it the color I actually perceived" or "fix what the camera could not do," can become risky. This also reminds us to let go. The eventual photograph isn't the point. The point is to be there for the flash of perception, and to be open to others, which will soon arise after one is gone.

IV.

The forms covered in *Looking and Seeing* and briefly explained here break down the visual into the visual. We begin with the Color as Color assignment, exploring full, direct experiences of color, photographing those flashes of perception to deliver equivalent images. Color as Color images are vivid, simple, and bright; without thing-ness or objectification; pre-concept and bold. They often overlap with other Level One assignments—Pattern, for instance, or Texture, or Space—but the predominate experience is of color as color.

The second assignment is a combination of Pattern and Texture, called Surface. In Surface, we begin to recognize how we know it is we see something, by seeing its surface: the pattern of a weave, of bricks, of fabric; the texture of grit, of fur, even of slick shininess. While pattern is often the easiest of the forms of perception to experience and capture, texture is trickier than it sounds. Here we are interested in texture we can see, not just know is there. Seeing texture requires light, often side light, to show us the surface we are seeing. Looking at a blank brick wall with low light reveals more pattern visually than texture, even if we "know" bricks are rough. It is only with side light that we can see the texture of the bricks and feel their roughness with our eyes. In this way, texture and pattern often overlap or coexist in the same shots; in particular, texture images almost always have pattern, while only some pattern shots have texture. The question is always what the primary perception was and if that got communicated, even as a lot of these perceptions overlap with color, space, or light.

Light as Light is the most complex of the assignments in *Looking and Seeing*, both technically and visually. Obviously, light exists nearly constantly; without it we could not see and definitely could not photograph. However, we want to explore light visually: how can we see light? As we have seen already, light helps us see texture, and in a larger-scale way, it helps us see shape and form. Light on Form is one part of the light assignment, noticing how side light helps us see the curve of a ball, for instance, which otherwise, visually, we only know to be there. We also explore back light and front light, the latter being taboo in photography because of its tendency to flatten subjects. However, we are interested in all visual perceptions of light, even ones that don't seem to reveal magic to us in an obvious way.

The second part of the light assignment points to another way we see light directly: when it is in contrast with shadow. Patch of Light/Patch of Shadow helps us see the patterns and contrast that make it possible to know the presence of light through its absence next to its presence.

The overall effect of noticing light is the bridge to Level Two, or this text *Heart of Photography*. Once we begin to notice how light shows us shape and form, we begin to notice shapes and forms again—the very objects we were not working with explicitly in Color as Color, and Surface. But now, with some training, we notice perceptual manifestations, not just "that statue with some light on it that shows us the texture/shape of it," but the feeling of what it is like to be in direct contact with that moment of perception containing those parts. We will explore a lot more in this volume what we mean by this direct contact, what implications it has for our practice and our life. But suffice it to say that the line between *Looking and Seeing* (Level One) and *Heart of Photography* (Level Two) is not as solid as we might make it out to be. Abstraction and form play with one another in light, in and out of appearance and concept. That is part of our exploration, beginning with light in Level One, and continues to be a part of Level Two in a big way.

The final two assignments in *Looking and Seeing* point to the core dharma teachings in Nalanda Miksang: Space and Dot-in-Space. Images that capture space let the eye float, relax without having to fix on one point, but also do not batter the eye around in too many directions. Natural occurrences of visual space happen most readily on beaches, in parks with wide open areas of grasses, and while looking at the sky. However, lest we get too conceptual, this, again, is visual space we can see, not the concept of distance between you and a far-off tree. This means even a concrete wall just a few feet from you can exhibit visual space, even the windshield of a car. Discovering and exploring visual space is a deep treasure.

Finally, Dot-in-Space is the last Level One assignment. Dot-in-Space is a many-layered teaching, one we explored quite deeply in *Looking and Seeing* and will dig into even more here. For now, we will simply say Dot-in-Space in a Level One way works with noticing the very form of how we experience vision itself: we cannot see a thing without something in contrast to it. In Level One, these experiences are more abstract and formal: a splash of red paint on a blue wall, a patch of shadow on a lit-up area of grass, two round shapes sitting on a surface.

Dot-in-space is really what carries us from Level One to Level Two: a flag against the sky, a cat against the window, a tree against the grass—these are all examples of dot-in-space in a Level Two way, which we explore here through various assignments. We open to the depths of dot-in-space: it isn't simply something against a background, but a deep way of experiencing the resonance and interdependence of all phenomena.

Our first volume, *Looking and Seeing*, contains many wonderful stories and exercises, as well as powerfully contemplative essays. We recommend that you pick it up in order to explore these teachings in a deeper way. In the meantime, if you want to continue the way of seeing, let's jump into the heart of perception together.

Tonglen: Exchanging Self For Other

Nalanda Miksang is a form of contemplative photography. In some ways, what this means is the practice allows us to apply our mind to topics we have a harder time finding insight into. Formal contemplation practice operates the same way: we pick topics, quotes, passages, concepts; it is hard for us to come to insight through thinking, and we practice applying our mind in a felt way. There are two contemplative practices in particular which emphasize relationships with others: *Tonglen* and *Maitri* (aka *metta*). If we truly want to connect, to be in touch, to be touched, we have to be vulnerable. Most of us associate vulnerability with weakness, exposure, or lack of protection. Nalanda Miksang is one way to work with being in touch and learning from experience (not from mental concept) the strength inherent in vulnerability, generosity, and connection; Tonglen and Maitri are two others.

People often find these complementary practices useful, and you don't have to be Buddhist to do them. The fundamental view of Tonglen and Maitri is working with relationships through kindness and compassion. This pairs well with the Nalanda Miksang understanding of appreciating the phenomenal world through direct experience—opening to a cat's meow, or the light on your daughter's hair. Through Tonglen and Maitri practice we are letting the soft-spot quality of someone's tears, or even their anger, touch us, even if it doesn't involve making an image of that flash of connection. The world pierces us, and we let it pierce us, so we can know it for what it is.

We provide many resources in our bibliography for formal instruction in Tonglen and Maitri/Metta practice. Here we will simply present how the view of both these practices complements Nalanda Miksang practice.

Tonglen is the practice of exchanging yourself for others, or beings who seem to be others. When you experience someone in a great deal of pain—for example, a newscast showing victims of a natural disaster, or a relative dying—that single contact, similar to one of Dorothea Lange's photographed gestures, helps you make contact with their humanness. Instead of distancing ourselves, which is what we often do, trying to get away from another person's pain as if it were a disease, we actually allow ourselves to contact it, to get in touch with it, to touch it. This is a wonderful practice to do if, while out photographing people and other sentient beings, you encounter something difficult or potent—for example, a person yells at you for photographing them, you see a dead bird, someone living on the street touches your heart in a painful way. Instead of focusing on "that person" yelling at "you," you can begin to develop a larger view: their yelling is their current manifestation of frustration of the human heart we all share. Vulnerability is both the problem and the solution: because we are touched, we need to get in touch.

After doing Tonglen for a while, especially combined with the view of seeing things as they are in Nalanda Miksang, we can really feel how much discomfort and exposure we can handle (hint: more than we think). In discovering that capacity, we also increase our room for joy. Fundamentally, we connect, make contact, are in touch and touched more deeply. Shambhala teachings say warriorship is needed in order to allow ourselves to be this open and raw, just as open and raw as we need to be to receive any flashes of perception, whether they are connections with stones or humans.

Maitri is a slightly related practice that focuses on generating loving-kindness. This is also a useful contemplative practice to do after photographing people and other sentient beings. It involves generating good feelings and thoughts; traditional examples include "May all beings be happy," and so on, and beaming those thoughts and good feelings out to beings, starting first with yourself and working your way out to people you've never met, people you are angry with, folks you see daily but do not know (Pema Chödrön calls them "the neutrals"), and those you generate love for easily (your pets or family or partner or best friend). While it may seem trite at first, this is not simply the idea of "wishing someone well"; it is actually a challenge for us to wish fundamental happiness and the roots of happiness for the boss we hate at work or the friend who misspoke.

The habitual patterns that preserve a sense of separation to protect us from who we perceive to be "others" are in direct conflict with our deep need and desire to connect, to touch, and to be in touch. Uprooting these patterns can seem challenging, because they are. By going into the heart of relationship, through direct perception, we begin to pierce not only the false distance between ourselves and others but the overall cocoon of habit that keeps us separate from our world. Waking up in this way is both refreshing and intimidating.

Nalanda Miksang gives us direct sips of the world of interconnection we are already constantly swimming in. Take your time, but keep connecting. Relationships are what help us stay in touch, as intimidating as they can seem.

Three Levels Of Perception
By Chögyam Trunpga
(From *True Perception*)

Perception can be categorized into three levels: experience, emptiness, and luminosity. At the first level, experience, perception is not meaningful self-confirmation, but the experience of things as they are. White is white and black is black. There is a kind of exuberant energy that goes along with the perception. You actually experience something as though you were it. You and the experience become almost indivisible when you experience something in that way. It's that kind of direct communication without anything between.

The second level is the perception of emptiness, which is the absence of things as they are. That is, things have their space; they always come with a certain sense of room. Despite the complexities or the overcrowdedness of our experience, things provide their own space within the overcrowdedness. Actually, that is saying the same thing: overcrowdedness is room, in some sense, because there is movement, dance, play. Things are very shifty and intangible. Because of that, there is a very lucid aspect to the whole thing.

The third level of perception is luminosity. Luminosity has nothing to do with any visually bright light; it is a sense of sharp boundary and clarity that does not have a theoretical or intellectualized reference point. It is realized on the spot, within the spaciousness. If there were no space, it would be unfocused; there would be no sharpness. But at this third level, in terms of ordinary experience, we have a sense of clarity and a sense of things as they are, seen as they are, unmistakably.

So there are three types of perception: the sense of experience, the sense of emptiness, and the sense of luminosity. With these three levels of perception, we are able to see all the patterns of our life. Whether the patterns of our life are regarded as neurotic or enlightened, we are able to see them very clearly.

Glossary

basic goodness: Akin to *bodhicitta*, or a basic open heartedness, basic goodness is a Shambhala teaching that points to the inherent goodness in all humans.

Chögyam Trungpa: Tibetan lama who escaped Tibet in 1959 and eventually came to North America, where he founded Shambhala. He died in 1986.

contemplation/contemplative: Using external media—words, cameras, flowers—as an object in order to directly experience our minds and the world around us.

flash of perception: The naturally occurring, quickly changing action of perception, which changes every millisecond and gives us a fresh experience in every moment.

meditation: Working directly with breath or other objects to engage the mind and become familiar with its workings.

Nalanda: Ancient Buddhist monastery and school in India. Also used as an umbrella term to describe the contemplative arts in Shambhala Buddhist contexts.

perception: Experience of the world and ourselves via our senses.

phenomenal world: The world as we directly experience it through perceptions.

phenomenology: The philosophy of perception and study of "things as they are."

resonance: A Taoist expression of the interdependence of all beings in our world. Akin to the waves of sound or water, each action has an effect on all else in positive or negative ways.

Shambhala: A school of Buddhism that comes through Chögyam Trungpa Rinpoche, based in the roots of Kagyu and Nyingma teachings of Tibet and a vision of enlightened society in which all humans recognized their basic goodness. Current leader is Sakyong Mipham Rinpoche.

Vajra Regent Ozel Tenzin: Declared main dharma heir to Chögyam Trungpa in 1976. Died in 1990. Oversaw the development of Miksang photography.

Way: Taoist expression of "things as they are."

Study Guide

DHARMA TEXTS

Chögyam Trungpa Rinpoche. *True Perception: The Path of Dharma Art*. Shambhala, 2008.

Chögyam Trungpa Rinpoche. *Shambhala: The Sacred Path of the Warrior*. Shambhala, 2007.

Sakyong Mipham. *The Shambhala Principle: Discovery Humanity's Hidden Treasure*. Harmony, 2014.

Sakyong Mipham. *Ruling Your World: Ancient Strategies for Modern Life*. Harmony, 2006.

OTHER RECOMMENDED READINGS

Aitken Roshi, Robert. *A Zen Wave: Basho's Haiku and Zen*.

Ates, Emma. *Contemplative Photo Therapy: Group Intervention for Youth with Anxiety Disorders*. Kindle, 2017.

Hayward, Jeremy W. *Sacred World: The Shambhala Way to Gentleness, Bravery, and Power*. Shambhala, 1998.

Karr, Andy and Michael Wood. *The Practice of Contemplative Photography: Seeing the World with Fresh Eyes*. Shambhala, 2011.

Loori, John Daido. *Zen of Creativity: Cultivating Your Artistic Life*. Ballantine Books, 2005.

Patterson, Freeman. *Photography and the Art of Seeing: A Visual Perception Workshop for Film and Digital Photography*. Firefly Books, 2011.

Saitzyk, Steve. *Place Your Thoughts Here: Meditation for the Creative Mind*. First Thought Press, 2013.

APPENDIX

Find Us Online

Nalanda Miksang has a presence in social media and on its websites. Please join us to play and learn further:

www.miksang.org
www.miksangwayofseeing.com

Social Media

Instagram and Twitter:
> @nalandamiksang
>
> @wayofseeing
>
> @heartofphotography

Facebook: Nalanda Miksang International Way of Seeing
> (also, location-based groups such as Miksang Texas)

Flickr: Miksang, Way of Seeing, and Miksang Teacher and Student Forum

Credits

About The Authors

John McQuade is one of the founders of Miksang Contemplative Photography, which he has presented for thirty years. He is the most senior teacher of the Nalanda Miksang school. John is a long time meditator, meditation instructor, and Shambhala Training director in the Shambhala tradition. He practices Taoist Qi-gong and writes on the contemplative arts. He holds an M.A in Phenomenology and a PhD in Social and Political Thought.

Miriam Hall is a contemplative arts teacher who lives in Madison, Wisconsin, and travels internationally to teach Nalanda Miksang, Shambhala Art, and contemplative writing. She is the second most senior teacher under John McQuade in the Nalanda Miksang School. She has been teaching these practices for over twelve years and deeply enjoys committing her livelihood to them. For more information on her offerings, visit www.herspiral.com.

www.ingramcontent.com/pod-product-compliance
Lightning Source LLC
Chambersburg PA
CBHW041027050726
47599CB00018B/1892